ORWELL
THE ROAD TO AIRSTRIP ONE

ORWELL
THE ROAD TO
AIRSTRIP ONE

IAN SLATER

Second Edition

McGill-Queen's University Press
Montreal & Kingston • London • Ithaca

© Ian Slater 1985
ISBN 0-7735-2622-6

Legal deposit fourth quarter 2003
Bibliothèque nationale du Québec

Printed in Canada on acid-free paper.

McGill-Queen's University Press acknowledges the support of the
Canada Council for the Arts for our publishing program. We also
acknowledge the financial support of the Government of Canada through
the Book Publishing Industry Development Program (BPIDP) for our
publishing activities.

First edition published 1985 by W.W. Norton and Company.
Book design by Jacques Chazaud.

Permissions are found on pp. ix-x.

National Library of Canada Cataloguing in Publication

Slater, Ian
Orwell: the road to airstrip one/Ian Slater. – 2nd ed.

Includes bibliographical references and index.
ISBN 0-7735-2622-6

1. Orwell, George, 1903-1950 – Criticism and interpretation.
2. Orwell, George, 1903-1950 – Political and social views. I. Title.

PR6029.R8Z785 2003   828'.91209   C2003-903574-3

For Marian,
Serena,
and Blair

CONTENTS

ACKNOWLEDGMENTS AND PERMISSIONS

I am grateful to the late Mrs. Sonia Orwell, the Orwell Archive at University College in London and to Ian Angus and his staff at the University College library. I would like to thank Professors Adrian Marriage and Robert Rowan, who, as my teachers, and later my colleagues, in the Arts One Program at The University of British Columbia, opened the door to the most interesting intellectual journey of my life. In addition, I'd like to thank Professors Alan Cairns, Robert Jackson, and George Feaver (also at The University of British Columbia) for their comments on an earlier version of the manuscript upon which Professor Peter Stansky, William Abrahams, and Professor Bernard Crick also graciously commented. Special thanks also are due to Thomas C. Wallace of W. W. Norton, Jane Lebow, and Professor Charles Slonecker.

Most of all, I am indebted to my wife, Marian, for her invaluable support in my work.

I wish to thank the following for giving me permission to quote from copyrighted material:

The estate of the late Sonia Brownell Orwell and Martin Secker and Warburg, Ltd. and Harcourt Brace Jovanovich, Inc. for permission to quote from Orwell's published works: *Down and Out in Paris and London,* copyright © 1933, copyright renewed 1961 by Sonia Pitt-Rivers, *Burmese Days,* copyright © 1934, copyright renewed 1962; *A Clergyman's Daughter,* copyright © 1935, *Keep the Aspidistra Flying,* copyright 1936, *The Road to Wigan Pier,* copyright © 1937, *Homage to Catalonia,* copyright © 1938, copyright renewed 1953, *Coming Up*

PREFACE TO THE
SECOND EDITION

Before Orwell, there was Eric Arthur Blair, a policeman in the service of empire who, at the age of twenty-nine, changed his name to George Orwell.[1] Not surprisingly, one often meets people who do not know Orwell's real name, and why should they? After all, he wanted his readers to know and remember him as Orwell.

While it is unusual these days to come upon someone who has never heard of George Orwell, many people, beyond knowing him as the author of *Nineteen Eighty-Four*, and perhaps *Animal Farm*, do not know much about him or why he is such an important figure in the literature of our times. In 2002 Christopher Hitchens wrote *Why Orwell Matters*. In *Orwell: The Road to Airstrip One* I have tried to show not only why Orwell matters now but why he will *always* matter. I have done this by discussing the wide range of Orwell's works, including some of his most famous essays. One of these, on Salvador Dali, begins, "Autobiography is only to be trusted when it reveals something disgraceful." This is vintage Orwell, at once insightful and—dare one say it, given much of the dour scholarship on Orwell?—entertaining. For those readers, especially students, who know Orwell only through his (course-assigned) novels, his essay style will probably come as a surprise. He was a much better essayist and columnist than novelist (the exception being *Animal Farm*). For those readers interested in politics, Orwell's deft and vivid descriptions of his experience in the Spanish Civil War and his brilliantly argued caution against losing the idea of objective truth are bracing and often surprising, as is the fact, reported by Hitchens, that it was Orwell who, on October 19, 1945, barely two months after one of the Big Three allies had dropped the atom bomb on Hiroshima, first coined the phrase "Cold War," preceding his division of the world into the three super-states of *Nineteen Eighty-Four*.

Hitchens' book is largely a skewering of critics who, wilfully or unwittingly, misquote Orwell for their own purposes, and it assumes that the reader is familiar with the British literati. Mine does not. While doing research at the Orwell Archive in London, I visited an English friend. Soon we were talking about Orwell. "No," she said, "I never read that book he wrote [*Nineteen Eighty-Four*] but I used to read him regularly in the *Trib* [the British socialist *Tribune*]." This comment drove home to me that there remain two very different audiences for Orwell's work. One, mainly British, largely recalls Orwell the journalist and essayist; the other, mainly North American—and to a large extent students—knows him almost solely as a novelist. In my discussion of Orwell's views I have tried to bring the two audiences together, and I hope that a better understanding of Orwell the novelist, essayist, and social/political commentator emerges. Given these two very different audiences, I have not assumed that the reader is familiar with all of Orwell's works or the previous scholarship on him and therefore have given references wherever I thought they might be helpful.

Specifically, I look at what Orwell has to say about what he saw as the major injustices of his time: imperialism, unemployment, the stultifying power of political orthodoxy, and the ever-increasing tendency of the state and society throughout the world to smother the individual. Orwell's work does not lend itself readily to a single-theme approach. Such an approach, the product of overspecialization, does not tell us enough about either Orwell or his work because it ignores his diversity. He writes as passionately about the first blush of spring in "Some Thoughts on the Common Toad" as about the concentration camps of Hitler and Stalin. With equal intensity he tells us, brilliantly, that "the imagination, like certain wild animals, will not breed in captivity," crankily, that "all tobacconists are Fascists!" and, usefully, how to prepare "A Nice Cup of Tea." Such diversity should not, of course, woo us into confusing the trivial with the important, but it does alert us that we need to look at more than one theme if we are to have a clear understanding of Orwell and some of his more engaging and irritating paradoxes.

"Airstrip One" is the name Orwell gave to England in *Nineteen Eighty-Four*, an easily translatable term for an area suggestive of a certain level of technical development in an otherwise drab, food-rationed country. He set the novel in post-war England because he wanted to make it clear that there was nothing inherently superior in the English-speaking world that would protect it against the threat of totalitarianism, and that a totalitarian state could triumph anywhere, "*if not fought against.*" (The italics are Orwell's.) This last point—one that Orwell made to an American fan—is crucial in understanding Orwell's most important work but has been either overlooked or dismissed by critics who have determined that there is no hope evident in the novel.

Indeed, one of the most persistent arguments about Orwell's dystopian novel is whether it is a relentless tome of despair or whether there is any hope that the totalitarian regime of Big Brother, Thought Crime, and Face Crime can be thwarted in our future. The answer is not merely a matter of literary conjecture but of imminent importance, given the already frightening number of totalitarian regimes at the beginning of the twenty-first century and the dire, well-founded predictions of books such as Robert Kaplan's *The Coming Anarchy* and Huntington's *The Clash of Civilizations*, written well before 9/11. For biographer Jeffrey Meyers (*Orwell: The Wintry Conscience of a Generation*, 2000), the problem with *Nineteen Eighty-Four* is that it "lacks a positive vision, for everyone in the novel finally betrays everyone else" and the suffering of the protagonist, Winston Smith ("Winston" as in Churchill, "Smith" as in the common man), "obliterates the novel's satiric wit, emphasizes his cowardice and betrayal, and suggests that the Socialist ideal of brotherhood will always be defeated" (Meyers, 287). Meyers' view has good company. I say more about this and the opposing view in the "Global Vision" section of *The Road to Airstrip One.*

There is not even agreement on whether *Nineteen Eighty-Four* is Orwell's best book. For a succinct and crisply written summary of the kind of debate that swirls around this question, I refer the reader to Erika Gottlieb's *The Orwell Conundrum* (Carleton University Press, 1992) where she suggests that if a novel conveys unrelenting despair, critics will classify it as a "flawed masterpiece" no matter what impact it has made on readers. Despite the array of tendentious literary arguments in favour of the "flawed masterpiece" theory, I am convinced that for some critics (not necessarily those in Gottlieb's book) such a conclusion reflects a dislike of Orwell's political ideas outside the novel, more than an appraisal of the work itself. I say this notwithstanding Orwell's agreement with writer and critic Julian Symons (recorded in Meyers) that the torture scenes in room 101 detracted from the novel. I agree with Symons that

Orwell was "interested in ideas rather than personal relationships." These ideas proved so powerful and interesting that the novel has been translated into more than sixty languages, Orwell having become so popular that, as John Rodden points out in *The Politics of Literary Reputation* (1989), "The 'puritanical' Orwell once satirized in a friend's novel as railing against the danger that 'scanty panties' posed to the stability of the English family was now the subject of feature stories in *Playboy* and *Penthouse*," with arguments for and against his warnings being made not only by intellectuals and editorialists but by political leaders from Margaret Thatcher to Vice-President Walter Mondale, former astronaut John Glenn, and social activist Jesse Jackson. Rodden concludes that the view that Orwell's work has evoked the fiercest "pro and anti-reactions of any writer since Marx" is correct.

George Orwell has so many enemies and admirers both on the right and on the left because he thought for himself and was unwilling to bend to orthodoxy, either social or political, in order to fit in. The point might seem obvious, but the battle never ends since all of us, seeking the comfort and consolation of friends and society at large, are constantly tempted to surrender individual integrity under group pressure. This theme runs like a vein of precious metal through all Orwell's works but in *Nineteen Eighty-Four* the neverending struggle between the individual and an omnipresent state strikes one with the force of a physical blow.

If *Nineteen Eighty-Four* lacks the elegant artistry of *Animal Farm*, it remains by far not only Orwell's most popular novel but the most influential one—at times influential in the most unexpected ways. A personal anecdote speaks to the point. In 1984 I was invited to a conference on Orwell at Lake Bled, Slovenia, which was then still part of northern Yugoslavia. Lake Bled is a stunning body of water with the backdrop of a castle high above it and the jagged sweep of Austria's Julian Alps beyond. Despite the natural beauty of the place, there were reminders of the drab and oppressive atmosphere of *Nineteen Eighty-Four*. With the exception of Romania, Hungary, Bulgaria and a few others, most of the Eastern Bloc countries had refused to attend. The man from Moscow eventually came after an initial refusal — one of the other eastern representatives whispered to me rather angrily that it was just like the apparatchiks in Moscow to refuse to attend what they obviously saw as a Western-plot conference, albeit in what was nominally a Communist country, and then finally send someone to check it out. At the beginning of the conference, after the obligatory two minute anti-U.S. hate session, we got down to discussing Orwell. The Moscow man—whom a number of the Eastern Bloc representatives believed had been sent to spy on them—immediately attacked what he said was Orwell's innocence and naivety, which was guaranteed to offend certain Orwell admirers, who think they understand realpolitik. He also said he deeply resented Orwell having characterized the "Soviet people as pigs" in *Animal Farm*. The celebrated Chinese author and physician Han Suyin, who was also attending the conference, called on me to reply and I explained that the pigs were not the Russian people but Stalin and his lieutenants. The Moscow man seemed a little nonplussed by this, but carried on. It was apparent that the eastern representatives were afraid of him and, indeed, throughout the conference, one noticed how deep the hatred of the Soviet system was. The current Czechoslovakian joke doing the rounds was that someone asked a Czech that if he had three wishes, what would they be? He said: "My first wish would be that China invade Czechoslovakia; my second wish would be that China invade Czechoslovakia, and my third wish would be that China invade Czechoslovakia." Why would he want that? To invade Czechoslovakia, the Chinese would have to cross Russia, resulting in the two totalitarian states fighting one another six times. People from the Eastern Bloc referred to *Nineteen Eighty-Four* as an extraordinarily accurate description of their life, both in the physical sense of the run down nature of Oceania and in the psychological sense, telling me stories of how the autonomous individual was an all-but-unknown species in the totalitarian Soviet domain. One of the representatives, Lennart Meri, an Estonian writer, had been hastily summoned from Estonia to Moscow just before the conference, having been issued a travel visa in a matter of days rather than the usual period of several months during which KGB security checks were normally made to evaluate the risk of defection. (Such measures were actually superfluous insofar as anyone who left the Soviet Union with a visa knew that if they did not return by the route and on the day specified, relatives and/or friends would pay the cost, usually by imprisonment.) Upon arriving in Moscow, Meri was told by an official at the Writers' Union that he was to leave in the morning for an Orwell conference in Yugoslavia, upon which Meri informed the official that he had not read any Orwell.

"You haven't read Orwell?" asked the union official in astonishment. "Everyone's read him."

"How could I?" answered Meri. "Orwell is banned." Momentarily flummoxed, the official instructed Meri to go to the basement where he would be given a number of books by Orwell that he was to read before the early morning flight to Bled. Chain-smoking, Meri pored over the books, knowing of course that it was impossible to read anything like a substantial amount of Orwell's work in such a short time. He knew about *Animal Farm* because he had heard it secretly on a BBC broadcast and was familiar with a few other of Orwell's works via the *samizdat* (works that circulate through this underground channel are typewritten, with a maximum of four copies being made at one time since the print on the fourth carbon copy is so faint it can barely be read). Late into the night, Meri proposed to the Writers' Union official that he be allowed to take the Orwell books to his hotel to read as much as possible before the flight. This was initially refused, but finally the official acquiesced on condition that someone accompany Meri to his hotel and collect the books early the next morning. The contempt Meri felt for the whole system was palpable.

On the last evening of the conference, Meri and I were talking in my hotel room and I gave him all my copies of the Orwell books I had used in preparation for my doctoral thesis. They were dear to me, marked up and thumbed through so many times that several had to be held together by scotch tape and elastic bands. They had become old friends, but I was happy to pass them on, until I detected hesitation in my Estonian friend which I understood, or thought I understood, to be a natural reticence to carry such dangerous contraband into the Soviet Union. I immediately told him that I understood his predicament and had no wish to embarrass him or place him in any danger. But I had entirely miscalculated the reason for his hesitation.

"No," he said. "It's one's moral responsibility to read such books." (I can still recall the frisson of admiration that passed through me in that moment.) "No," he continued thoughtfully, "I was just calculating how many hours I will have on the plane between Bled and Belgrade and between Belgrade and Moscow—how long I will have to read."

Later I was invited to give an address at the Communist Youth Palace in Belgrade, speak at the University, see the film of *Nineteen Eighty-Four*, and join a panel discussion about the film. There was great excitement about the forthcoming screening and I was told that there would be a tremendous fight for seats. So I turned up early, and indeed the theatre, filled with the pungent smoke of Turkish tobacco, was jam-packed. It was, for Belgrade, the premiere performance of *Nineteen Eighty-Four*—the original, made in 1955. I was told that it was the first time it had been shown in Yugoslavia, though I suspect some of the Inner Party members had already seen it. I remember that it was very well-translated. The line that got the best response came when Julia enters her and Winston Smith's hide-away, carrying a package. Winston sniffs, and, eyes wide with surprise, declares, "It's coffee...real coffee."

The theatre just about came apart because at that time Yugoslavia was going through yet another strikingly similar austerity period and "Coffee, real coffee!" was the very phrase used by coffee-starved Yugoslavs.

At the panel discussion, the mood was so crushingly pessimistic that I felt obliged to try to add a little hope to the proceedings. I read aloud one of my favourite passages from Orwell in an attempt to convey the fact that, as dismal as *Nineteen Eighty-Four*'s totalitarianism is, Orwell did hold out some hope for the future, arguing that if we have courage enough to fight against totalitarianism, it need not take us over. The passage I read was from Orwell's essay, "Some Thoughts on the Common Toad," written in 1946:

At any rate spring is here, even in London, N.1, and they can't stop you enjoying it. This is a satisfying reflection. How many a time I have stood watching the toads mating or a pair of hares having a boxing match in the young corn, and thought of all the important persons who would stop me from enjoying this if they could. But luckily they can't. So as long as you are not actually ill, hungry, frightened or immured in a prison or a holiday camp, spring is still spring. The atom bombs are piling up in the factories, the police are prowling through the cities, the lies are streaming from loud-speakers, but the earth is still going round the sun, and neither the dictators nor the bureaucrats, deeply as they disapprove of the process, are able to prevent it.

Immediately an editor from the Yugoslav journal *Nim* turned to me and said: "They're working on it."

I was impressed by the bravery of the organizers of this event, particularly at their daring to have a conference and panel discussion on Orwell. When, before I began my speaking engagements (I cringe at the memory), I asked an embassy official if there was any possible danger to me from the official Communist regime for comments I might make, he said, "Well, of course not. It is, however, a very risky business for them." I learned that the entire editorial staff of a major newspaper had just been fired because officials said they were becoming too liberal.

At the end of the discussion, I had intended to congratulate the panel on their courage in raising such issues in their country at that time during the Cold War and to say that this boded well for the future. But I decided not to, for the obvious reason that it might invite further retaliation against critics of the regime, even though Yugoslavia, under Marshall Tito, had become the least intolerant country in Europe's Communist orbit. At that moment, I was reminded of what Orwell had warned about—that such a system can quickly suborn you into abetting the regime through your own acts of self-censorship. In the same way I noticed that as my comments were being translated for the audience, the interpreter was very careful to preface each translation with, "Professor Slater says this ... Professor Slater's view is so and so," in order to create a safety moat between himself and my remarks.

I exchanged a few postcards with Lennart Meri over the next few years and I sent him a copy of the first edition of this book. But I did not hear any more of him until one hot summer's day, while holidaying on Gabriola Island, one of the Gulf Islands near Vancouver, I happened to be watching a TV newscast of the momentous unraveling of the Soviet Union following the fall of the Berlin Wall. Among the first of the breakaway republics, during a time when the danger of such an act was still acute and evident to all, was Estonia, and on the screen they showed the new president of Estonia: Lennart Meri. Naturally, I was thrilled, and his words in that hotel room in Bled years before raced back to me. During one of my telephone conversations with him since then, he told me he had had to move a number of times during the change from Lennart Meri the writer to Lennart Meri the president. But, he said, while like most of us he had had to get rid of some things during each move, "I know exactly where the Orwell books are on my shelf." For an Orwell aficionado, that's about the best ending to *Nineteen Eighty-Four* that you could wish for.

Orwell's reputation was riding high when, in the early nineties, a counterattack was launched by critics who charged Orwell with being an informer. This is the infamous story of "the list," a case which I believe, despite some admittedly disturbing elements, was a literary molehill blown up to mountainous proportions after the discovery of a quarto notebook in which Orwell, as quoted in Hitchens' book, had written down what he had once described as "a list of crypto-Communists & fellow-travellers which I want to bring up to date." The list, which came to public notice in Bernard Crick's *George Orwell: A Life* (1980), contains about 170 names, 35 of which Orwell is said to have passed to a friend who worked in the Information Research Department (IRD), which has been ominously referred to as a semi-secret division of the British Foreign Office. However, as Timothy Garton Ash points out, "Robert Conquest, who worked in the Information Research Department ... explains how, far from being part of an English secret police, the department's job was to show up the Soviet one." In the relative comfort of our post-Cold War environment, Orwell's action might seem shocking to some. And, as Ash points out in his review of Peter Davison's monumental *The Complete Works of George Orwell*, "it *is* unsettling to see the labeling, 'Jewish?'(Charlie Chaplin) and 'English Jew' (Tom Driberg), even if other names have 'Jugo-Slav,' 'Polish,' 'Anglo-American,' and so on"—despite Orwell having often written against anti-Semitism. On the other hand, while the list of names, without Orwell's racial descriptions attached, was passed on to the IRD during the Cold War, it was a time, as Ash points out, when "there really *were* Soviet agents in British intellectual life [my italics]." And one should remember that Orwell was neither a pacifist (a position he respected if didn't agree with) nor a fence-sitter, unlike so many Western intellectuals who are often, in Kipling's memorable phrase, "makin' mock o' uniforms that guard you while you sleep."

For those interested in a ringside seat to the kind of debate that Orwell's work continues to generate I suggest they follow (click onto) the argument that has been going on between Louis Menand, a professor of English at the City University of New York, writing in the *New Yorker*, and Leon Wieseltier of the *New Republic*. Menand, in a journalistic sweep that would not pass muster in any freshman's essay, declares, "Almost the only thing Orwell's posthumous admirers [sic] have in common, besides the button ["Orwell Was Right"], is anti-communism." How does Menand know this? Did he take a poll? I think many people, particularly those who have read some of

Orwell's earlier novels and/or his journalism, admire him not so much for his anti-communism as for his uncommon understanding of poverty and unemployment. Surely unemployment, along with imperialism, Fascism, and communism, was one of the four great issues of the twentieth century and, the way things look at present, will remain one of the great issues of the twenty-first.

It is almost impossible to get people, especially academics and intellectuals who have never experienced it, to fully understand the exhausting complexity of poverty and unemployment. Poverty, to most people, is viewed in extraordinarily simplistic terms—you have no money, you collect unemployment insurance, and you live simply and awfully. Orwell, in *Down and Out in Paris and London, The Road to Wigan Pier* and his classic essay "How the Poor Die" (which my children's pediatrician years ago told me was required reading for all his medical students) conveys not only the smells and inhumanity of this other world but the complex maneuvering required to get through each day. He is talking about not only the subservient behaviour demanded by an omnipresent bureaucracy in a welfare state, or the shock of suddenly being laid off ("downsized"), but the host of individual decisions required of an often malnourished, and therefore benumbed, individual trying desperately to think in order to hang on to whatever shreds of dignity he or she still has. I talk about this in the second part of this book under the heading "England."

In yet another criticism of Orwell, Menand argues that "the point is not that Orwell made things up. The point is that he used writing in a literary, not a documentary, way: He wrote in order to make you see what he wanted you to see, to persuade." But Menand then quotes Orwell as freely admitting in his essay "Why I Write" that "every line of serious work that I have written since 1936 has been written, directly or indirectly, *against* totalitarianism and *for* democratic Socialism, as I understand it." Orwell repeatedly warned his readers of his political bias so that they could better judge his arguments — surely preferable to those journalists who, while effecting political neutrality, write in obeisance to a hidden agenda.

Menand also states that while Orwell was against colonialism (a subject I deal with in the first chapters of this book) he was not in favour of "national self-determination," concluding, "If this is anti-imperialism, make the most of it." He fails, however, to entertain the possibility of other kinds of regimes between colonialism and immediate self-determination. Has he not read Kaplan's *The Coming Anarchy* or any of the other seemingly endless stream of reports of the disasters that, for example, have followed on the heels of rapid decolonization in West Africa? These have been so catastrophic that, to take just one case, the locals, including government bureaucrats, in post-colonial Sierra Leone begged the British major in charge of a salvage mission to "re-colonize us." Rapid "national self-determination" has proven to be an unmitigated disaster in many countries, so that Orwell's hesitancy about it, along with his descriptions of what a future totalitarian society might look like, is remarkably prescient.

Another attack Menand launches against Orwell is prefaced by his statement that Orwell found Hitler "personally appealing." This is true, Orwell admitting in 1940 that "I have never been able to dislike him [Hitler]." What Menand, in a classic case of quoting out of context, fails to mention is that in the same paragraph (from Orwell's review of *Mein Kampf* in 1940) Orwell adds, "I have reflected that I would certainly kill him if I could get within reach of him." What Orwell is telling us is a deeper and disturbing truth, namely that Hitler, who was democratically elected to power, appealed to great numbers of people because, in Orwell's view, he had a "Christ crucified" appeal, looking like a "martyr, the victim ... the self-sacrificing hero who fights single-handed against impossible odds. The attraction of such a pose," Orwell continues, "is of course enormous; half the films that one sees turn upon some such theme."

On the other hand, Menand is quite correct when he points out that Orwell was far better as a social and political critic than in coming up with solutions to the problems he analyzed so astutely and succinctly. I deal with this subject throughout this book. And Menand is right again in his criticism of Orwell's ignorance about America and in pointing out that Orwell, like most of us, could be quite nasty at times. Menand reminds us that Orwell was not only a middle-class intellectual who was contemptuous of the middle class and intellectuals but a "Socialist whose abuse of Socialists—'all that dreary tribe of high-minded women and sandal-wearers and bearded fruit-juice drinkers who come flocking toward the smell of "progress" like bluebottles to a dead cat'—was as vicious as any Tory's."

By now we are well aware that Orwell was neither saint nor sinner, but what matters is the enormous impact of his writing. This is the result of his ability, like all good novelists, to extrapolate from his personal experience into the world at large. Scholars and others have expressed both puzzlement and, on the part of people who lived in Stalinist Russia, amazement at how Orwell was so successful in capturing not only the oppressive wholeness but the depressing particularity of their daily existence. One Jewish intellectual expelled from Russia told me that "this [1984] is my life."

This recalls the reception of Stephen Crane's *The Red Badge of Courage* by veterans of America's bloodiest war. They were so taken by his realistic battle scenes that they had assumed he had fought in the Civil War, until someone realized that at the time (1861-65) Crane did not exist, not having been born until 1870. "Then how did you know all that stuff?" veterans reportedly asked him, to which he reputedly replied, "I played football." No doubt his answer was somewhat tongue-in-cheek, but the point made was that, quite apart from being an acute observer, he had extrapolated from the moments of sheer fright he had experienced during the onrush of an opposing team in the rougher game of his time. This, and other experiences as he was growing up, had been put to good use in the novel.

In Orwell's case it was not only the experience of being hunted by the Communist secret police in Barcelona during the Spanish Civil War that helped him create the terror exerted by O'Brien and the Inner Party in *Nineteen Eighty-Four* but also his experience as a young boy at boarding school. This connection is mentioned throughout *The Road to Airstrip One*.

In the final section, "The Global Vision," I write that Orwell "told his friend Julian Symons that he looked forward to going to America upon his recovery to report on the Deep South." Symons told me this over lunch in Vancouver in the spring of 1981 and added, with a puzzled look into the middle distance, that he had told this to at least one prominent biographer of Orwell and several others "but they've never used it. I don't know why." His comment was not delivered in the throw-away tone of someone who thought Orwell's plans to be the unrealistic whim of a dying man but was stated with a seriousness that clearly implied that Orwell, however ill he was, really intended to go to America and do a kind of *Road to Wigan Pier* on the Deep South, should he, improbable as it seemed, cheat death one more time, as he had on several occasions before, the most dramatic of these being when he survived after being shot through the throat by an enemy sniper during his time fighting in the Spanish Civil War. With regard to Orwell's interest in the Deep South it is worth recalling (as described in Michael Shelden's *Orwell* [1991]) that after recovering from an earlier serious bout of illness, Orwell in 1934 had approached Eugene Saxton, Harper's visiting editor-in-chief, asking whether the American publishing house would commission him to do a biography of Mark Twain. Orwell was not given the commission (his first novel, *Burmese Day,* had not yet been published) but in 1943 he penned a long essay on Mark Twain in which he wrote about the essence of frontier life. It was this life, as Hitchens points out, that, despite the myths surrounding its legend, evoked for Orwell a part of the world where a man's destiny was not settled by his social position at birth. Meyers also mentions Orwell's interest in the Deep South, albeit briefly.

So it is not surprising that in 1949, the now-famous Orwell, flush with the royalties from the sales of *Nineteen Eighty-Four* in addition to those from the sales of *Animal Farm,* might have thought seriously about the possibility of visiting the United States. I suggested to Symons that Orwell's conversations with him about visiting America had been largely ignored because for many it would have involved thinking outside the Orwellian paradigm, particularly for those who see in *Nineteen Eighty-Four* the despair of a dying man who, devoid of any hope of recovery, had transferred this "hopeless" prognosis into his last novel. To have considered Orwell's plans to visit the Deep South seriously would have meant upsetting the neat theories that Orwell's certainty of his death precluded any hope in the novel. Such theories ignore, of course, Orwell's contention, with which I agree as a fellow novelist, that it is virtually impossible to write a novel, the marathon as well as the most anarchical of literary forms, without a modicum of hope.

But it should be noted that as I write this I have learned that in Barcelona the residents of the Barri Gotic (Gothic Area) have complained that in the Plaça George Orwell, security cameras overhead continue to invade their privacy.

ORWELL
THE ROAD TO AIRSTRIP ONE

INTRODUCTION

In 1948 George Orwell thought that *Nineteen Eighty-Four* might sell ten thousand copies. How wrong he was. The book, in the parlance of the trade, "took off." In a year it had sold almost half a million copies and thirty-five years later, in January 1984, it again became a bestseller, topping *The New York Times* paperback bestseller list, with over fifty thousand copies a day—in both hardcover and paperback—being sold in the United States alone.

Then, in May 1984, the discovery in London of a cache of radio scripts and letters by Orwell from the time he was working for the B.B.C. during the Second World War injected even more interest in him—for the discovery alone has reaffirmed for us that, good as it is, *Nineteen Eighty-Four* is but the final work in an intellectual journey that was often more fascinating and impressive than the book at the journey's end. *Orwell: The Road to Airstrip One* retraces this journey, concentrating on those conditions that Orwell believed could lead us into the nightmare world of totalitarian superstates in which most of us would be subservient to a minority ruling by deception and terror. The book also examines Orwell's ideas about how such a world might be prevented. It is not a biography, but I hope it will complement any such account.

While I was doing research at the Orwell Archive in London, I visited an English friend at her home in East Dulwich. Soon we were talking about Orwell. "No," she said, "I never read that book he wrote [*Nineteen Eighty-Four*] but I used to read him regularly in the *Trib* [*Tribune*]." This comment drove home to me the point that there still remain two very different audiences for Orwell's work. One, mainly British, largely recalls Orwell the journalist and essayist as well as the novelist; the other, mainly North American, remembers him almost solely as a novelist, the man who wrote *Nineteen Eighty-Four* and *Animal Farm*. In my discussion of Orwell's views, I have tried to bring the two audiences together, and I hope that a better understanding of Orwell the novelist and social and political commentator will emerge.

Specifically, I look at what Orwell has to say about imperialism, unemployment, the stultifying power of political orthodoxy, and the ever-increasing tendency of the state and society throughout the world to smother the individual. I have chosen these themes, which represented to Orwell the major injustices of his time, because Orwell's work does not lend itself readily to a single-theme approach. Such an approach, the product of overspecialization, does not tell us enough about either Orwell or his work because it ignores his diversity. He writes as passionately about the first blush of spring in "Some Thoughts on the Common Toad" as about the concentration camps of Hitler and Stalin. With equal intensity he declares, brilliantly, that "the imagination, like certain wild animals, will not breed in captivity,"[1] crankily, that "all tobacconists are Fascists!"[2] and then just as easily holds our attention with advice on how to prepare "A Nice Cup of Tea." Such diversity should not, of course, woo us into confusing the trivial with the important, but it does alert us to the fact that we need to look at more than one theme if we are to have a clear understanding of Orwell and some of his more engaging and irritating paradoxes.

Because of the existence of what I believe are two very different audiences, I have not assumed that the reader is familiar with all of Orwell's works or the previous scholarship on him and therefore have given references wherever I thought they might be helpful.

I

BURMA

CHAPTER 1

"In Moulmein, in Lower Burma, I was
hated by large numbers of people."[1]

T HAT SENTENCE IS IMPOSSIBLE TO IGNORE. LIKE SO MANY OF
Orwell's. It is what an editor calls a "grabber" and it tells us
two things immediately: that Orwell was a writer who knew how to
get a reader's attention in a hurry and that he must have *done* something to be hated by so many Burmese. What was it? The quick
answer to that is that for five years, in his early twenties, he was a
policeman in the service of Empire. The more intriguing answer is
how he came to experience imperialism at first hand—how he got to
Burma and what made him do things for which he hated himself as
much as he said the Burmese hated him.

Eric Arthur Blair (Orwell's real name) was born in 1903 at Moti-
hari in India, where his father, Richard Blair, worked in the Opium
Department of the Indian Civil Service. He was the second of three
children, one sister being five years older than he and another sister
five years younger. At one time his maternal grandfather had been a
teak merchant in Burma.

In 1907, when he got leave, Richard Blair took his family back to
England. When he returned to India some months later, his wife,
Ida, and the children remained in England at Henley-on-Thames.
Toward the end of 1911, the first year of the reign of George V and
the year of Richard Blair's final return to England, Mrs. Blair took
the advice of some Anglo-Indian acquaintances and sent eight-year-
old Eric to St. Cyprian's, a private school in Sussex. One of the
attractions of the school was that its "old boys" often ended up in
Eton, Harrow, or one of the other socially and academically prestigious public schools.*

* In the United States "public" schools are public and free of charge, but in England
the term refers to large, privately owned schools largely supported by school fees.

Blair's only close friend at St. Cyprian's, Cyril Connolly, remembers the shy young Eric as "one of those boys who seem born old."[2] The school, writes Connolly:

was typical of England before the last war; it was worldly and worshipped success, political and social; though Spartan, the death-rate was low, for it was well run and based on that stoicism which characterized the English governing class and which has since been underestimated. "Character, character, character," was the message which emerged when we rattled the radiators or the fence round the playing fields and it reverberated from the rifles in the armoury, the bullets on the miniature range, the saw in the carpenter's shop and the hoofs of the ponies on their trot to the Downs.
   Not once or twice in our rough island's story,
   The path of duty was the way to glory
was the lesson we had to learn and there were other sacred messages from the poets of the private schools: Kipling or Newbolt.
   Muscle-bound with character the alumni of St. Wulfric's [St. Cyprian's] would pass on to the best public schools, cleaning up all houses with a doubtful tone, reporting their best friends for homosexuality and seeing them expelled, winning athletic distinctions—for the house rather than themselves, for the school rather than the house, and prizes and scholarships and shooting competitions as well—and then find their vocation in India, Burma, Nigeria and the Sudan, administering with Roman justice those natives for whom the final profligate overflow of Wulfrican character was all the time predestined.[3]

Though critical of the school, Connolly concludes that St. Cyprian's was efficiently run and overall had benefited him greatly. Blair remained convinced to the end of his life that the school did him irreparable harm. Years later, writing as George Orwell, he would recall how he had been beaten and humiliated as an eight-year old for bed wetting and how capricious cruelty was an integral part of the learning process—especially for poorer boys like Blair who belonged to the lowest of the school's castes and were often humiliated over clothes and petty possessions.[4] Unlike Connolly and the other well-to-do boys, Blair had come from a relatively poor middle-class Anglo-Indian family. They could not afford to pay the full tuition, and it was arranged that young Blair would be accepted as a reduced-fee student. It was hoped that he would make up for this by working hard and would bring honor to St. Cyprian's by winning a scholarship to one of the renowned public schools. The "secret" of

---

The term *private school,* as used in England, means a privately owned and financed but usually smaller school. The state-run schools are known either as "state schools" or as "maintained schools."

his reduced-fee status was frequently thrown at him by the headmaster, who joined the headmistress in never letting young Blair forget that as "one of the poor but 'clever' boys," he was there on sufferance. The effect of all this on Blair was to produce in him a resentful but fearful submissiveness:

Whenever one had the chance to suck up, one did suck up. . . . I accepted the codes that I found in being. Once, towards the end of my time, I even sneaked to Brown [the deputy headmaster] about a suspected case of homosexuality. I did not know very well what homosexuality was, but I knew that it happened and was bad, and that this was one of the contexts in which it was proper to sneak. Brown told me I was "a good fellow," which made me feel horribly ashamed. Before Flip [the headmistress] one seemed as helpless as a snake before the snakecharmer. She had a hardly-varying vocabulary of praise and abuse, a whole series of set phrases, each of which promptly called forth the appropriate response. There was *"Buck* up, old chap!", which inspired one to paroxysms of energy; there was "don't *be* such a fool!" (or, "It's path*e*tic, isn't it?"), which made one feel a born idiot; and there was "It isn't very straight of you, is it?", which always brought one to the brink of tears. And yet all the while, at the middle of one's heart, there seemed to stand an incorruptible inner self who knew that whatever one did—whether one laughed or snivelled or went into frenzies of gratitude for small favours— one's only true feeling was hatred.[5]

The result was that Blair seldom, if ever, rebelled. His burning resentment of the pressure to conform would last all his adult life, infusing the memories of his early school days with an extraordinary and intense bitterness. Were his memories a "gross distortion," as Bernard Crick asks in his biography of Orwell?[6] Distortion or not, Blair believed that he was made to feel different as a way of forcing him to work especially hard in the scholarship class and became convinced that according to the

"armies of unalterable law," . . . the schoolmasters with their canes, the millionaires with their Scottish castles, the athletes with their curly hair . . . , I was damned. I had no money, I was weak, I was unpopular, I had a chronic cough, I was cowardly, I smelt. This picture, I should add, was not altogether fanciful. I was an unattractive boy. St. Cyprian's soon made me so, even if I had not been so before. But a child's belief in its own shortcomings is not much influenced by facts. I believed, for example, that I "smelt", but this was based simply on general probability. It was notorious that disagreeable people smelt, and therefore presumably I did so too. Again, until after I had left school for good I continued to believe that I was preternaturally ugly. It was what my schoolfellows had told me, and I had no other authority to refer to. The conviction that it was *not possible* for me to be a success went deep enough to influence my actions till far into adult life. Until I was about thirty I always planned my life on the assumption not only that any major undertaking was bound to fail, but that I could only expect to live a few years longer.[7]

Despite his hatred of the school—indeed largely through his fear of it—Eric Blair at thirteen followed the traditional expectation of his Edwardian school and won a scholarship to Eton in 1916 as England, her enthusiasm still high, entered the second year of the First World War. He was able to take up residence at Eton in 1917, when places became available because of the increasing enlistment of Etonians in the army following the disastrous losses in France.

Whatever his feeling about his earlier school, its fervent patriotism during the war years had rubbed off on Blair and would stay with him. His first published work, "Awake! Young Men of England" (which came out in October 1914, when he was still a pupil at St. Cyprian's), is an unabashed call to arms. Two years later, at Eton, despite his remark to his friend Connolly that whatever the military outcome of the great war, England would lose and his rejection of "the war, the Empire, Kipling, . . . and character,"[8] he wrote another equally exuberant and patriotic poem, "Kitchener." The poems were an early sign of a strong sense of patriotism, of being an Englishman, no matter what. This patriotism would repeatedly surface through Blair's and Orwell's (as he was later called) more pessimistic, and at times Hobbesian, view of a world where men's actions were motivated solely by the lust for power.

Despite frequent and pervasive intellectual opposition to the *idea* of war, the daily experience of witnessing patriotism, the reading of honor rolls in Eton's chapel, and the like, left Blair and the others who were too young to fight with a feeling of guilt and an emotional envy that he said would never leave them.

Despite the publication of "Kitchener," Blair did not distinguish himself academically at Eton, beginning a slacking-off period that he had promised himself after the enforced rigors of St. Cyprian's scholarship class; yet it was there that he became a voracious reader, memorizing Shaw, Chesterton, and A. E. Housman, among others. He did gain some notoriety, however, as a leader in the rebellious schoolboy atmosphere that prevailed at Eton in the mixed emotional climate of the immediate postwar period. Recalling at a later time this period of disillusionment, during which he had joined fellow Etonians on November 11, 1918, in demanding the resignation of the school's commander of the Officer Training Corps, Orwell would refer to himself as "an odious little snob." Though he was probably not much different in his snobbery than some other Etonians, there is ample evidence that he was telling the truth about his attitudes—from making disparaging remarks about his parents to the mean and flashy cynicism that he displayed upon being instructed in the Anglican catechism before being officially confirmed in the Church of England.[9]

In truth, Blair's cynicism belonged more to the head than the heart, more to his polemical streak than to his patriotic one. Later he would write:

Those years, during and just after the war, were a queer time to be at school. . . . For several years it was all the fashion to be a "Bolshie," as people then called it. England was full of half-baked antinomian opinions, . . . and of course the revolutionary mood extended to those who had been too young to fight, even to public schoolboys. At that time we all thought of ourselves as enlightened creatures of a new age, casting off the orthodoxy that had been forced upon us by those detested "old men."[10]

The tameness of the schoolboy's revolutionary stance in Blair's case is revealed in his decision in 1922, at age eighteen, to join the Indian Imperial Police. It was an unusual choice for Etonians, who, if they sought a career in the overseas Empire, usually chose the more prestigious Indian Civil Service. It is true that Blair's family could not have afforded to send him to university without scholarships—even if he had wanted to go—but his decision to be a policeman stemmed largely from his being tired of school. He wanted instead to go out into the world outside of academe in which some of his contemporaries (including Cyril Connolly) from the exceptional 1916 Election, or class, would remain before distinguishing themselves in the world of arts and letters. The author George Orwell would not become known in that world for another ten years, and the impression Blair left among his contemporaries at Eton was that of a youth who, though friendly and active enough in the school's activities, was never intimate with anyone. His reticence about his private life and thoughts had already placed him nearer to the periphery of camaraderie than at its center—without, rather than within.

In 1922 Blair left England as Probationary Assistant Superintendent of Police for Burma, which, although it was considered the poorest province in the Indian service, was the region where his family had so many roots. Because he had been unable to fight for England in the war, perhaps he hoped that some of the humiliation could be worked off in the service of Empire. Although he had declared himself against Empire and many of the ideas of Kipling (who seemed to represent imperialism) he greatly admired Kipling as a writer—particularly favoring *Kim*—and we have to be careful not to make too much of a young man of nineteen who joined an organization that he had recently criticized—a common enough hypocrisy.

In October 1922 Blair, like so many young administrators of Empire before and after him, began "the voyage out." His entry into Empire was little different from that of all those others who, in the words of E. M. Forster, would

go forth into a world that is not entirely composed of public school men or even Anglo-Saxons, but of men who are as various as the sands of the sea; into a world of whose richness and subtlety they have no conception. They go forth with well-developed bodies, fairly developed minds, and undeveloped hearts. And it is the undeveloped heart that is largely responsible for the Englishman abroad. An undeveloped heart—not a cold one. . . . For it is not that the Englishman can't feel—it is that he is afraid to feel.[11]

In Burma, "the tall, thin, and gangling"[12] Blair could not help but feel for the Burmese, who, he believed, were being shamefully exploited; but he also felt a pressure exerted against the expression of any such feeling, a pressure to conform to a guilt-ridden solidarity among the whites that stemmed, Blair believed, from the imperialists' efforts to hide their knowledge that it is clearly "wrong to go and lord it in a foreign country where you are not wanted."[13]

Despite enjoyable periods such as the Kipling-inspired romance of his tours of Mandalay, where he underwent early training, Blair was clearly unsuited for the life of an imperialist in Burma. He had acquired the reputation of being an outsider, of not mixing very well with the other Europeans, of not wanting to join in with the almost obligatory activities at one's club that were so much a part of the imperialist's life. Moreover, he was even unhappier in the outposts of Empire than he was in Mandalay, for in the field he was to come face to face with the realities of police work—not just the harsh jungle climate but the ambivalence of implementing British rules on Burmese subjects despite the official ideal of minimum interference with local custom. Of this time Orwell would write,

I had begun to have an indescribable loathing of the whole machinery of so-called justice. . . . The Burmese themselves never really recognized our jurisdiction. The thief whom we put in prison did not think of himself as a criminal justly punished, he thought of himself as the victim of a foreign conqueror. The thing that was done to him was merely a wanton meaningless cruelty. His face, behind the stout teak bars of the lock-up and the iron bars of the jail, said so clearly. And unfortunately I had not trained myself to be indifferent to the expression of the human face.[14]

Blair never did get used to what he believed was the "monstrous intrusion" of the British, and though he did not speak of his sympathy for the Burmese, this sentiment made it hard for him, unlike his colleagues, to fit into the imperialist structure. In the face of what he felt was the white man's code of silence in the East, his sense of shame found release in ineffectual rebellions in his off-duty hours.

From the more civilized society of Mandalay to the mosquito-ridden isolation of Myaungmya in the Irrawaddy Delta, to Twante in the Hanthawaddy district, where as sub-divisional police officer his duties in the mangrove- and oil-rich region could include anything from a murder investigation to ensuring routine surveillance of known criminals, Blair was considered "somewhat eccentric." It became known, for example, that he attended the religious services of Karens converted to Christianity and spent his spare time talking with Buddhist priests. He was, in the words of one of his fellow officers, "obviously odd man out with other Police Officers, but longing, I think, to be able to fit in."[15] His eccentricity stayed with him even when he moved out of the swampy terrain of the Delta in 1925 to the much more agreeable climate of Insein near Rangoon, where he had the opportunity of enjoying a more normal and civilized existence only ten miles from the capital. Indeed, in public he seemed the typical imperialist policeman, even turning up at the club each evening, but in private he continued to indulge his empathy with those over whom he had power.

Between 1926 and 1927 Blair was stationed at the port of Moulmein, where there was a relatively large white population, and later at Katha, a small town in Upper Burma. It was Katha which, despite its much better climate, would become the model for Kyauktada, the sweltering outpost town of *Burmese Days*, his first novel. After falling ill in Katha, he asked for leave six months early and left Burma for England, arriving home in August 1927.

When I came home on leave in 1927 I was already half determined to throw up my job, and one sniff of English air decided me. I was not going back to be a part of that evil despotism. But I wanted much more than merely to escape from my job. For five years I had been part of an oppressive system, and it had left me with a bad conscience. Innumerable remembered faces—

faces of prisoners in the dock, of men waiting in the condemned cells, of
subordinates I had bullied and aged peasants I had snubbed, of servants and
coolies I had hit with my fist in moments of rage (nearly everyone does these
things in the East, at any rate occasionally: Orientals can be very provok-
ing)—haunted me intolerably.[16]

In the early years of his long pilgrimage to rid himself of his imperialist guilt and as part of his latent desire to become a writer, Blair
wrote *Burmese Days* in the summer of 1932 while on holiday from a
teaching post at a private school for boys. The book, published first
in America by Harper Brothers because of fears about possible libel
actions in England, came out in October 1934.[17] Blair had begun
using the name Orwell in 1933 (Orwell is the name of a river near to
the house where Blair lived in Suffolk), a change that was itself an
attempt to break free of the past. As Peter Stansky and William Abrahams have said in *Orwell: The Transformation* (1979), it was the
beginning of what Samuel Hynes rightly calls an "imaginative identity"—a new beginning for Blair.[18] Though by temperament he was
in the tradition of the nineteenth-century liberal-radical writers like
Hazlitt, Cobbett, Dickens, and Gissing[19] in attacking what he saw
as the injustices of the established social and political order—in this
case the imperialist exploitation of the Burmese—Orwell at this point
was in the early stages of his long search for the right form. This
search reflected the increasing social and political tensions that had
been growing in England during Blair's absence in the Twenties.
Orwell would be propelled into this world through his bitterness
and disillusionment over Burma. He would later list as the "four
great motives for writing": "1. Sheer egoism. . . . 2. Aesthetic enthusiasm. Perception of beauty in the external world. . . . 3. Historical
impulse. Desire to see things as they are. . . . 4. Political purpose . . .
Desire to push the world in a certain direction, to alter other people's
idea of the kind of society that they should strive after."[20]

Orwell goes on to acknowledge how these motives must necessarily conflict at times but concedes that his strongest inclination at that
time was to follow the dictates of egoism and aestheticism, claiming
that "in a peaceful age I might have written ornate or merely descrip-
tive books" and remembering: "[Once,] I wanted to write enormous
naturalistic novels with unhappy endings, full of detailed descriptions and arresting sentences, and also full of purple passages in which
words were used partly for the sake of their sound. And in fact my
first complete novel, *Burmese Days,* which I wrote when I was thirty,

but projected much earlier, is rather that kind of book.[21]

Orwell did not live in a peaceful age, however, and even the purple, or aesthetically inspired, passages of *Burmese Days* were to be countered by a new impulse among writers in the crisis-marked Thirties. The impulse was that of "political purpose"—to attack the mounting problems of the day with a new and dynamic realism. To be silent was to collaborate with those of the old reactionary order, who were to be held responsible for many of the postwar problems as well as for the war itself. Orwell's own political purpose in his first novel was nothing more than to convince the reader that imperialism is morally wrong.

Whatever positions writers and social commentators in the crisis-ridden Thirties were taking, whether they were poets like Auden and Spender, who were sympathetic to the Marxist stance, or novelists like Greene and Waugh, who were sympathetic to the Catholic side, the significant fact was that they were taking positions. Like many of Auden's poems, they were saying that society had to be changed and the artist should do as much as possible to effect that change.

By writing *Burmese Days,* Orwell (recently returned from Burma) would breathe the same spirited air but he was not to belong to what has been called the "Auden Group" or to any other group. He belonged to himself. As in Burma, he would become the odd man out, for although he was like other writers in his belief in greater freedom as part of society's general improvement, he also maintained that freedom for a writer meant "the freedom to criticize and oppose" not just the opposing side but also your own.[22] Sympathetic to the new mood of commitment, he was opposed to the power of both its social and its political orthodoxy, which could so easily use appeals for unity—against Fascism, for example—to corrupt the truth and stifle a dissenting opinion. This theme of the individual versus the group, which was to culminate in *Nineteen Eighty-Four,* first found voice in *Burmese Days*—his testament to the power of imperialism's orthodoxy over the individual in an outpost of Empire.

Burmese Days is set in Kyauktada, a small and "fairly typical Upper Burma town, that had not changed greatly between the days of Marco Polo and 1910, and might have slept in the Middle Ages for a century more if it had not proved a convenient spot for a railway terminus. In 1910 the Government made it the headquarters of a district and seat of Progress—interpretable as a block of law courts . . . a hospital, a school and one of those huge, durable jails which the English have built everywhere between Gibraltar and Hong Kong."[23] The protagonist of the novel is John Flory, who was said to have been called George Orwell in one of Blair's early drafts of the book.[24] Flory is a timber merchant of about thirty-five whose youth has been sapped by the trials of living in Kyauktada. The only other Europeans in the population of four thousand—odd are the heavy-set, middle-aged Macgregor, deputy commissioner of Kyauktada district; Mr. Lackersteen—also middle-aged—the alcoholic manager of a timber firm; Lackersteen's wife, whose complaints against the natives are as frequent as Macgregor's anecdotes; Westfield, the soldierly district superintendent of police; Maxwell, a young forest ranger with a blood lust; and Ellis, another timber merchant, whose dialogue is nearly always offensive to someone and whose vehemence against the natives is without respite. Later in the novel, the Lackersteen's niece, Elizabeth, and Verral, an arrogant young cavalry officer, appear.

The plot revolves about the attempt of a corrupt native magistrate, U Po Kyin, to gain favor in the eyes of his British superiors and thereby make himself eligible for membership in the hitherto all-white Kyauktada Club. To do this, however, U Po Kyin must first rid himself of an unwitting competitor, Dr. Veraswami, an Indian doctor and good friend of John Flory. U Po Kyin's scheming is often inspired by a clumsy kind of inventiveness: for example, at one point he uses an ex-mistress of Flory to disgrace him publicly—thus diminishing Flory's worth in the eyes of Elizabeth Lackersteen, with whom Flory has fallen in love and whom he plans to marry. Although Flory hopes to reinstate himself in Elizabeth's heart, his plans are dashed by U Po Kyin's intrigue, along with Dr. Veraswami's hopes of joining the Club.

More important to the story than U Po Kyin's attempt to gain prestige, however, are Flory's thwarted attempts to preserve a sense of right and wrong in an outpost of Empire where questions of morality are often buried beneath concerns about "hanging together" in the face of a much larger, if subservient, population. The success of U Po Kyin's scheming, Flory's love–hate feelings about Burma in general, and his special hatred of imperialism and what it does to ruler and ruled alike, combine to cause the sensitive Flory to give up the battle between his conscience and the pressures of the small white community. In a state of consummate alienation from his original environment, he commits suicide.

The story unfolds in the oppressive tropical climate of the Burmese jungle; indeed, the jungle becomes the central metaphor for the seemingly uncontrollable forces that encroach upon one's sense of individuality. From the very beginning of the book, Orwell creates an atmosphere of an irrepressible natural force of evolutionary struggle: "By the roadside, just before you got to the jail, the fragments of a stone pagoda were littered, cracked and overthrown by the strong roots of a peepul tree. The angry carved faces of demons looked up from the grass where they had fallen. Nearby another peepul tree had twined itself round a palm, uprooting it and bending it backwards in a wrestle that had lasted a decade."[25] We are constantly made aware that climate and vegetation play an important part, not only in aging a man more rapidly than in England, but in forming his political beliefs and behaviour. As Flory walked down to the Club,

the heat throbbed down on one's head with a steady, rhythmic thumping, like blows from an enormous bolster. . . . In the borders beside the path swaths of English flowers—phlox and larkspur, hollyhock and petunia—not yet slain by the sun, rioted in vast size and richness. The petunias were huge, like trees almost. There was no lawn, but instead a shrubbery of native trees and bushes—gold mohur trees like vast umbrellas of blood-red bloom, frangipanis with creamy, stalkless flowers, purple bougainvillea, scarlet hibiscus and the pink Chinese rose, bilious-green crotons, feathery fronds of tamarind. The clash of colours hurt one's eyes in the glare.[26]

In the midst of this luxuriant growth, this undisciplined riot of color, this disorder, which reflects nature's overindulgence, a concomitant sapping of a man's will occurs. There is a lack of discipline evident in Flory's increasing degeneracy, his gin-swilling before breakfast, his refusal to shave, and the gradual erosion of his integrity. His behavior constitutes a personal revolt against order, an order so often mirrored in the artificially created and highly ordered polity about him. It is a revolt that can find no other way of expressing itself beneath the omnipresent stares of his fellow imperialists than by a studied slovenliness. On the one hand, it vulgarly asserts the remnants of his individualism, and on the other, it asserts his desire to be at one with the immediate environment of an unrestrained jungle.

The naturalistic image of the jungle continues to be dominant throughout the story, even in the final moments before Flory's suicide, when he desperately pleads with Elizabeth: " 'Do try and understand. Haven't I told you something of the life we live here?

The sort of horrible death-in-life! The *decay*, the loneliness, the self-pity?' "[27] (The italics are mine.)

Burmese Days is atypical of the main body of Orwell's work. Revealing his impulse for the aesthetic as well as his commitment to attacking an "oppressive system," it relies more heavily on the naturalistic than on the mechanistic metaphor that is so often present in later works such as *The Road to Wigan Pier* and *Nineteen Eighty-Four*, in which the imagery of the machine is savagely and depressingly dominant. The book is typical, however, in its fundamentally moralist stance and in its treatment of individuals as embodiments of different world views. Most typical of all is the way in which Orwell paradoxically concentrates on the most deviant individual of a group in order to draw a picture of the conformist. In *Burmese Days*, the conformist is the stereotype imperialist who justifies exploitation of the natives through a firm conviction that he is superior in all respects.

Like Orwell, who believed that "no man, in his heart of hearts, believes that it is right to invade a foreign country and hold the population down by force,"[28] Flory believes that imperialism is at root an evil system. In his battle to retain his integrity within this system, he finds solace only in his friendship with Veraswami. Even so, he is always painfully aware of the distance between men, even between friends. If it is the "hideous birthmark" on his face that is the daily symbol of his alienation from his fellow Europeans, it is a fundamental difference in outlook that marks his disagreements with Veraswami. Whereas Veraswami is an Indian who looks down on the Burmese and passively accepts the British presence as an "advance," Flory sees it as an outrage against the Burmese. Yet when Veraswami is nominated for membership in the white man's club, in a grudging response to a Rangoon directive, Flory buckles under the pressure of his fellow Englishmen and fails to stand up for his Indian friend.

Although Flory's later support of Veraswami's nomination testifies to a latent integrity, it also reveals the seesawing nature of the tensions within him. At the same time that he desperately wants to stand up for the principle of equality between whites and natives, he just as desperately feels the need to belong to his own kind. No matter how much he might ridicule the conventions of his fellow Englishmen, he knows that within those conventions there is a comradeship and sense of security that are essential if one is to survive in a foreign clime. Each time he approaches the club, which is the focal point of events for the white community in Kyauktada, Flory recognizes that there is a price to be paid for such survival and the currency is hypocrisy. To him the most scurrilous hypocrisy of all is the way in which the whites justify their blatant exploitation of the natives: their claim that the latter are so backward that the white man is morally obliged to help them "develop" their natural resources and to fulfill the larger imperative to bring progress to ungodly peoples.

Essentially, Orwell sees imperialism as a parasitic venture of the colonialist upper classes to create jobs for their sons as well as to maintain and increase their power at home. Accordingly, Orwell (through Flory) describes the imperialists as constituting "a kind of up-to-date, hygienic, self-satisfied louse," and, presaging his sustained and spirited attack upon one of the most pervasive metaphors of his time, decries what he believed to be the guise of the "slimy *white man's burden* humbug." (The italics are mine.) This, he says, perpetuates the fiction that the white man establishes empires to better the natives instead of robbing them. Such a fiction is not the sole property of missionaries, but is tenaciously held by all whites as an excuse for their unwanted presence.[29]

Such hypocrisy, says Flory, leads to a perpetual feeling of guilt that generates a never-ending attempt by the whites to rationalize their actions and is at the heart of the imperialists' ill treatment of the natives.[30] Orwell gives us examples of how the moral hypocrisy of imperialism corrupts Flory, having him sign the notice at the Club that postpones discussion of Veraswami's election. Though ashamed of his action, Flory gives in to the "kind of spurious good-fellowship between the English and this country. . . . Hanging together, we call it. It's a political necessity." Later, when Veraswami says to Flory that if he, Flory, really disapproved of Empire he would surely make his views public, Flory answers, "Sorry, doctor . . . I haven't the guts. I 'counsel ignoble ease.' . . . It's safer. You've got to be a pukka sahib or die, in this country. In fifteen years I've never talked honestly to anyone except you. My talks here are a safety-valve, a little Black Mass on the sly."[31]

Flory's talks with Veraswami are not an effective enough safety valve, nor is his gin swilling. It is Flory's acute awareness of his own guilt and the hypocrisy of the white community in general, expressed in their choice of self-justifying imagery, that leads him to spend as much time as he can among the natives and to confess to Elizabeth during their visit to the bazaar, "I try—just sometimes, when I have the pluck—*not* to be a pukka sahib."[32] With this in mind and remembering that Flory was called Orwell in an early draft of *Burmese Days*, it is interesting to note a particularly revealing report on Orwell's service in Burma:

But if in public he conformed to what was expected of him at Headquarters and the Club, in private he could indulge his eccentricities. Beadon, who came out to see him one day when he was living at Insein, found his house a shambles, with "goats, geese, ducks and all sorts of things floating about downstairs." Beadon, who prided himself on his own neat house, was "rather shattered," and suggested to Blair that perhaps he might bear down on his houseman. The suggestion was shrugged aside: he quite liked the house as it was. Beadon changed the subject—was it true, as he had heard, that Blair was attending services in the native churches? Yes, it was true; it had nothing to do with "religion," of course, but he enjoyed conversing with the priests in "very high-flown Burmese" (Beadon's phrase); and he added in his sardonic (or leg pulling) way that he found their conversation more interesting than that he was forced to listen to at the Club. Whereupon he took Beadon off for a farewell drink—at the Club!—before he set off for Rangoon.[33]

In his quest to expiate his guilt, Flory does not attack only the traditional, often missionary-inspired, idioms and metaphors that had often been used to justify imperialism as a moral responsibility of the white man; he also ridicules those images that were almost entirely derived from an amoral and nonreligious belief in the white man's allround superiority in the natural order of things. Examples of this belief abound throughout the novel, as when Mrs. Lackersteen irritably proclaims, "Really I think the laziness of these servants is getting too shocking. We seem to have no *authority* over the natives nowadays, with all these dreadful Reforms, and the insolence they learn from the newspapers. In some ways they are getting almost as bad as the lower classes at home." In another case the timber merchant Ellis vehemently asserts, "The only possible policy is to treat 'em like the dirt they are. . . . *We are the masters.*" Elizabeth, too, displays her particular sense of superiority when, after Flory has pointed out to her that statistically it is really more natural to have a brown skin than a white one, she concludes, "You *do* have some funny ideas."[34]

Just as Flory dismisses the idea that European skulls are supposedly more sensitive to sunstroke than those of the natives, Orwell would later write:

But why should the British in India have built up this superstition about sunstroke? Because an endless emphasis on the differences between the "natives" and yourself is one of the necessary props of imperialism. You can only rule over a subject race, especially when you are in a small minority, if you honestly believe yourself to be racially superior, and it helps towards this if you can believe that the subject race is *biologically* different. There were quite a number of ways in which Europeans in India used to believe, without any evidence, that Asiatic bodies differed from their own. Even quite considerable anatomical differences were supposed to exist. But this nonsense about Europeans being subject to sunstroke and Orientals not, was the most cherished superstition of all. The thin skull was the mark of racial superiority, and the pith topi was a sort of emblem of imperialism.[35]

Out of such observations as this there emerged one of Orwell's most celebrated warnings: that "once you have the habit" of using phrases invented by someone else, such as "the white man's burden," without examining the appropriateness of the image, then "if thought corrupts language, language can also corrupt thought" because a bad habit spreads through imitation. He went on, "When you think of something abstract [such as imperialism] you are more inclined to use words from the start, and unless you make a conscious effort to prevent it, the existing dialect will come rushing in and do the job for you, at the expense of blurring or even changing your meaning.[36]

At this point it should be noted that Orwell's tendency to think of imperialism as a "selfsatisfied louse," more or less synonymous with exploitation and always turning a profit rather than (as others have claimed) being an economic burden on the home country, involves sweeping assumptions, to say the least. In constantly reflecting the belief that economic imperialism was synonymous with imperialism as a whole, Orwell succumbed in part to that habit which he warned us about. The likeness he saw in this instance between economic imperialism and imperialism excluded the possibility of sincerity among those who claimed the moral obligation of the white man's burden.

Orwell knew better, but apart from Macgregor, the generally amiable deputy commissioner, he chose not to suggest that any of those in Kyauktada might have been moved by a genuine belief that they were spreading civilization. If nothing else could convince him, his parents' finances should have provided him with ample evidence that not all imperialists were out for rapacious gain and alerted him to the fact that, as John Atkins points out, even with the added benefit of servants, "British officials in Burma," [were often] as much victims of circumstances in their way as the Burmese themselves."[37]

However, the importance of noting Flory's simplistic assumptions about the nature of imperialism is that they reflect both the frustrations and the confusion of a sensitive individual when confronted by the orthodoxy of the pukka sahib's code in an outpost of Empire; and while Orwell ignores the possibility of the benevolent imperialist in his novel, the fact that nowadays such phrases and images as "the white man's burden" can no longer be used to camouflage the profit motive, however small or large a part it played, is due very much to Orwell and those like him who were prepared to attack what they saw as the habitual invocation of the metaphor. Further, his attack in general upon the language used to rationalize the exploitation of a foreign country also shows that Orwell was already well aware of the dangers of living with the lies of *unconscious* propaganda—in this case the slogans of imperialism. Flory warns of a time to come when "all the gramophones [will be] playing the same tune"— the same slogans.[38] It is against this possibility that Flory fights and loses.

Flory's alienation from the imperialist system stems in part from his difficulty in living outside the comforting, security-assuring customs of a more industrialized society like Britain. At home in a pub one could seek private consolation among friends for the improprieties of one's public behavior, but for Flory there is no such consolation, and his guilt stays with him. At one point he wants to help his friend Veraswami, who is under insidious attack from U Po Kyin, but he does not offer assistance, "for he knew the uselessness of interfering in Oriental quarrels. No European ever gets to the bottom of these quarrels; there is always something impervious to the European mind, a conspiracy behind the conspiracy, a plot within the plot."[39]

In Orwell's view, even if one does act, there is no easy way of discussing the right or wrong of the situation because "one of the Ten Precepts of the pukka sahib" is "to keep out of 'native' quarrels." The observance of this precept, the lack of opportunity to speak one's mind or even to simply "admit that we're thieves and go on thieving without any humbug,"[40] not only stems from but reinforces what Orwell calls the pukka sahib's code. The code, designed to ensure solidarity among the whites, is particularly strong in a small outpost   . of empire where the white minority does not have the benefit of a large garrison. This was especially true at the time of Orwell's stay in Burma, "[in] remote locations where violence prevailed and during a time when the British in the 'backward tracts' were making a desperate stand against any rumours of aspirations for freedom which might have come from Rangoon through educated Indian missionaries and British reformers."[41]

For all the moral outrage upon seeing a subject people consciously exploited by his own race, Flory is no stranger to the quest for solidarity. Well before a native attack upon the Club, Flory, counselling "ignoble ease," expresses to his friend Veraswami his fear of being alienated from his fellows. Orwell believed that this fear permeated all the white men's lives and resulted in their submission to five chief "beatitudes" of the pukka sahib's code, even if, like Flory, they did not believe in it. The five chief beatitudes are:

> Keeping up our prestige,
> The firm hand (without the velvet glove),
> We white men must hang together,
> Give them an inch and they'll take an ell, and
> *Esprit de Corps*.[42]

Such a code creates a sense of group safety, as well as serving to buffer the cultural shock of newcomers from England like Elizabeth Lackersteen. The observance of such a code in the Club also offers some refuge for those imperialists like Flory who feel alienated from the world at large. Whatever its failings, including its hypocrisy, the Club is at least a place to meet, to read newspapers from home, to reminisce. Here even Flory, who is painfully conscious of his facial birthmark—the stark physical symbol of his alienation—can seek relief in the ginandtonic rituals of apparent normality (the gin being added to the bittertasting tonic, or antimalarial quinine water, to make the water more palatable). The danger, however, is that like the occasional drink that turns to habit, what was once a temporary refuge can become a permanent way of life. In his temporary effort to avoid censure from the rest of the white community, the once-occasional visitor becomes a permanent captive of the Club's hypocrisy:

> It is a stifling, stultifying world in which to live. It is a world in which every word and every thought is censored. . . . You are free to be a drunkard, an idler, a coward, a backbiter, a fornicator; but you are not free to think for yourself. Your opinion on every subject of any conceivable importance is dictated for you by the pukka sahibs' code.
> In the end the secrecy of your revolt poisons you like a secret disease. Your whole life is a life of lies. Year after year you sit in Kipling-haunted little Clubs, whiskey to right of you, *Pink'un* to left of you, listening and eagerly agreeing while Colonel Bodger develops his theory that these bloody Nationalists should be boiled in oil. You hear your Oriental friends called "greasy little babus," and you admit, dutifully, that they *are* greasy little

babus. You see louts fresh from school kicking grey-haired servants. The time comes when you burn with hatred of your own countrymen, when you long for a native rising to drown their Empire in blood. And in this there is nothing honourable, hardly even any sincerity. For, *au fond,* what do you care if the Indian Empire is a despotism, if Indians are bullied and exploited? You only care because the right of free speech is denied you. You are a creature of the despotism, a pukka sahib, tied tighter than a monk or a savage by an unbreakable system of tabus.[43]

The result, particularly in a small community like Kyauktada, is that the whites, through fear of being ostracized, become the stereotypes of imperialism, daily reinforcing (and so perpetuating) prejudices. The alternative to this life, where acceptance is sometimes bought at the price of selfrespect is to opt out—as Flory finally does by committing suicide, his secret world of books and unuttered thoughts having failed to console him.

Nevertheless, Flory is the exception, and the stereotypes survive. They go on moving like puppets in time to an unchanging tune, for what Orwell shows us is that the strength of imperialism—at least at the local level—lies not in a readiness to change, but in an unchanging allegiance to the pukka sahib's code. Because of every man's need to be accepted by his fellows, because, in Flory's words, "it would be better to be the thickest-skulled pukka sahib who ever hiccuped over 'Forty years on,' than to live silent, alone, consoling oneself in secret, sterile worlds," Orwell feared that the world wherein "every word and thought is censored" would grow unimpeded and through force, culminate in the massive, all-embracing specter he would later write about in *Nineteen Eighty-Four.*[44] Here, through the proliferation of the gramophone mind of club-like Inner Party existence, group pressure would be *continually* mobilized to force the individual into adhering to the official line.

Among his descriptions of the stereotypes in *Burmese Days,* Orwell's portrait of Mrs. Lackersteen has special significance in that it draws attention to how pressure is aggressively exerted by the women as well as by the men. It illustrates U Po Kyin's recognition of the "power of European women" in the imperialist structure. Mrs. Lackersteen's authority and influence over much of Mr. Lackersteen's action is exerted through her "burra memsahib" expectations. Mrs. Lackersteen does not nag her husband with her prejudices; she simply makes it known that she holds certain unalterable beliefs about the natives and expects her husband to support these views at all times. In this context Mr. Lackersteen is representative of all those imperialists who really did not care about politics at all, but nevertheless perpetuated some of imperialism's evils for no other reason than they were afraid of their wives. In front of his wife, Lackersteen enthusiastically announces to the Club members that he will blackball any native nominated for membership. Knowing that his wife constantly suspects him of drinking, "he felt that a display of sound sentiment would excuse him."

Lackersteen could always be replied [sic] upon for sound sentiments in a case like this. In his heart he did not care and never had cared a damn for the British Raj, and he was as happy drinking with an Oriental as with a white man; but he was ready with a loud "Hear, hear!" when anyone suggested the bamboo for disrespectful servants or boiling oil for Nationalists. He prided himself that though he might booze a bit and all that, dammit, he *was* loyal. It was his form of responsibility.[45]

In the presentation of such characters Orwell makes a contribution to our understanding of how the imperialism of his time produced social as well as political stereotypes. It is the restraint placed upon the Mr. Lackersteens by wives like his and by all the clubs in the Empire that helped guarantee the stability of Empire at the grass roots because they did not question traditional norms.

While Flory is only too conscious of the possibility (never far away in the outposts of the Empire) of falling victim through loneliness to an "inner secret life," he is just as aware of how marriage may not improve matters. On the contrary, he knows that life may be worse beneath the debilitating power of someone like Mrs. Lackersteen, "some damned memsahib, yellow and thin, scandalmongering over cocktails, making kit-kit with the servants, living twenty years in the country without learning a word of the language." It is such a woman who, through silent coercion, prevents her husband from even uttering, let alone practicing, his capacity for tolerance. Instead, through the medium of the evil eye, she cajoles him into supporting her supremacist philosophy. Indeed, it is the final despair of the novel that Elizabeth Lackersteen, rather than becoming someone who would help Flory "to live with nothing hidden, nothing unexpressed," ends up, after her marriage to Macgregor, as yet another dull stereotype of imperialism: "Her servants live in terror of her, though she speaks no Burmese. She has an exhaustive knowledge of the Civil List, gives charming little dinner-parties and knows how to put the wives of subordinate officials in their places— in short, she fills with complete success the position for which Nature had designed her from the first, that of a burra memsahib."[46] This, together with the pressure applied on the individual by the club, calls to mind the observation that the ruling elite of *Burmese Days* differs from that of *Nineteen Eighty-Four* only "in one important respect, . . . [namely, that] it maintains its solidarity not by physical power, but solely by the strength of an amazingly inflexible public opinion."[47]

Apart from the social prohibitions that were in force at the local level, Orwell argued that the reluctance of *officials* to discuss imperial policy stemmed from the fact that although every Anglo-Indian functionary was haunted by a sense of guilt, he usually concealed it because to be overheard might damage his career. He recalls a night aboard a train in Burma when he met a stranger, a white educational officer. After each had decided "that the other was 'safe,' " they talked for hours in the darkness, damning the Empire; but "in the haggard morning light when the train crawled into Mandalay, we parted as guiltily as any adulterous couple."[48] It has been charged that Orwell's conclusion that Anglo-Indians were afraid to criticize the Empire is exaggerated. Even allowing for the fact that during his time in Burma the white communities in outlying districts tended to band together more than usual in the face of increasing political unrest, it does seem that Orwell's own reticence to speak freely about the administration in Burma, not uncommon among young subalterns, led him to believe that all officials acted as he did.[49]

Whether or not it is overdrawn, Flory's reluctance to criticize imperialism among his fellow whites is revealing in that it alerts us to one of the main themes running through *Burmese Days:* despite the division of the whites into two main parts—the civil servants like Macgregor, Westfield (the police officer), and Maxwell (the divisional forest officer) and the entrepreneurs like Ellis, Lackersteen, and Flory—all of them behave as if they had the same occupation, that of a bureaucrat. This is especially evident when, in response to Rangoon's directive that "in those Clubs where there are no native members, one at least shall be co-opted," Ellis, though not a bureaucrat, complains bitterly, " 'They've [Rangoon has] no right to dictate to us when we're off duty.' "[50] The fact that Rangoon sent such a directive pertaining to clubs shows how even the central authorities of the imperialist structure considered the Club at Kyauktada—and, indeed, all clubs—as an appendage of the administration. Even Flory, who irritates the others by saying "some Bolshie things sometimes,"[51] unhesitatingly acts in unison with his fellow members when the Club is besieged by natives quite rightly demanding retribution after Ellis has struck and blinded a native youth. In this, the climactic irony of the book, it is Ellis, the man who most opposes Flory, who provides Flory with the chance to win the white community's friendship and admiration. Flory saves the Club from being overrun by first swimming down the river—not against it—and then quietly organizing a small police detachment to thwart the angry mob.

The scene in which Ellis canes and blinds the Burmese boy, arousing the mob's fury, almost certainly owes something to the following incident described by Dr. Maung Htin Aung:

> One afternoon, at about 4 P.M., the suburban railway station of Pagoda Road was crowded with schoolboys and undergraduates, and Blair came down the stairs to take the train to the Mission Road Station, where the exclusive Gymkhana Club was situated. One of the boys, fooling about with his friends, accidentally bumped against the tall and gaunt Englishman, who fell heavily down the stairs. Blair was furious and raised the heavy cane that he was carrying, to hit the boy on the head, but checked himself, and struck him on the back instead. The boys protested and some undergraduates, including myself, surrounded the angry Englishman. . . . The train drew in and Blair boarded a first-class carriage. But in Burma, unlike India, first-class carriages were never taboo to natives, and some of us had first-class season tickets. The argument between Blair and the undergraduates continued. Fortunately, the train reached Mission Road Station without further incident, and Blair left the train.[52]

In *Burmese Days* the irony of Ellis having indirectly created such an opportunity for Flory to win the respect of his fellow whites is compounded by the fact that Flory's heroic action stems not from supporting the exploited natives, with whom he normally sympathizes, but results instead from him instinctively succumbing to the inviolable rule of the pukka sahib's code—that white men must stick together. Conditioned by their everyday existence in Kyauktada, "none of them [the whites] thought to blame Ellis, the sole cause of this affair; [and] their common peril seemed, indeed, to draw them closer together for the while."[53] Consequently, if most characters in *Burmese Days* appear to be stereotypes of imperialists, this is not so much a reflection of Orwell's hostility toward imperialism or of a lack of imagination as of his view of imperialism as an experience that forces people at the local level to conform to a rigid code of behavior because of a need to feel collectively secure. It is, at worst, the mind-set of a garrison; at best, the outlook of a small town.

Thus, Orwell argues that the life of an imperialist molds you, whether you like it or not, into a straight-jacket of conformity. In his view, no matter how independently you start out, the pressures and needs of mutual dependence as a way of guaranteeing a modicum of security and simple companionship make escape from the resulting "stifling, stultifying world" all but impossible. Indeed, the idea of escape seems so hopeless that when Flory can no longer tolerate the tension between the dictates of his conscience and his opposing inclination to live according to the Club's code—"with the stream of life, not against it"[54]—he shoots himself.

In considering Flory as an example of a man torn between the individual need to act morally and the group's pressure on him to conform, it is worthwhile looking at a later essay of Orwell's, "Shooting an Elephant," which was inspired by his experience as a police officer in Moulmein, Lower Burma, where "I was hated by large numbers of people." The conclusion of the essay, in which Orwell describes how he was called upon to execute an old elephant who had temporarily gone berserk and destroyed some native property, is a fine example of how even *outside* the club group pressure was at work, how the secret world of the individual and the requirements of institutional imperialism continued to clash: "All I knew was that I was stuck between my hatred of the empire I served and my rage against the evil-spirited little beasts who tried to make my job impossible. With one part of my mind I thought of the British Raj as an unbreakable tyranny, as something clamped down, *in saecula saeculorum*, upon the will of prostrate peoples; with another part I thought that the greatest joy in the world would be to drive a bayonet into a Buddhist priest's guts." Going to find the by-now passive elephant, Orwell is followed by an ever-growing crowd. Although he initially decides not to destroy the elephant, who is now "peacefully eating" and looks "no more dangerous than a cow," upon looking around at the "immense crowd, two thousand at the least and growing every minute," he suddenly realizes

that I should have to shoot the elephant after all. The people expected it of me and I had got to do it. . . . And it was at this moment, as I stood there with the rifle in my hands, that I first grasped the hollowness, the futility of the white man's dominion in the East. Here was I, the white man with his gun, standing in front of the unarmed native crowd—seemingly the leading actor of the piece; but in reality I was only an absurd puppet pushed to and fro by the will of those yellow faces behind.

Orwell thus argues that "when the white man turns tyrant it is his own freedom that he destroys" and that "in every crisis he has got to do what the 'natives' expect of him."[55] He shows how the acts of those in authority can not only be modified by subjects' expectation, but can actually be changed into a gesture of subjection rather than one of dominance. The pressure exerted on the imperialist official by a subject's expectations on such occasions could overrule that official's personality to the extent that it didn't matter in the end whether the assistant district officer was Eric Blair or "John Smith"—both would react in pretty much the same way.

It is this very predictability of the whites' master–slave behavior toward the natives that more than anything else, characterizes the stereotypes drawn from Orwell's imperialist experience in Burma and offers an early indication of his later rich-versus-poor view of the world.[56] In this view, conformity's victory over Flory would be repeated again and again, and it is the novel's pessimistic pronouncement that despite individual exceptions, the imperialist–totalitarian mentality would triumph over all who dared to challenge it. As one commentator noted, "The white society of Upper Burma, as Orwell portrays it, is the earliest prototype of the ruling elite of Oceania which he described fourteen years later in *Nineteen Eighty-Four*."[57]

In particular, *Burmese Days* shows us that what Orwell calls the "secret world" of conscience is not sufficient to counteract an individual's guilt of willful hypocrisy in the outside world. It shows how the unavailability of alternatives to the stereotyped code of behavior sometimes leads to personal tragedy. Such tragedy failed to make any difference to the administration of imperialism, however, because imperialism's code was pervaded by the sense that no one was irreplaceable and by the belief that all whites must follow in the same way the same code of behavior, when dealing with the natives, whether in shooting an elephant or in confronting an angry mob. Any deviation might encourage the ruled to question the infallibility of the rulers, and (more dangerously) cause the rulers to question their own infallibility.

The assumption of replaceability, together with the mandatory *esprit de corps*, often created an óverwhelming feeling of being totally submerged by a changeless conformity—even if one was only *slightly* deviant from the norm. This conformity was so oppressive that it left such an individual with only two alternatives— either to capitulate totally to the system or to withdraw totally. Partial withdrawal, especially in a small outpost—a small town—like Kyauktada, was impossible. Orwell sees the larger problem in this situation of the autonomous individual doomed to an anxiety-ridden existence, torn between what his conscience tells him is right and the expediency that is nurtured by the need for brotherhood. It is a theme that he would never leave, and it is this sense of hopelessness in such circumstances that gave birth to his haunting fear of (and later obsession with) totalitarianism. In *Nineteen Eighty-Four* we would see the ultimate triumph, not of minorities, as among the white population of Kyauktada, but of the mass, the petty imperialists of self-interest. For them as well as for the white minority in Kyauktada the sense of security is guaranteed by the growth of order and predictability but threatened by the deviant individual who dares mirror their own fears and doubts about the justice of the system they serve.

In Flory's case it was mainly a battle against "living the lie . . . that we're here to uplift our poor black brothers instead of to rob them." Orwell's experience of how this lie, the basis of imperialism as he saw it, "corrupts us in ways you can't imagine"[58] became the seed from which one of his most arresting and pervasive ideas would grow: that "to be corrupted by totalitarianism one does not have to live in a totalitarian country. The mere prevalence of certain ideas can spread a kind of poison that makes one subject after another impossible for literary [and ultimately other] purposes."[59] Orwell explains how the pressures to conform are so powerful that quite apart from forcing exploited and exploiter alike to conform to a bureaucratically imposed set of norms, the imperialist experience permeates not only the nine-to-five life of a colonial bureaucrat, but every hour of every day in the lives of all those who come in contact with it. That is why you cannot escape it.

One of those norms, of course, is the attitude, not only of male officials but of their wives, toward the natives. When Mrs. Lackersteen says of them, "In some ways they are getting almost as bad as the lower classes at home,"[60] she invokes the widespread analogy between natives and the English working class. This, together with the whites' frequent comparison of natives to children, seriously influenced many imperialist perceptions of nonwhite communities throughout the British colonies.[61] It was his recognition of the pervasiveness of the native–working class analogy that later led Orwell to make some of his best contributions on the nature and role of class differences. These contributions came after, but grew out of, his simplistic conclusion that "the English working class . . . were the symbolic victims of injustice, playing the same part in England as the Burmese played in Burma."[62]

Before leaving *Burmese Days* and Orwell's views of imperialism, I would like to discuss what this first novel tells us about Orwell as political and social commentator. The first thing that becomes apparent from his criticism is that the young Orwell was potentially a better journalist and essayist than he was a novelist. He has the polemicist's thrust, guided by a journalistic penchant for the exaggerated lead paragraph, which grabs the reader's attention. More interested in situations than in characters, he uses the latter, like chess men, as representatives and victims of group attitudes. It is an approach that can quickly classify opposing forces in the short space of journalism but dulls the sense of nuance so vital to the more literary device of the novel. Sociological categories, "characteristics rather than characters,"[63] as one commentator points out, are what we see, and, of course, these are easier to deal with if one has a didactic purpose in mind.

Beyond the portrayal of Flory as victim, there is a blind eye in *Burmese Days* to the exception among the "oppressors," an unwillingness to look beyond mere category to an individual of honorable intent—to the Fielding-like character in Forster's *A Passage to India,* for example. Instead, through Flory's eyes we get the impression that all imperialists are bad, just as in Flory's view of the world you are either a failure or not a failure. There is no middle ground: you are either in or out. Orwell's protagonist could never accept that there is a middle ground where it is possible for the moral man to win contentment by working for improvement within an imperfect system. It is a position that Orwell himself could not accept in his own role of imperial policeman and that predisposed him to the simplistic master–slave, rich–poor world view of his early writings.

Unfortunately, because Blair—the "odd man out"—ignored the middle position, Orwell's subsequent pronouncements on imperialism ignore the possibility of guilt-free, happy imperialists such as one of his former colleagues, who stated, "I loved Burma and the Burman and have no regrets that I spent the best years of my life in the Burmese police."[64] The ultimate rejection by Flory of compromise, and his penchant for the sweeping master–slave generalizations, stem from Orwell's habit of assuming that his experience was typical—in this case that his experience in the outposts[65] would have been duplicated in the headquarters of Empire. As a result, there is little or no attempt to suggest that Flory's criticisms of imperialism, so forthrightly stated that they gain the force of a condemnation of all imperialists, are really applicable only to imperialism at the *local level* rather than to imperialism as a whole. Devoid of such qualification, the master–slave view, not only of imperialism but of the world in general, would travel back to England with Eric Blair in August 1927.

II

ENGLAND

CHAPTER 2

For blair, on leave from Burma in the fall of 1927, the need to "expiate" the "immense weight" of imperialist guilt, allied with his lifelong desire to be a writer, precipitated a decision that he would not return to be a part of that "evil despotism." He resigned his commission in the imperial police, determined that he had need to go as far as Burma to find tyranny and exploitation. Here in England, down under one's feet, were the submerged working class, suffering miseries which in their different way were as bad as any an Oriental knew . . . it was in this way that my thoughts turned toward the English working class."[1]

The poor and the English working class had, of course, existed when Eric Blair left for Burma, and evidence of poverty and working-class conditions had abounded even for a relatively sheltered King's Scholar at Eton. In 1921, the year before he left for the Far East, there had been a general strike and the birth of the "dole," and in 1922 unemployment already exceeded 1.5 million.[2] There is no reason, however, to assume that Blair the schoolboy was either very conscious of or concerned with the obviously worsening situation in Britain.

Six years later, however, the evidence in England of physical and psychic exhaustion following World War I had a profound effect on him. In one of his first articles as a professional writer, he claimed that whereas before World War I England had been "the winner; today she is the loser. There we have in two words the source of all the evil."[3] The evil was unemployment; the losers the unemployed. After Burma, beginning his pilgrimage of expiation, he wanted to join the losers: "I wanted to submerge myself, to get right down among the oppressed."[4]

The nineteen-year-old Blair who had left England five years before in 1922 had not wanted to be an anti-imperialist or to rub shoulders with the poor. This had been the youth who had not only written "Awake! Young Men of England!" but had, after "his first adventure as an amateur tramp," concluded that while he was "very proud" of the "adventure" he would not repeat it.[5] The Eric Blair who came back from Burma would repeat it, and so would Orwell—no longer as a schoolboy looking at the world of tramps and unemployed from afar, but as an adult going among the lower classes from a sense of duty rather than adventure. He would repeat it in an England where the collapse of the postwar boom amid the dramatic rise in England's trade deficit (exports declining by 47.9 percent in 1921, compared with 1920), the beginning of protective tariffs, the hunger marches of the unemployed, the stringent economies proposed by the Geddes' committee, and the coal and general strikes of 1926 had left a bitter legacy. The dole, in particular, which J. B. Priestley reported as characterizing the "fourth" England,[6] had long ceased to be regarded simply as a legislative agent of relief. Instead, it had become a way of life, a symbol of hated charity by both those who needed it and those who did not. A symbol of society's failure to provide jobs for all those willing to work, it fuelled the growing belief that men's lives were controlled by uncontrollable forces.

Blair noticed that "the word 'unemployment' was on everyone's lips," which "was more or less new to me after Burma."[7] Still, while unemployment may have been more or less new to him, the feeling that new social forces were at work in the breakdown of the old order was not. In literature the new forces were already at large, passionately dedicated to social improvement, despite the prominence of the aloof "art for art's sake" approach to life exemplified by writers such as Virginia Woolf and James Joyce.[8] Although he had been away as a policeman in the jungles of Burma, Blair was no stranger to the aesthetic tendency (witness his lavish naturalistic descriptions in *Burmese Days*) and indeed, he would retain this tendency: "I could not do the work of writing a book, or even a long magazine article if it were not also an aesthetic experience." Even so, only two years after *Burmese Days* was published, Orwell was already expressing his own growing disdain for the aesthetics' intent to divorce themselves from the political realm: "On the last occasion when *Punch* produced a genuinely funny joke, which was only six or seven years ago, it was a picture of an intolerable youth telling his aunt that when he came down from the University he intended to 'write.' 'And what are you going to write about, dear?' his aunt inquires. 'My dear aunt,' the youth replies crushingly, 'one doesn't write *about* anything, one just *writes.*' This was a perfectly justified criticism of current literary cant. At that time, [the end of the Twenties] even more than now, art for art's sake was going strong. . . . 'Art has nothing to do with morality' was the favourite slogan. . . . To admit that you liked or disliked a book because of its moral or religious tendency, even to admit noticing that it *had* a tendency, was too vulgar for words."[9]

Out of the oscillating battle between realism and aestheticism—conflicting impulses that were often evident in different works by the same writer (for example, in Joyce)—the Thirties in England emerged as the decade of commitment to social and political causes.[10] Such commitment, which was particularly noticeable among the young, was not confined to writers; and despite the pessimism born out of the National (Liberal/Labour/Conservative) Government's inability to do much about the ravages of an economic depression begun in the Twenties and the feeling that there was an increasing "paralysis of foreign policy," there was generally a hopeful if angry introspection.[11] In the *Evening Standard*'s celebrated cartoons by David Low, the mood was not apathetic but caustic. Neither Mussolini and Hitler's menace on the one hand (representing the crisis from without) nor Ramsay MacDonald's vacillation on the other (reflecting the crisis of economic depression within) was spared slashing satire. In this climate, in which force seemed to be overwhelming reason and the League of Nations' principle of collective security floundered in the face of the dictators' arrogant aggression, there was on the literary scene a number of young poets, including Auden, Spender, Lewis, and MacNeice, who gravitated toward Marxist or near-Marxist positions. John Strachey's widely influential book *The Coming Struggle for Power,* published in 1932, warned that in the face of fascism, communism was the only alternative. By 1934, the year that *Burmese Days* was published, the *Left Review,* formed in response to the central committee of the International Union of Revolutionary Writers in Moscow, issued its call "for militant Communism and against individualism and metaphysics in the arts,"[12] and the growing interest in the Russian experiment gained new respectability with the publication in 1935 of Sidney and Beatrice Webb's two-volume *Soviet Communism: A New Civilization?*[13] (Later, the question mark after this title was dropped.)

George Bowling, the insurance-salesman protagonist of Orwell's fourth novel, *Coming Up For Air* (1939), also recalls the mood of the time. Like so many of the demoralized and demobilized soldiers of World War I, Bowling had made the bitter discovery that the "fit country for heroes to live in" that former Liberal Party prime minister David Lloyd George had envisioned was a land of rampant unemployment. He comments that "It's very strange, the things war [World War I] did to people."[14] He recalls how a few years before he had been a young grocery clerk in Lower Binfield, a quiet English country town; then suddenly he was in uniform and soon in the officer class, "more or less keeping my end up among a crowd of other temporary gents. . . . And—this is really the point—not feeling it in any way strange. Nothing seemed strange in those days . . . there was a temporary feeling about everything."[15]

Just as suddenly as he had joined the Army, Bowling was discharged and out of work. Though trying to recapture the memory of a surer age by returning to Lower Binfield, he tells us that he is not in nostalgic search of an ideal time. Indeed, he admits that life wasn't "softer" before the First World War: "Actually it was harsher. People on the whole worked harder, lived less comfortably, and died more painfully"[16]; but the redeeming feature of life then was the "feeling of security"—above all, a "feeling of *continuity*. . . . All of them [knew that they had to die and a few of them even knew they faced bankruptcy], but what they didn't know was that the order of things could change."[17] (The italics are mine.) Bowling understands that much anxiety is relieved if one can face the idea of death with the knowledge that "the things you care about are going to survive."[18] The loss of such conviction in the Thirties and the futility of Bowling's own "backward" journey to Lower Binfield in search of the old certainties is revealed when he remembers how "the war and the feeling of not being one's own master overshadowed everything. . . . If the war didn't happen to kill you it was bound to start you thinking. After that unspeakable idiotic mess you couldn't go on regarding society as something eternal and unquestionable, like a pyramid. You knew it was just a balls-up."[19]

This feeling of the postwar period lingered, for even as the England of the Twenties recovered slightly, it was assaulted anew in 1929—

two years after Blair had returned from Burma—by the shock waves of the Wall Street crash in America. This helped to push Britain's unemployment to 2.5 million in 1930 as the country entered the Great Depression, and the realization that the old prewar order was never to return grew even more pervasive, particularly among young writers.[20]

The year 1931 saw a revolution in Spain, the fall of Manchuria to the Japanese, and in England a series of crises that, amid increasing unemployment, a drain on gold, and the fall in the British pound, culminated in the resignation of the second Labour government under Prime Minister Ramsay MacDonald. To the Labour cabinet's "utter stupefaction,"[21] this was immediately followed by the formation, on August 24, under MacDonald's leadership, of the National government, a coalition of Labour, Liberal, and Conservative members. Apart from the sharp division this caused in the Labour Party, the divisions between Left and Right were made worse by the National government's subsequent attempts to cut wages and unemployment pay drastically. For the most part, the middle classes had rallied to the government's side, responding to calls at year's end to "buy British," in an effort to shore up the weakened pound. Something of a patriotic determination to go along with the austerity cuts even reached the working class (who were by no means solidly Labour).[22]

Part of the austerity program also called for a reduction of pay in the armed services. In the Navy this meant a pay loss of approximately 25 percent, with the loss incurred by the enlisted men proportionally much higher than that of the officers. The result was that on September 15, 1931, there was a "mutiny," called a "strike," aboard the Atlantic Fleet in Cromarty Firth. Although it ended quietly, it helped to move the government to introduce the "Incitement to Disaffection Act"[23] a year later. It was in this climate of emergency, under pressure from the Conservative majority, that the recently formed National government called for an election in October of 1931.

The result was an overwhelming victory for the National government, which won 556 seats—472 of them Conservative, as against only 46 seats for Labour. It was in essence a Conservative victory "under false colours," and "Once again, whatever the popular tides of feeling since the war, they [the Conservatives] were in power. . . . The old ministers were back, the humdrum figures of the Twenties, without even the need of seeking the new blood."[24] For many in

England it was not so much a vote of confidence as the lack of any viable alternative.[25] In any event, the collapse of the Labour government was a devastating blow for the leftist reformers who had hitherto placed so much faith in the Labour Party. Recalling how *New Signatures*, an anthology of poetry, was "related to the political events," one of its founders, John Lehmann, writes:

By the time of the General Election in 1931 I was already sufficiently converted [to Socialism] to share to the full the consternation and gloom that settled on all our circle at the collapse of the Labour Government. . . . But even as I reached this point of intellectual conviction, I began to move away from it, further to the left. The discredit of Labour made even staunch supporters of the Party in Bloomsbury mutter that perhaps more radical measures of Marxism were necessary to defeat reaction and stop the drift towards a new war.[26]

Despite Lehmann's attraction to socialism, most members of the intelligentsia had not yet moved to the left, indeed they had not moved in any direction. As more and more writers made the commitment to political and social purpose, however, the direction would be "forward from liberalism" towards a "general radical revolutionary leftism."[27] By 1933, having made such political commitments, Michael Roberts could write for his fellow anti-capitalists in the preface of *New Country*, another influential anthology, "I think, and the writers of this book obviously agree, that there is only one way of life for us: to renounce the (capitalist) system now and live by fighting against it. It is time that those who conserve something which is still valuable in England began to see that only a revolution can save their standards."[28]

Although in most cases it was writers who articulated the Left's disillusionment with the old order, such disillusionment was widespread in other quarters as well. The growing impatience of the young in general toward the older members of society, who, they believed, perpetuated the old political order, was especially noticeable because of the missing generation that had been killed in the war, a generation that might have acted as a kind of buffer between the experience of the old and the impatience of the young.

As a manifestation of their forward-looking view, and in more charitable extensions of what Orwell later called the "curious hatred of old men,"[29] the younger writers, now preoccupied with revolt against the authority and orthodoxy of the old order, inclined not only "towards a world view, social consciousness," but towards "a platonic affection for the proletariat."[30] Into this world came Eric Blair, his nascent affection for the proletariat an inverse measure of his own disillusionment with the old order.

Yet Blair's entry into the postwar world of young writers was very different than most. Whereas the conflict between youth and the old order had largely come about through the disorder and uncertainties of a world war, Orwell's dislike of the old order had other origins. The ex-policeman's disillusionment was not nurtured in the trenches of France, where a holocaust had been "conducted mainly by old men . . . with supreme incompetence,"[31] but by the old order's imperial stance in Burma, where Flory describes the war as having merely "rolled on like a storm beyond the horizon."[32] Again unlike so many other postwar writers, Blair, upon his return to England, had "no interest in Socialism or any other economic theory."[33] In "Why I Write" (1946), Orwell says that although his time in Burma had taught his something about imperialism, it had not given him "an accurate political orientation."[34] All he had at that time in the way of a political belief was a self-confessed "anarchistic theory" that viewed all government as evil and divided the world up into the oppressed, who were always right, and the oppressors, who were always wrong.[35]

Blair's irrevocable political orientation was to come in 1936–37, during the civil war in Spain. The course of events during this crucial period "turned the scale and thereafter I knew where I stood."[36] Nevertheless, between the time he resigned from his job in Burma and his trip to Spain, where he would fight with the Republicans, Orwell vented his disillusionment with the old order, his anger and guilt, by conducting an investigation of (and indulging a fascination with) poverty and unemployment.

In 1928, after a failing apprenticeship as a struggling poet in the Portobello Road and occasional sorties into London's East End as the tramp P. S. Burton, the aspiring writer went to Paris. Here (still under the name Blair) he wrote his first professional piece, "Censorship in England". It appeared in *Le Monde* and was followed by articles about unemployment in England, tramps, and Burma, published in *Progrès Civique*. During the period 1928–29, in Paris, Blair was a dishwasher for a time, was hospitalized with pneumonia, and wrote several unpublished short stories and two unpublished novels—all of which he later destroyed. At the end of 1929 he returned to England and tried his hand at writing reviews, poems, and documentary sketches. With few exceptions these were all published between March

1930 and August 1935 in *Adelphi,* the "scurrilous [socialist] rag" Blair had used for target practice in Burma.[37]

By January 1933 *Down and Out in Paris and London* had been published, although earlier T. S. Eliot had rejected it at the London publishing firm of Faber and Faber and a depressed Blair had left it with a friend with instructions to "throw it away." The book was saved, of course, though Blair requested that it be published pseudonymously, "as I am not proud of it."[38] Thus, the name George Orwell was used for the first time.

It has been claimed that the name change was not of much importance, given Blair's desire to hide his authorship of a book he said he did not care for. I don't agree, for it seems clear that as a first step for someone trying to shuck off an old way of life—someone who wants to immerse himself in the ranks of the poor and who speaks of being welcomed as a fellow down-and-out by a workman as a "kind of baptism"[39]—a new name is important, a new beginning; and though Blair's selection of the name Orwell out of a final list of four (P. S. Burton, Kenneth Miles, George Orwell, and H. Lewis Allways)[40] was more or less pressed on him by his impatient publisher, the fact of his changing his name and using the pseudonym until his death, remains—even though he never made the shift in a court of law.

The argument that the name change was not particularly important rests largely on Orwell's assertion that "I have no reputation that is lost by doing this and if the book [*Down and Out*] has any kind of success I can always use the same pseudonym again."[41] This is fair enough, but it hardly closes the door on the possibility that for Blair there were other good reasons for a name change that he didn't care to explain to his publisher—hardly an uncommon occurrence for an author, as for anyone else—and it is hardly playing silly psychological games to suggest that a man who was by general agreement extraordinarily reticent about such details did not care to give detailed explanations for taking a new name for a new career. He was no longer just a writer, but an author.

In any case, whatever the reasons and despite the fact that he was still known to his friends as Eric Blair, the name change occurred and the private Blair became the public Orwell; and although he had not as yet even nominally affiliated himself with any party, he had been convinced even before the name change that only his descent into the abyss would exorcise his imperialist guilt. He wrote, "What

I profoundly wanted, at that time, was to find some way of getting out of the respectable world altogether. . . . Once I had been among them [the "lowest of the low"] and accepted by them, I should have touched bottom, and—this is what I felt: I was aware even then that it was irrational—part of my guilt would drop from me."[42]

Nevertheless, Blair was rational in that he understood that if you are to exorcise your guilt successfully, as Orwell only partially succeeded in doing by "writing it out" in *Burmese Days,* you need to rid yourself of the cause of that guilt, not merely its symptoms. You need more than a new name; you need a philosophy that will prevent you from repeating the old mistakes—in Orwell's case, the exploitative attitudes and acts of the imperialist. He recalls, "I wanted to see what mass-unemployment is like at its worst. . . . This was necessary to me as part of my approach to Socialism, for before you can be sure whether you are genuinely in favour of Socialism [or any replacement system], you have to decide whether things at present are tolerable or not tolerable, and you have got to take up a definite attitude on that terribly difficult issue of class."[43] Thus, although Blair knew that he did not want a prolongation of the days when he wore the policeman's uniform—when "those straps under the boot give you a feeling like nothing else in life"[44]—and he had formulated his "anarchistic theory" of government, Orwell was not yet sure what system should replace the one that Blair had spurned. The following years of poverty and semipoverty—in which he was *through choice* a struggling writer, tramp, tutor (1930–31), a schoolmaster (1932–33), a bookshop assistant (1934), and a storekeeper (1936)—were in effect an apprenticeship. It was a period of distillation for some of Blair's generalized, albeit firmly held, convictions about exploitation—most specifically about the working class and the poor in England. He was mostly influenced in the way he went about descending into the world of the poor by the earlier investigations of Jack London. He believed that the American's investigation of the poor in the East End of London, recorded in *The People of the Abyss* (1903), "still has sociological value" and regarded London's book, *The Road,* describing the American's experiences, as "brilliant."[45]

Of the beginning of his voluntary descents into the lower classes Orwell writes, "I knew nothing about working-class conditions. I had read the unemployment figures but I had no notion of what they implied . . . All this was outside the range of my experience."[46] Of course, Orwell was not alone in his ignorance or confusion about

what the unemployment figures really meant; for although econo-
mists and historians can tell us in retrospect that otherwise useful
economic indicators in the interwar period were "up," large sectors
of the population, particularly the 2.5 million unemployed, were
"down." Even among those whose material well-being was improved,
there were many for whom the effects of increased material benefit
were negated by pervasively depressing social conditions.[47]

Orwell's determination to penetrate the statistical abstraction known
as "poverty" began with the experiences he recorded in *Down and
Out in Paris and London* (1933). His investigation reached a high
point in 1936 with his journeys into the depressed coal-mining areas
of northern England at a time when the country's unemployment
figure stood in excess of 2.1 million and 23.9 percent of those receiv-
ing the dole had been out of work for more than a year.[48]

Orwell would meet these statistics face on, particularly in Wigan
(where in 1933 one man in three had been on the dole), and would
record his experiences in *The Road to Wigan Pier* (1937), a work commissioned by his publisher, Victor Gollancz. Orwell's choice of the
title is significant in that Wigan, being inland in Lancashire, has no
pier—the phrase "Wigan Pier" being a wry comment by those workers unable to afford a holiday in Blackpool.[49] Very few could afford
Blackpool in 1936.

CHAPTER 3

Women generally do not get to the top power positions in British society, but neither do the lower classes. It was the lack of social revolution there in the 19th century—and bitter class distrust and hatred still aflame today—that is the basic cause of economic problems that even she [Prime Minister Thatcher] is not beginning to solve. Co-operation among the social classes is virtually non-existent.[1]

THIS IS A JOURNALIST REPORTING IN ENGLAND IN 1981. How sadly Orwell would have agreed. If you care about equality at all, you must first confront poverty and your views of it head on. That means understanding the details of poverty: with all the best intentions in the world, the world can't be bettered by people for whom poverty remains as something abstract —something out there—merely seen in passing. That is what Orwell tells us in his writings of the decade before the Second World War.

While he did not shy away from the possibility of bloody change in his assault against poverty and the class system, Orwell clearly preferred the removal of privilege in society through effecting a fundamental shift in power through the pressure of public opinion, rather than through arms. Thus, "Revolution does not mean red flags and street fighting, it means a fundamental shift of power. Whether it happens with or without bloodshed is largely an accident of time and place. Nor does it mean the dictatorship of a single class."[2] Certainly he did not see violence as a preordained *policy* of a revolution— only, like war, as a sometimes unavoidable, if necessary, evil; and at the same time that he believed that the "structure" of society must be changed "from below"—with violence if absolutely necessary— he also believed just as strongly in first trying the democratic process even in times of war.

Above all, he would come to believe that the real beginning of revolution, of overthrowing privilege, lay not only in changing the social "structure," but in changing oneself. An attack upon the class system really began with an attack upon one's own class prejudices, and that, as he demonstrates in *The Road to Wigan Pier,* is the most difficult revolution of all: "For to get outside the class-racket I have got to suppress not merely my private snobbishness, but most of my other tastes and prejudices as well. I have got to alter myself so completely that at the end I should hardly be recognizable as the same person. What is involved is not merely the amelioration of working-class conditions . . . but a complete abandonment of the upper-class and middle-class attitude to life."[3] Such were the motivations behind Orwell's descent into the world of the poor and his unexpected discovery of those details of poverty that both inhibit the urge for revolution and perpetuate the baser forms of poverty.

"He wanted to go down . . . submerge himself—to *sink,* as Rosemary had said. . . . He liked to think about the lost people, the under ground people, tramps, beggars, criminals, prostitutes . . . beneath the world of money . . . where failure and success have no meaning; a sort of kingdom of ghosts where all are equal, . . . where you could lose yourself for ever."[4] This is how George Orwell described Gordon Comstock in his third novel, *Keep the Aspidistra Flying,* published in April 1936. Comstock is a struggling young poet and assistant bookseller in London. The passage occurs not long after Comstock has spent the night in jail, an incident that is based on an incident in the author's own life. Orwell had already described this overnight detention in his essay, "Clink," and it is a striking example of Orwell's penchant for conscripting his experience for use in his fiction.[5] Satisfying his perverse desire to be down and out, Comstock quickly discovers that "the first effect of poverty is that it kills thought" because "he had learned what it means to live for weeks on end on bread and margarine, to try to 'write' when you are half starved, to pawn your clothes, to sneak trembling up the stairs when you owe three weeks' rent." Above all, he finds out that although poverty may free you from the restraints and responsibilities expected and imposed by the respectable "world of money," you do not escape from money pressures "merely by being moneyless." Ironically, you are as much a "slave" to money as you would be in "the servitude of a 'good' job"— a situation from which Comstock tries to escape.[6]

The discoveries of Gordon Comstock come directly from Orwell's experience. Apart from his intermittent descent into the world of the down-and-out between 1928 and 1931, when he, too, was trying to write on very limited means, Orwell's most sustained experience of poverty, after a particularly prolific but commercially unprofitable period of writing in 1928–29, was a ten-week period in Paris in the fall of 1929. When his savings from the Burma period had all but disappeared, he worked as a *plongeur* (dishwasher) in both a luxury hotel and a small restaurant. His most important discovery about poverty in this transitional period was that being poor, which "you thought . . . would be quite simple . . . is extraordinarily complicated." He describes how the drive to keep up appearances, to maintain dignity, creates a need for "secrecy" that can be met and maintained only by a habitual and often expensive practice of lying: "You stop sending clothes to the laundry, and the laundress catches you in the street and asks you why; you mumble something and she, thinking you are sending the clothes elsewhere, is your enemy for life." In the same way as Comstock in London studiously avoids meeting acquaintances in the pub, being too poor to buy a round, Orwell, writing of his Paris period, tells how "you have strayed into a respectable quarter, and you see a prosperous friend coming. To avoid him you dodge into the nearest café. Once in the café you must buy something, so you spend your last fifty centimes on a glass of black coffee. . . . Once [*sic*] could multiply these disasters by the hundred. They are part of the process of being hard up."[7]

Along with the myriad connivances that the requirements of dignity force upon you, there is the sheer exhaustion that afflicts those who have always been poor and must work long hours for little pay. Describing the *plongeur* as "one of the slaves of the modern world, . . . no freer than if he were bought and sold," working between sixty and a hundred hours a week, Orwell notes that "he lives in a rhythm between work and sleep, without time to think, hardly conscious of the exterior world."[8]

It is not surprising that living in an industrialized world, we most often think of such conditions as being the lot of the city worker, but in Orwell's second novel, *A Clergyman's Daughter* (1935), he reminds us that the superficially idyllic country setting can camouflage an equally debilitating life. Using his own experience in the hop fields as a basis for the novel, Orwell writes of Dorothy Hare, the reverend's daughter, an amnesiac who has drifted off into the "hard up" worlds of the seasonal agricultural worker in Kent and the unemployed in London. He tells us that although she was happy in the hop fields, the work literally stupefied her. In London Dorothy is not working but experiences again the blurring of her perceptions, "the dazed witless feeling she had known on the way to the hop fields." Now the almost constant lack of cover, which is the lot of many unemployed, causes her condition to worsen, and "all the while it is as though everything were a little out of focus, a little unreal." Even for the *plongeur* who is employed, "the world, inner and outer, grows dimmer till it reaches almost the vagueness of a dream."[9]

The dream is not a nightmare, because it is accompanied by extreme "apathy."[10] The point that the novel makes clear is that fatigue through overwork, on the one hand, and lethargy through undernourished inactivity, on the other, often converge. Whether the world of poverty and unemployment is transitional or not, "the best intellects will not stand up against it. . . . You can't command the spirit of *hope* in which anything has got to be created."[11] The result of Dorothy Hare's experience in her slave-like labor of the hop fields was that "more and more she had come to take her curious situation for granted, to abandon all thoughts of either yesterday or tomorrow. . . . It narrowed the range of your consciousness to the passing minute."[12]

Orwell shows us how these petty details of poverty, all but insignificant in themselves, accumulate and how the resulting complexity of living from day to day drains the poor of all energy, which is already low because of lack of food. Whether or not being poor is caused by unemployment, or by low wages accompanied by long, dull, exhausting hours of work, the job of satisfying hunger and finding shelter leaves no time for anything else—hence Orwell's remark that *plongeurs* never thought of forming a union or going on strike because they simply had no leisure for it.[13] Furthermore, from his living with miners in Wigan he was quick to see that after travelling time to and from the actual work face where payment begins and "washing up" time had been accounted for, some miners had less than four hours a day free time.[14] This is an instance of how, with his eye for the concrete detail, Orwell alerted his readers to the qualifications one has to place on official statistics—for example those that give the impression that miners work only seven and a half hours a day.

Orwell's conclusion is simply that tired, poor people are unlikely to resist exploitation, let alone to revolt. This means that such a revolt would most likely have to be instigated and led by middle-class intellectuals who had more free time than the poor. The assumption that revolution is unlikely to come from the poor gains strength from Orwell's observation that together with the boredom of the unemployed comes "the great redeeming feature of poverty: the fact that it annihilates the future."[15] If concern for the future is gone, so is any motive for resistance.

The annihilation of the future is largely possible because the need to satisfy immediate and essential needs makes the present the only thing worth thinking about. The resulting lack of anxiety about the future, says Orwell, gives way to a sense of relief—almost of pleasure—gained from knowing that you have reached bottom and have not gone to pieces. This is the world of the proles in Nineteen Eighty-Four. However, in this case, as we shall see later, it is precisely because they have nothing more to lose that they hold the only hope, weak though it is, of humanity surviving in a world of Big Brother.[16]

If the future is annihilated, what of the past? No matter how much hunger may exclude worry about the distant future, the past is embedded in memory and is not annihilated. Does it not present the poor with at least the idea—the possibility—of an alternative way of life as a solution to their poverty? In short, why do the lessons, the models of action in history, from the revolt of Spartacus to the French Revolution and on, fail to move the poor to action? Why is it for such people, standing about on the dole, permitting apathy to take hold, that stories of past revolts of people against their rulers fail to excite even the dream of a way out? The answer is to be found in one of the most important insights of A Clergyman's Daughter, found in the part of the novel that clearly draws on Orwell's experience as a private school teacher in 1932–33. He writes, "Dorothy had not realized till now how hard it is for children who come from poor homes to have even a conception of what history means. . . . These children came from bookless homes and from parents who would have laughed at the notion that the past has any meaning for the present."[17]

According to Orwell, because the poor do not read books, they do not have a sense of history. Because they do not have a sense of history, they are ignorant both of other ways of life and of blueprints for action to attain them.[18] With this in mind, there is little difference in Orwell's extrapolation from the particular to the universal, between the miners in Wigan who do not read books and know of an acute housing shortage only "when we were told about it"[19] and the proles in Nineteen Eighty-Four who so docilely accept their wretched condition because the history books have been written by the ruling class. Orwell believed that in both cases the lack of history condemns the underprivileged to a largely unquestioning and servile acceptance of an apparently immutable world of "them" and "us."

Orwell's emphasis on the lack of history among the poor, however, cannot be taken to mean that he thought the poor so abysmally ignorant as to be incapable of recognizing their plight or so mentally deficient that they could never envisage a better future. Travelling by train past a row of slum houses in the wintry and dismal slag-heaped industrial North, he saw a woman in a sacking apron and clogs trying to clean a clogged drainpipe. The woman, "her arms reddened by the cold," looked up at the passing train with the

exhausted face of the slum girl who is twenty-five and looks forty. . . . I saw it, the most desolate, hopeless expression I have ever seen. It struck me then that we are mistaken when we say that "It isn't the same for them as it would be for us" . . . that people bred in the slums can imagine nothing but the slums. For what I saw in her face was not the ignorant suffering of an animal. She knew well enough what was happening to her—understood as well as I did how dreadful a destiny it was to be kneeling there in the bitter cold, on the slimy stones of a slum backyard, poking a stick up a foul drain-pipe.[20]

The point Orwell makes is that despite the vague notion that there must be something better, the lack of *models* for realizing a better future disposes the poor to adapt to circumstances rather than to try to change them.

This tendency to adapt rather than to challenge "them" is particularly evident in *The Road to Wigan Pier* when upon investigating the chronic and severe unemployment in the North, Orwell notes that because conditions were more or less the same for millions of the unemployed and their dependents, a sense of relative deprivation was lessened. Consequently, "you have populations settling down, as it were, to a lifetime on the P.A.C. [Public Assistance Committees]. . . . Take, for instance, the fact that the working class think nothing of getting married on the dole."[21]

The dole hardly makes for contentment, however, even after settling down to poverty has been achieved[22]; and the contrary assumption made by well-fed critics of the poor, that living on the dole spawns a contented and rampant laziness among its recipients (who thus become unwilling to improve their situation), is vigorously attacked by Orwell. Such an assumption led critics of the poor to the use of the term "unemployable"—designating unwillingness rather than incapacity. For Orwell this assumption is grossly exaggerated, if not simply wrong, in most cases. Drawing on his association with the down and out, he suggests that quite apart from the money, the unemployed among the poor—far from being contentedly lazy—worry as much as, if not more than anybody else about not having work. He argues that this is not just because for every statistical unemployed worker there are often several dependents also suffering, but also because the illiterate man, having little or no other means of expression save his work habit, needs work "even more than he needs money."[23] This questions whether the dole, or its modern equivalent, will in fact keep people (as C. L. Mowat claims it did in the "hungry thirties") "on the safe side of discontent and thoughts of revolution."[24] Ironically, Orwell maintained, it was not the dole, but what the dole could *now* purchase that accounted for the fact that despite the grinding poverty of the interwar years, the working class "neither turned revolutionary nor lost their self-respect."[25]

The fact that the underprivileged had not risen up against the privileged, despite the initial postwar "wave of revolutionary feeling," was due, he said, to the advent of cheap luxuries that mitigated the humiliating conditions of poverty.[26] This helps to explain how, as Orwell noted earlier, people were able to accept the dole as a way of life rather than simply as a temporary condition.

Today, in the face of the outsider's ignorance of how the minds of the poor or unemployed work, the number of television aerials cluttering the already cluttered slum disposes many an observer to regard the proliferation of luxuries among the poor as evidence of a parasitic irresponsibility; but to the insider the truth is that when you are depressed by poverty the same logic applies to appliances as it does to food, that is, you do not want the ordinary (that is all around you); what you want is the *extraordinary*—you want escape. As Orwell writes, "When you are unemployed, . . . bored and miserable, you don't *want* to eat dull wholesome food. You want something a little bit 'tasty' "—hence his scorn for Lady Astor's advice to the poor on how to economize with cheap but nutritious food. With more disturbing implications for our times, he adds that "an aspirin is much better as a temporary stimulant than a crust of brown bread."[27]

In particular, Orwell discerned how postwar mass production resulted in the luxury often being cheaper than the necessity. The effects of mass production among the poor were most noticeable in the appearance of relatively cheap clothes, which, Orwell claimed, combined with movies to make the greatest contribution to the mitigation of poverty.[28] Ironically, as coal miners were thrown out of work by postwar industrial advances in equipment that relied less and less on coal, the work-filled life of a miner's wife was simultaneously being eased by the advent of the rayon industry.[29]

Among the cheap luxury items that provided (in Orwell's view) some respite for the poor in Britain between the world wars and "averted revolution," is gambling. Orwell notes it as an agent of hope, "something to live for" amid the squalor of economic deprivation. Calling it "the cheapest of all luxuries," he notes that gambling "has now risen almost to the status of a major industry. Consider for instance the Football Pools, with a turnover of about six million pounds a year, almost all of it from the pockets of working-class people" and how "when Hitler re-occupied the Rhineland . . . the threat of war aroused hardly a flicker of interest locally [in Yorkshire] but the decision of the Football Association to stop publishing their fixtures in advance (this was an attempt to quell the Football Pools) flung all Yorkshire into a storm of fury."[30]

Beyond viewing gambling as an agent of hope lies the deeper conviction among the poor that life itself is dependent on chance and not on planning. This is expressed by Boris, the garrulous waiter in *Down and Out in Paris and London* who tells Orwell, the dishwasher, "Waiting is a gamble. . . . You may die poor, you may make your fortune in a year. . . . You never know when a stroke of luck is coming."[31] Again, the lack of a conception of history plays its part, because in not providing the poor with an historically identifiable villain, it moves them instead to look for other answers to explain their underprivileged world. One answer is to believe in luck. (Another is religion, which will be discussed later.) One can revolt against an identifiable villain but one cannot revolt against luck. In any event, as Orwell's journey to Wigan suggests (though he notes, "It goes against the grain to say this"), the poor know that while "ideally, the worst type of slum landlord is a fat wicked man, preferably a bishop, who is drawing an immense income from extortionate rents, . . . actually, it is a poor old woman who has invested her life's savings in three slum houses, inhabits one of them, and tries to live on the rent of the other two—never, in consequence, having any money for repairs."[32] How can one revolt against old ladies who cannot afford repairs?

Orwell was aware, of course, that belief in luck was not confined to the poor; but he saw that despite the indulgence of the upper and middle-classes in buying the "odd" raffle ticket and "occasional" drink, these classes held a disdainful view of the poor's preference for luxury over necessities. They saw the unemployed's preference for luxury not as a measure of their need to relieve the constant crushing boredom of unemployment, but as evidence of the lack of the will to work, even though, as Orwell has shown, work was greatly desired by the unemployed—not only for the money it could bring, but as the sole measure of personal worth.

Again, as with the pukka sahibs and memsahibs of *Burmese Days,* hypocrisy is hidden in language. Although the upper and middle classes are attracted to luxury, to gambling, as are the poor, their indulgence is likely to be camouflaged by the use of "non-poor" words. Thus, Reverend Hare in *A Clergyman's Daughter,* desperately trying to maintain the old prewar lower-middle-class style "with one thumb in the belt of his cassock, . . . frowned abstractedly. . . . His broker had advised United Celanese. Here—in Sumatra Tin, United Celanese and numberless other remote and dimly imagined companies—was the central cause of the Rector's money troubles. He was an inveterate gambler. Not, of course, that he thought of it as gambling; it was merely a lifelong search for a 'good investment.' "[33]

Unless we are aware of such verbal camouflage, we are apt to underrate or simply not notice the importance of the belief in "luck" in Orwell's work.[34] The institutionalization of this belief by the rulers in *Nineteen Eighty-Four* is captured in the following example of Orwell's ability to extrapolate from firsthand experience to the universal. Describing the passage of Winston Smith, the protagonist, through a working-class ("proles") area, he uses his British experience—even down to the Cockney accent—as a blueprint for the Britain of 1984:

It was nearly twenty hours, and the drinking-shops which the proles frequented ("pubs," they called them) were choked with customers. From their grimy swing doors, endlessly opening and shutting, there came forth a smell of urine, sawdust, and sour beer. In an angle formed by a projecting housefront three men were standing very close together, the middle one of them holding a folded-up newspaper which the other two were studying over his shoulder. Even before he was near enough to make out the expression on their faces, Winston could see absorption in every line of their bodies. It was obviously some serious piece of ["low level"] news that they were reading. He was a few paces away from them when suddenly the group broke up and two of the men were in violent altercation. For a moment they seemed almost on the point of blows.

"Can't you bleeding well listen to what I say? I tell you no number ending in seven ain't won for over fourteen months!"

"Yes, it 'as, then!"

"No, it 'as not! Back 'ome I got the 'ole lot of 'em for over two years wrote down on a piece of paper. I takes 'em down reg'lar as the clock. An' I tell you, no number ending in seven—" . . . They were talking about the Lottery. Winston looked back when he had gone thirty metres. They were still arguing, with vivid, passionate faces. The Lottery, with its weekly pay-out of enormous prizes, was the one public event to which the proles paid serious attention. *It was probable that there were some millions of proles for whom the Lottery was the principal if not the only reason for staying alive.* It was their delight, their folly, their anodyne, their intellectual stimulant. Where the Lottery was concerned, even people who could barely read and write seemed capable of intricate calculations and staggering feats of memory. There was a whole tribe of men who made a living simply by selling systems, forecasts, and lucky amulets. Winston had nothing to do with the running of the Lottery, which was managed by the Ministry of Plenty, but he was aware (indeed everyone in the Party was aware) that the prizes were largely imaginary. Only small sums were actually paid out, the winners of the big prizes being non-existent persons.[35] [The italics are mine.]

Here, in a description of a world where even the most common anodyne of television has ceased to provide escape from the drabness, fear, and inherent inequality of a police state, the most significant lines are those which testify to the fact that the proles' faith in the lottery is more important than actual evidence of riches. What was the agency of hope for the starving sweepstake ticket holder in Wigan Pier[36] has become the *sole repository* of hope for the proles. Like everyone else, they have lost their belief in a personal immortality as a reward for the trials of existence in the totalitarian state, and so in a world of such patent inequality, the only recompense, the only "believed in" equality, is that afforded by the hand of chance.

Although in his last novel Orwell sees gambling and cheap ginhouses as a deliberate policy of Big Brother in containing any proletarian discontent, he dismisses the idea that in interwar Britain gambling, along with other cheap palliatives, was an astute manoeuver by the governing class to keep the poor and unemployed quiet. He believes instead that although revolution was undoubtedly "averted" by the advent of cheap luxuries, their appearance was, in the main, the "unconscious" result of the interaction between postwar supply and demand. Furthermore, he writes that what he had seen of the governing class does not convince him that they were intelligent enough to conceive, let alone execute, any such "bread and circuses" plan.[37]

But if Orwell viewed the servility-producing "weapon of unemployment"[38] as simply the result of the vicissitudes of the world market rather than a willful policy of governing elites, he did hold the more privileged population responsible for the continuance of existing inequalities. Here, we move from Orwell's consideration of those aspects of poverty that "cowed" the revolutionary spirit to his consideration of those upper- and middle-class attitudes that he believed perpetuated poverty itself, attitudes that would culminate in the grossly unfair world of Big Brother, in which 85 percent of the population are deliberately kept poor. Orwell argued that the practice of maintaining poorly paid "useless work" jobs (as in the provision of nonessential services) in order to keep the poor too busy for revolution was the indirect result of what he considered the rich person's "deep-seated fear of the mob [the poor]." He argues that at the very root of this pervasive fear, and thus at the root of class structure, is the belief that quite apart from money, "there is some mysterious fundamental difference between rich and poor, as though they were two different races"—such as whites and natives in Burma or men and "animals" in England.[39]

Unsophisticated as this view was, Orwell saw a direct connection between it and the servility he believed was endemic to the capitalist system and the class prejudices "which generally persist from birth to death," prejudices from which everyone claims "that he, in some mysterious way, is exempt."[40] He feared that those people who continued to believe that there is a fundamental difference between rich and poor at birth would not only perpetuate present inequalities but might well prefer "any injustice" sooner than letting the mob loose or allowing the poor time to plan and eventually present a challenge to privilege. "The mob (the thought runs) are such low animals that they would be dangerous if they had leisure." An intellectually honest rich man, writes Orwell, will admit that "poverty is unpleasant, in fact, since it is so remote, we rather enjoy harrowing ourselves with the thought of its unpleasantness. But don't expect us to do anything about it. We are sorry for you lower classes, just as we are sorry for a cat with the mange, but we will fight like devils against any improvement of your condition. We feel that you are much safer as you are." This, writes Orwell, is the attitude of those well-to-do "intelligent, cultivated people" who side with the rich for no other reason than that they believe that more liberty for the poor is less liberty for them.[41] This suggests how easily the existence of privilege, including greater freedom for some than for others, can be rationalized by appealing to the social Darwinism of the commercial mind—to the winner–loser, profit-and-loss view of the world that pervades the marketplace. Here, liberty can be thought of as being no less subject to the laws of scarcity than the supply of bread. That is, lack of freedom for some can be excused by those who have more freedom by encouraging acceptance of the analogy between "liberty" and "goods," as if liberty were somehow a "non-renewable resource" and there were only so much to go around. The danger is that this view can be used to justify a *willful* reduction in liberty.

The fear of an undisciplined rabble storming the bastions of privilege, which encourages the use of force against strikers, demonstrators, and the like, is itself perpetuated, Orwell claims, for no other reason than that the rich, including those with potentially "liberal opinions," never mix with the underprivileged and so never question their subliminal fear of the mob.[42]

Though Eric Blair in 1928 was not rich or even well-to-do, he was a member of the somewhat privileged "lower-upper-middle class," and he well understood fear of the mob, because he had it himself. His first real contact with the poor—his first attempt to get "inside" the world of poverty before he wrote *Down and Out in Paris and London*—is recorded in *The Road to Wigan Pier*, when he talks about his entry into a lodging house in Limehouse Causeway. The passage is a dramatic representation of the transition from Eric Blair to George Orwell, who suddenly realizes that Blair's class-bred fear could not stand up against his experience with the down-and-out.

Heavens, how I had to screw up my courage before I went in! It seems ridiculous now. But you see I was still half afraid of the working class. I wanted to get in touch with them, I even wanted to become one of them, but I still thought of them as alien and dangerous; going into the dark doorway of that common lodging-house seemed to me like going down into some dreadful subterranean place—a sewer of rats, for instance. I went in fully expecting a fight. The people would spot that I was not one of themselves and immediately infer that I had come to spy on them . . . they would set upon me and throw me out—that was what I expected. I felt that I had got to do it, but I did not enjoy the prospect.

Inside the door a man in shirt-sleeves appeared from somewhere or other. This was the "deputy", and I told him that I wanted a bed for the night. My accent did not make him stare, I noticed; he merely demanded ninepence and then showed me the way to a frowsy firelit underground. There were stevedores and navvies and a few sailors sitting about and playing draughts and drinking tea. They barely glanced at me as I entered. But this was Saturday night and a hefty young stevedore was drunk and was reeling about the room. He turned, saw me, and lurched towards me with a broad red face thrust out and a dangerous-looking fishy gleam in his eyes. I stiffened myself. So the fight was coming already! The next moment the stevedore collapsed on my chest and flung his arms round my neck. "'Ave a cup of tea, chum!" he cried tearfully; "'ave a cup of tea!"

I had a cup of tea. It was a kind of baptism. After that my fears vanished. Nobody questioned me, nobody showed offensive curiosity; everybody was polite and gentle and took me utterly for granted.[43]

Though Orwell did not go to the lodging house as a rich man, the truth that this episode in Blair's descent to the poor makes clear is that there is no "mob." This is not to contradict the obvious fact that the "poor" are clearly identifiable as a group, but Blair challenged the widespread notion that the poor constitute an actively hostile group. Orwell saw firsthand that there is no collective and conscious anti-rich plot—or even anti-rich sentiment—no group of conspirators who are ever ready to attack those who are clearly more privileged (or even those with public schoolboy accents who are marginally more privileged). When the world is divided by the poor into "them" and "us," this only denotes recognition of a money barrier, not permanent hostility toward the more privileged classes. Indeed, Orwell saw this recognition as an abjectly servile act,[44] an acceptance of the status quo—not a challenge to it.

So when Orwell talks of the working class as a revolutionary "class," it is in terms of *potentially* revolutionary spirit—not of a "mob" straining at the leash. It was only in emergencies, such as during World War II, that Orwell could see any real possibility of the potential revolutionary becoming active, when "somewhere near a million British working men [in the Home Guard] now have rifles in their bedrooms and don't wish to give them up."[45]

Blair's descent into poverty not only taught him that there was no revolutionary "mob" as such, but that the reason there was none was that those who are *in* a subordinate class are not necessarily *of* it. As a *plongeur* in Paris, his eye for the concrete detail saw not only how the swing door between kitchen and dining room effectively divides rich from poor, but also how the shadow of "caste" moves in and out with the waiters as the latter move between the world of their origin and the world of their aspirations:

It is an instructive sight to see a waiter going into a hotel dining-room. As he passes the door a sudden change comes over him. The set of his shoulders

alters; all the dirt and hurry and irritation have dripped off in an instant. He glides over the carpet, with a solemn priest-like air. . . .
The waiter's outlook is quite different [from that of the rest of the workers]. He too is proud in a way of his skill, but his skill is chiefly in being servile. His work gives him the mentality, not of a workman, but of a snob. . . . between constantly seeing money, and hoping to get it, the waiter comes to identify himself to some extent with his employers. . . . Our staff, amounting to about a hundred and ten, had their prestige graded as accurately as that of soldiers, and a cook or waiter was as much above a *plongeur* as a captain above a private.[46]

Orwell noted that the waiter's movement between the cursing, filthy world of the kitchen and the clean, subdued world of the dining room was daily so rapid and frequent that there was literally a constant tension between "coming" and "going" between the two worlds. This tension, he believed, was not conducive to solidarity with fellow workers who are permanently behind the swing doors.

Orwell was starting to recognize the importance of *status,* seeing how even in the world of the lower classes it was the desire for social standing, as much as for money, that ensured the continuance of some men's privilege through other men's servitude and helped create "this perpetual uneasiness between man and man, from which we suffer in modern England"[47]—and in the world. In pursuing the implications of the drive for status, he would pass from Eric Blair's grasp of the essentially *economic* divisions between individuals to George Orwell's growing understanding of the *social* divisions between them. As he admitted when he began his pilgrimage among the down-and-out, he had no notion of what unemployment figures implied, but "above all I did not know the essential fact that 'respectable' poverty is always the worst."[48] Though in this passage he meant "respectable" to refer to all those who worked, he was about to discover how much worse "respectable" poverty was for the middle class and how in their terror of it, how in fearing their loss of status as well as money, they perpetuated inequality.

In terms of Orwell's books during the interwar years, this recognition of the distinction made between the "respectable" poor and all others who were poor marked a definite shift from his preoccupation with the unemployed and poor working classes in *Down and Out in Paris and London* (1933) to the impoverished middle classes of *A Clergyman's Daughter* (1935), *Keep the Aspidistra Flying* (1936), and *Coming Up For Air* (1939). It was a shift from the master–slave, rich–

poor concept of *Down and Out in Paris and London* to the view that "to Dr. Goebbels' charge that England is still 'two nations,' the only truthful answer would have been that she is in fact three."[49] The third nation was that of the middle classes, the home of Eric Arthur Blair.

Paradoxically, for Orwell the middle classes were both the hope and the despair of any desire for social reform. As a member of the middle classes himself and one who sought to reform society by eliminating the gap between privileged and underprivileged, Orwell, as we know, did not believe that such reform need necessarily be violent;[50] but he did believe that the success of any movement aiming to remove differences between rich and poor had to be dependent upon a coalition of working-class *and* middle-class interests. He considered the middle class indispensable to any such enterprise because it includes "practically the whole of the technocracy . . . without which a modern industrial country could not exist for a week." With typical Orwellian irony he correctly pointed out that this middle class had largely been ignored as a revolutionary force by middle-class advocates of the "proletarian revolution"—an "old fashioned" concept that predated the rise of the modern technocrats.[51] In Orwell's view, however, there was a major impediment within the middle classes to any blue collar–white collar coalition. Superficially, this impediment was their snobbishness towards the working classes, but such snobbishness was merely symptomatic of the drive for wealth and status. For the American reader such differences between middle class and working class may seem exaggerated; but this was England in the thirties, not contemporary America.

Orwell does not suggest that the drive for status is confined to the middle or upper classes. He notes in *The Road to Wigan Pier,* for example, that "one of the most desolating spectacles the world contains" is the trade union official who, though chosen to represent the working class, ends up on the bourgeois side because he sees his position as a way of stepping up in the world. Orwell believed that such drives for wealth and status are much stronger in the middle classes, yet ironically it was in the working-class districts of the North that he was "struck by the profound differences that are still made by *status.*" In Wigan he stayed with a miner who had *nystagmus,* a disease of the eyes that is fairly common in miners. The miner, who could barely see across his room, had been paid a pitifully small pension for nine months, but now the colliery was talking of reducing even this by half. The importance of status was driven home to Orwell in the atmosphere of cap-touching servility that surrounded the miner's grateful receipt of his miserable pension. Orwell writes of the "petty inconvenience and indignity of being kept waiting about, of having to do everything at other people's convenience" that he sees as being "inherent in working-class life."

A member of the bourgeoisie may also have to suffer certain inconveniences, but they are not visited upon him with the same sense of discrimination, for even when he is on the verge of starving, he has certain rights attached to his "bourgeois status." This status, Orwell adds, carries with it an expectation of civility and deference,[52] but for a working man it is different: "A thousand influences constantly press a working man down into a *passive* role. He does not act, he is acted upon. He feels himself the slave of mysterious authority and has a firm conviction that 'they' will never allow him to do this, that, and the other." He recalls how once, while picking hops, he asked the grossly underpaid pickers why they had not formed a union. He was immediately told that " 'they' would never allow it." When he asked who "they" were, he reports, "nobody seemed to know; but evidently 'they' were omnipotent."[53]

For Orwell this subservience in the presence of authority explained why although the English working class had a flair for organization, they "do not show much capacity for leadership." It was, he believed, a capacity to which the person of bourgeois origin is more educated, so that "in almost any revolt the leaders would tend to be people who could pronounce their aitches." He laments the fact that despite his efforts against it, even communist miners in Wigan insisted upon calling him "sir" and that although he and they were friends, all of them knew that he was essentially a "foreigner" in their midst. Therefore, he writes, "whichever way you turn this curse of class difference confronts you like a wall of stone." Reflecting upon such experiences Orwell concludes, "Everyone, barring fools and scoundrels, would *like* to see the miner better off [and] in a sense it is true that almost everyone would like to see class distinctions abolished"; but he argues, using his own case as an example of the general problem, while "it is easy for me to say that I want to get rid of class-distinctions, . . . nearly everything I think and do is a result of class-distinctions. All my notions—notions of good and evil, of pleasant and unpleasant, of funny and serious, of ugly and beautiful—are essentially *middle-class* notions . . . the products of a special kind of upbringing.[54]

It was this *special kind of upbringing*, including its emphasis on status as well as wealth, that Orwell saw as the chief obstacle to any bluc collar–white collar coalition. In particular, it explained for him why the middle class "have always tended to side with the capitalist class and against their natural allies, the manual workers." Such unnatural identification with the exploiters, argued Orwell, was largely the result of "an educational system *designed* to have just that effect."[55] (The italics are mine.) This education constituted the "largest item" of middle-class expenditure,[56] making the search for status (to keep the aspidistra flying) much more pervasive than it was in the working class. He believed that it perpetuated the social and economic gaps between the two classes and directed attention away from the central fact that "poverty is poverty, whether the tool you work with is a pick-axe or a fountain pen." The fact that poverty is not a unifying force between classes is reflected in Orwell's celebrated remark that "the essential point about the English class-system is that it is *not* entirely explicable in terms of money." He gives the example of a naval officer and a grocer, who may have the same income but "are not equivalent persons" and "would only be on the same side in very large issues . . . possibly not even then" to illustrate his point that a "caste-system" exists within the middle classes.[57] For families who knew theoretically how to act, and yearned to act, like the upper classes, the sacrifices made for middle-class rent, clothes, and school bills in order to maintain a semblance of upward mobility formed an unending nightmare.[58] This theme runs through all three novels of the English period.

Describing his lower-middle-class neighbourhood, George Bowling, the insurance salesman in *Coming Up For Air,* declares that its long line of stucco, semidetached row houses, with such pretentious French names as Mon Abri, Mon Repos, and Belle Vue constitute nothing more than "a prison with the cells all in a row." In each house, argues Bowling, the breadwinner lives in fear of the "boss," the "sack," and is "*never* [psychically] free except when he's fast asleep and dreaming that he's got the boss down the bottom of a well and is bunging lumps of coal at him." The reason for the fear, "the basic trouble with people like us," says Bowling, "is that we all imagine we've got something to lose." Most of the people on Ellesmere Road, this insurance salesman tells us, harbor the belief that they own their own houses, even while they are burdened by payments that keep them awake at night. This fear that some misfortune will make payments impossible, says Bowling, only bolsters the "illusion that we . . . have what's called 'a stake in the country.' "[59]

Of course, not all of the struggling middle classes were so bound to the upper class in terms of debts owing; but whatever the degree of sacrifice involved, the common result of the illusion of a stake in the country was a lack of empathy for the working class, who were not party to the same misapprehension. Even Bowling, who is so disdainful of the fear on Ellesmere Road, says cavalierly, "There's a lot of rot talked about the sufferings of the working class. I'm not so sorry for the proles myself. Did you ever know a navvy who lay awake thinking about the sack? The prole suffers physically, but he's a free man when he isn't working."[60] This remark reflects Orwell's more general point in *The Road to Wigan Pier* that if you "suggest to the average unthinking person of gentle birth who is struggling to keep up appearances . . . that he is a member of an exploiting parasite class, . . . he will think you are mad." Such a person, says Orwell, will point to a number of ways in which he considers himself much worse off than the worker. Furthermore, such a person does not see the working class as "a submerged race of slaves" but as "a sinister flood creeping upwards to engulf himself . . . and his family."[61]

For such people the "mob" of *Down and Out in Paris and London* is a reality. Bowling's claim of "free" navvies, many of whom no doubt worried as much about feeding their families as did the lower-middle-class breadwinners of Ellesmere Road, is obviously a Great Depression–bred exaggeration. Nevertheless, a theme that pervades *Down and Out in Paris and London* and *The Road to Wigan Pier* is the marked difference in anxiety that Orwell notices between those with "nothing" and those with "something" to lose. Such anxiety explains why "there is much more *consciousness* of poverty" in the middle classes.[62] The obvious question, then, given the level and pervasiveness of middle-class anxiety, is why doesn't the middle class dream of "bunging lumps of coal" at the boss become a reality? Why didn't the struggling inhabitants of Ellesmere Road overthrow the big landlords of the "Hesperides Estate"? Why wouldn't such sustained anxiety eventually explode in revolution?

The most obvious answer is that, its privations notwithstanding, the aspirations of the middle class, like those of the waiters in *Down and Out in Paris and London,* are aligned with those of the rich, and Bowling's comment that every man on Ellesmere Road "would die on the field of battle to save his country from Bolshevism," because he believes in the "illusion" of achieving "a stake in the country," goes some way toward explaining the reluctance of the middle class to rebel. This does not explain, however, why Orwell finds it quite easy to imagine, in *The Road to Wigan Pier,* that this middle class, even when totally disillusioned and "crushed down to the worst depths of poverty . . . [would still remain] bitterly anti–working class."[63] Certainly, the maintenance of bitter anti–working class feeling in such circumstances has much to do with the maintenance of "status." No one likes to "come down in the world," no matter what class he or she is in.[64] This is hardly surprising, but what is the underlying cause of the *tenacity* with which the middle classes cling to their status, the cause of what Orwell calls that "strange and sometimes 'heroic-snobbishness' that is found in the English middle classes"?[65]

For Orwell this tenacious snobbery not only qualifies the Marxist belief expressed by Ravelston in *Keep the Aspidistra Flying* "that ideology is [simply] a reflection of economic circumstances," but constitutes a serious impediment to social reform, insofar as it prevents the alliance of potential allies in the overthrow of privilege. In Orwell's work the underlying cause of tenacious snobbery in the middle classes is the "educational system." More specifically, it is the English "private" and "public" (as opposed to state) schools system that Orwell saw as "designed" to thwart a middle- and working-class alliance.[66] Recalling how as a teenager he was himself a snob—"but no worse than other boys of my own age and class"—Orwell comments on how successful the English public school education is in training one in the subtlest forms of class distinction. He notes how you quickly forget the scholastic curriculum soon after leaving school, "but your snobbishness, unless you persistently root it out, . . . sticks by you till your grave."[67]

In *Keep the Aspidistra Flying,* Comstock, a member of the shabby but genteel "middle-middle classes" in which proportionately "huge sums" were sacrificed to education, was sent to private schools. Like Eric Blair he discovered that nearly all the boys were richer than he and that he had to "suffer snobbish agonies such as a grown-up person can scarcely even imagine."[68] In such schools both boys learned to hate poverty. Comstock voices Orwell's recollection of the countless humiliations caused by having relatively poor parents, of how the phrase "your parents wouldn't be able to afford it . . . pursued me throughout my schooldays." Orwell remembers bitterly "the contempt for foreigners and the working class, an almost neurotic dread of poverty, and, above all, the assumption not only that money and privilege are the things that matter, but that it is better to inherit them than to have to work for them."[69]

Given the almost neurotic fear of poverty, it comes as no surprise that for Comstock the first seven months of his encounter with poverty "were devastating. They scared him and almost broke his spirit." Comstock realizes, however, that for the middle class to which he belongs, it is "not poverty but the down-dragging of *respectable* poverty that had done for them." Like George Bowling," he had never felt any pity for the genuine poor. It is the black-coated poor, the middle-middle class who need pitying."[70]

But why had "*respectable* poverty . . . done for them"? Orwell gives part of the answer in his description of how Comstock (and Orwell himself), determined to break out of the moneyed world, suddenly gives up a "good job." The immediate result of even this descent into poverty is that his family and relatives think that "Gordon must have gone mad,"[71] even though his descent was voluntary. Together with Bowling's description of life on Ellesmere Road, the relatives' reaction is a reflection of Orwell's general point that because of the *expectations* of the middle-class family, the prospect of poverty produces much more *psychic* trauma in middle-class individuals than in those of the "lower" classes.[72] What Comstock "realized," both in the middle-class school and "more clearly as time went on, was that money-worship has been elevated into a religion. Perhaps the only real religion—the only really *felt* religion—that is left to us. Money is what God used to be. Good and evil have no meaning any longer except failure and success. Hence the profoundly significant phrase, to *make good*."[73]

Similarly, Comstock's growing cynicism mirrors the bitter parody of I Corinthians 8 that prefaces the novel: "And though I have all faith, so that I could remove mountains, and have not money, I am nothing." For Orwell the sense of virtue and self-worth that once emanated from the belief of the faithful in future rewards for present decency now shifts aimlessly under the push of expediency. Such a world is very different from the world of pre–World War I Britain described in *Coming Up For Air* in which, for George Bowling's parents, "good and evil would remain good and evil . . . [and] they didn't feel the ground they stood on shifting under their feet."[74] In the world of relative right and wrong, however, Gordon Comstock finally comes to believe that "money *is* virtue . . . and poverty *is* crime."[75] (The italics are mine.) Again, Comstock's experience mirrors Blair's at St. Cyprian's, where material possession was "mixed up in people's minds with the idea of actual moral virtue."[76]

When such a belief is nurtured by the snobbishness of middle- and upper-class schools, it is not surprising that the middle class grows away from, and not closer to, the working class or that the young Eric Blair felt "in the air I breathed that you were no good unless you had £100,000"[77] and was taught that the working class were to be despised.[78]

Of course, Orwell came to despair of snobbish attitudes in himself and others that because they "generally persist from birth to death,"[79] perpetuate the divisions between men. On the other hand, he then argues, in a typically Orwellian stance, that you cannot blame the middle class for maintaining such attitudes: that to a middle-class parent such snobbishness is "necessary" for so long as vulgar accents will doom children to inequality of opportunity.[80] Indeed, the inconsistency between Orwell's theoretical call for equality through "a uniform educational system for the early years" that would "cut away one of the deepest roots of snobbery"[81] and his practical concern for his son's education is to the point. As late as 1948, in a letter to Julian Symons, he writes of his son, Richard,

I am not going to let him go to a boarding school before he is ten, and I would like him to start off at an elementary school. If one could find a good one. It's a difficult question. Obviously it is democratic for everyone to go to the same schools, or at least start off there but when you see what the elementary schools are like, and the results, you feel that any child that has the chance should be rescued from them. . . . I remember in 1936 meeting John Strachey in the street— then a C.P. [Communist Party] member or at least on the staff of the [Daily] Worker— and him telling me he had just had a son and was putting him down for Eton [Orwell's school]. I said, "How can you do that?" and he said that given our existing society it was the best education. Actually I doubt whether it is the best, but in principle I don't feel sure that he was wrong.[82]

It is important to remember this if we are to understand more clearly what Orwell meant, in his criticism, by an educational system "designed" to keep the middle class closer to the rich than the poor. That is, he believes that the "design" is not one maliciously *imposed from above;* rather, it is prompted by the impulse for self-defense in the middle class rather than by any upper-class vindictiveness. The middle classes, as Orwell views them, are caught between rich and poor and are merely trying to stay closer to the rich. Thus, they take care to absorb and maintain upper-class manners and traditions[83]— for example, in keeping their children at school much later than the working class, to whom "the notion of staying at school till you are nearly grown-up seems merely contemptible and unmanly."[84] It is Comstock's frustration with the defensive posture of his class that moves him to exclaim of his family that "They had never had the sense to lash out and just *live,* money or no money, as the lower classes do."[85]

It was this defensive posture of the middle classes, expressing the fear that they had "something to lose" and could fall prey to the "sinister flood creeping upwards," that accounted for Blair's expectation of a fight when he first descended into the world of the poor below Limehouse Causeway. It was the presence of this posture that led Orwell to suggest that it is from the poorer sections of the middle class, "the shock absorbers of the bourgeoisie" who are *forced* into close contact with the working class, that "the traditional upper class attitude [of "sniggering superiority"] towards 'common people' is derived."[86] The suggestion that upper-class attitudes are as much derived from the middle class as imposed upon them by the upper class is not only a claim of a symbiotic relationship between the two classes, but, more importantly, does much to explain Orwell's dismissal of upper-class conspiracy theories. He believed that despite often harshly felt internal divisions, England was still a family in a way that other countries were not. He maintained that although ignorance and inefficiency were rife in the hierarchy of the country, wickedness was not.[87]

Still, Orwell did not hold the upper classes completely blameless in the perpetuation of inequality, and in the case of the educational system, he singled out the powerful influence exerted in middle-class schools by the example of upper-class hierarchy. Further, as part of his conviction that the middle class is educated against the working class, he held the upper classes guilty of actively creating an acceptance of inequality through what he calls "deliberate incitement to wealth-fantasy." Such incitement, he claimed, was made possible through the "completely shameless" snob appeal of upper-class–owned, youth-oriented, and "political vetted" publications of his day, such as the widely read *Gem* and *Magnet*. He believed that we are much more influenced by novels, films, and serial stories than we admit and that "the worst books are often the most important because they are usually the ones that are read earliest in life." In "Boy's Weeklies" he says,

It is quite clear that there are tens and scores of thousands of people to whom every detail of life at a "posh" public school is wildly thrilling and romantic. They happen to be *outside* that mystic world of quadrangles and house-colours, but they yearn after it, day-dream about it, live mentally in it for hours at a stretch. . . . Recently I offered a batch of English papers to some British legionaires of the French Foreign Legion in North Africa; they picked out the *Gem* and *Magnet* first.[88] [The italics are mine.]

Based upon his experience as a schoolteacher in two private schools (1932–33), Orwell notes that unlike the rich "public" school boys, who stopped reading the likes of *Gem* and *Magnet* when they were about twelve, the middle-class private school boys kept reading them, "still taking them fairly seriously when they were fifteen or even sixteen." He reports that the basic political assumptions of such publications are that "nothing ever changes" (including inequality) and that foreigners and the working class are "funny." In such publications when working class people are not "comics," they are "semi-villains," and such things as "class friction, trade unionism, strikes, slumps, unemployment, Fascism and civil war" are never mentioned.[89]

It could be argued that any ill effects that this kind of "deliberate incitement" can have among the poorer classes (by raising expectations that cannot be fulfilled under the existing system) are mitigated by other mass publications stressing that being poor but honest is a happier fate than being rich and dishonest. Not surprisingly, Orwell was against such mollification as much as he was against incitement to wealth. He wrote that although "in any form of art designed to appeal to large numbers of people, it is an almost unheard-of thing for a rich man to get the better of a poor man, . . . this business about the moral superiority of the poor is one of the deadliest forms of escapism the ruling class has evolved." Such escapism, while not a deliberate attempt to perpetuate exploitation, is a "sublimation" of the "*real* facts" of inequality and of class struggle. Film magnates and press lords, he notes, "amass quite a lot of their wealth by pointing out that wealth is wicked."[90]

Although disturbed by the role of mass publications in contributing to the acceptance rather than the questionning of widespread economic disparities, Orwell was equally concerned with the way such publications foster the unquestionning acceptance of hierarchy—of disparities in power. Elsewhere in "Boy's Weelies" he wrote: "Nearly all the time the boy who reads these papers—in nine cases out of ten a boy who is going to spend his life working in a shop, in a factory or in some subordinate job in an office—is led to identify with people in positions of command ... above all with people who are never troubled by shortage of money."[91] Whether or not they informally derived many of their examples of the outside world from such papers, pupils' identification with the hierarchy of the rich, with an apparently unchanging and unchangeable world of authority patterns, was particularly marked in the more formal middle-class educational system. Of learning his early winner–loser catechism at St. Cyprian's, Orwell recalls:

Life was hierarchical and whatever happened was right. There were the strong, who deserved to win . . . and there were the weak who deserved to lose and always did lose, everlastingly.
I did not question the prevailing standards, because so far as I could see there were no others. How could the rich, the strong, . . . the powerful be in the wrong? It was their world, and the rules made for it must be the right ones. . . . It was not easy, at that date, to realize that in fact it *was* alterable.[92]

Such training exacerbated middle class–working class divisions, provided a pool of willing middle-class administrators like former Assistant Superintendent Blair to administer the Empire, and encouraged the view, as expresses in *Burmese Days*, that natives were no better than the working class. Such education also seriously qualified hopes that Britain's new wartime militias would be the "'nucleus' of genuinely democratic army," let alone the nucleus of revolution. Orwell certainly did not hold much hope for such an army, for he believed that so long as "nearly everybody who has been to a private school has passed through the O.T.C." and so long as the bourgeoisie form the pool of officer recruitement, "every increase" in military strenght effectively meant an increase for "the forces of reaction."[93]

An ominous synthesis of the effect of the educational system and what Orwell believed was the failure of religious belief [94] to sustain the old beliefs in absolute right and wrong emerges. Orwell shows how such training, with its unquestioning obedience to those in power and its celebration of relative right and wrong, at once nurtured and was nurtured by the "cult of realism," or the cult of "power worship." He held firmly to the idea that the "modern cult of power worship" was inextricably bound up with the failure of the belief in immortality, "with the modern man's feeling that life here and now is the only life."[95] When generations like those of young Comstock and young Blair see that because "good and evil have no meaning except failure and sucess,"[96] power is money, and "God is money," then it is hardly surprising that they see Power taking the place of God. This, of course, is precisely the religion of *Nineteen Eighty-Four*, in which the interrogator O'Brien asserts, "We are the priests of power,"[97] and the implications of power-worship for the perpetuation of, and increase in, inequality would be most dramatically discussed by Orwell.

Following his criticism of the English educational system, his repeated concern about the decline in religion, and how both contributed to the feeling that "might is right," the question that naturally presents itself is what Orwell would put in their place. Given the fact that he was so critical of the educational system and that he did not wish the belief in life after death to return,[98] did he have anything with which to fill what he called the "big hole" that had been left by the disappearance of a belief in the hereafter,[99] which, for all its faults, had set moral limits and had given meaning to "the belief in human brotherhood"?[100] Did he have a nonreligious system *designed* to replace the current educational system—one that would combat inequality rather than perpetuate it?[101] The answer is yes, he did. In *Nineteen Eighty-Four* O'Brien, while interrogating Winston Smith (the symbol of union between the privileged, "Winston," and the underprivileged, "Smith"), asks,

"Do you believe in God, Winston?"
"No."
"Then what is it, this principle that will defeat us [the "priests of power"]?"
"I don't know. The spirit of Man."[102]

For Orwell this spirit was the idea of human brotherhood, and "unless we can reinstate the belief in human brotherhood without the need for the next world to give it meaning, . . . we are moving towards . . . something more like the Spanish Inquisition, and probably far worse, thanks to the radio and the secret police."[103]

Orwell did not want to reinstate the Church's influence, for he believe that because the ideas of submission to God and of human control over nature are felt to be inimical, the Christian churches are on the whole hostile to reform, especially to "any political theory tending to weaken the institution of private property."[104] The system that Orwell chose as having the best chance of salvaging civilization through the propagation and manifestation of the spirit of brotherhood was "democratic socialism." In this system the main goal of life is not the pursuit of money and power by those who no longer believe in the heavenly paradise as a reward for the kind of heroic and pathetic perseverance demonstrated by the Pithers in *A Clergyman's Daughter*.[105] The goal of this system, to which Orwell turned "more out of disgust with the way the poorer sections of the industrial workers were oppressed . . . than out of any theoretical admiration of a planned society,"[106] is the attainment of a "world state of free and equal beings." In such a state private possessions such as clothes and furniture would be kept by the individual but the means of producing such "private" possessions would belong to the state.[107] As such, "Socialism is in the last analysis an optimistic creed," and its adherents hold "the earthly paradise to be possible."[108] It reflects the concept of a society "in which men know they are mortal and are nevertheless willing to act as brothers."[109]

Early in 1936 Orwell presented this vague vision—troubled though he was by its inadequacies—in the hope that it might mobilize the sense of decency that he believed we all have in common but hardly ever exert.[110] With this vision he sought to give the lie to Dorothy Hare's despairing conviction at the end of *A Clergyman's Daughter* that "either life on earth is a preparation for something greater and more lasting, or it is meaningless, dark, and dreadful."[111] Orwell's vision would darken in the torture chambers of *Nineteen Eighty-Four*, but in its more optimistic days it was to do away with the kind of exploitation that had bred Dorothy's despair, and as such, socialism for Orwell in *The Road to Wigan Pier* was to mean nothing less than "justice, . . . common decency[112] . . . and liberty."[113]

What needed to be done, said Orwell, was to "reinstate" the belief in brotherhood, the belief that no matter what differences exist between us, we are responsible for each other: "We have got to be the children of God, even though the God of the Prayer Book no longer exists."[114] If we do not act as members of one family, the divisions between people will widen into the yawning chasms of totalitarianism. Orwell did not believe that the spirit of brotherhood was dead but that it lay dormant—hence his use of the word *reinstate*. The way to do this politically, so that it might have the power to do good, was to turn to the socialist movement, which had traditionally appealed to the spirit of universal brotherhood as a basis for a fairer distribution of work and its rewards. Even in this there were problems.

CHAPTER 4

ORWELL BELIEVED THAT IN MATTERS OF PROPERTY FEW MEN "will behave any better than they are compelled to do."[1] Even so, because he was convinced that most people do not want to see English miners exploited or foreign proletarians held down by force, he maintained that the injustices of exploitation, like poverty, existed more from economic maldistribution than from a willful lack of decency.[2]

Accordingly, his idea of socialism arose largely from the simple view that "the world is a raft sailing through space with, potentially, plenty of provisions for everybody; [and] that we must all cooperate and see to it that everyone does his fair share . . . and gets his fair share of provisions." To Orwell this basic proposition of socialism was so "blatantly obvious" that "no one could possibly fail to accept it unless he had some corrupt motive for clinging to the present system." Corrupt motives (as in matters of property) aside, he believed that socialism's failure to appeal to the masses, particularly those without property, was due largely to the use of ideological cant. This spawned a widespread ignorance of what socialism could mean in everyday life.[3] It was to remove this widespread misunderstanding of what socialism meant that Orwell devoted much of his writing after visiting Wigan in 1936.

He claimed that the problems of production and consumption, of "wasted surplus" and "unemployment," which caused and perpetuated inequality, would not exist in a socialist economy, provided that common ownership of the means of production was founded upon "nationalized industry, scaled down incomes," a "classless educational system," and "political democracy." Writing at a time when he believed that the establishment of socialism in England and winning World War II were mutually dependent, he outlined how these prerequisites might be achieved. In summary, he said that: (1) *nationalization* essentially meant that "nobody shall live without working" but that previous owners and managers would be kept on as state employees. Small traders, particularly farmers, would be allowed to go on as before but a limit would be placed on land ownership of around fifteen acres. The ownership of land would be forbidden in urban areas. (2) while an expectation of equal *incomes* was unrealistic, a minimum wage based solely on the amount of consumption goods available would come into effect and would probably require rationing. Monetary incentives would be necessary, but as in the ownership of land by smallholders, a limit would be set. This limit would be based on a "maximum normal variation" of ten to one. This variation would allow "some sense of equality."[4] (3) Regarding *education* his system maintained that all children would have to attend *some* school up to the age of twelve—after which time they would be separated into more-gifted and less-gifted student categories. The main thrust of educational policy would be to erect a "uniform" system for the early years, so as to "cut away one of the deepest roots of snobbery."[5] To begin this, the autonomy of the public schools ("festering centres of snobbery") would be abolished and state-aided students, selected solely on the basis of ability, would flood the universities. This would do away with expensive public (i.e., private) school education, which was, in effect, a tax that the middle class paid for the right to make inroads into upper-class professions. The "vast majority" of England's ten thousand private schools "deserve[d] nothing but suppression," because not only did they exist solely because of snobbery but their educational level was generally very low. In *all* three areas the prime concern was a shift in emphasis "from privilege to competence."[6]

Beyond these few concrete proposals we learn more about Orwell's ideas for moving away from poverty and unemployment toward greater equality by noting not so much what he thought socialism should be, but what he thought it should not be. He claimed that in order to remove the "current distaste for Socialism," one had to get "inside the mind of the ordinary objector to Socialism." This meant that "paradoxically, in order to defend Socialism it is necessary to start by attacking it."[7] This belief is particularly evident, as we shall see, in Orwell's celebrated and often vindictive attacks upon the Left and leftist intellectuals, and it explains why he is often viewed as being a critic of socialism as much as he was its advocate.

Although Orwell was aware that the difference between socialism and capitalism went well beyond mere differences in technique,[8] he would have immediately understood the Russian joke that the difference between capitalism and communism is that whereas under capitalism man exploits man, under communism it is the other way around. In the same spirit, believing that "beyond a certain point . . . Socialism and Capitalism . . . merge into one," he warned that "Socialism *in itself*"[9] may not be any improvement over capitalism and that "it cannot be said too often . . . that collectivism is not inherently democratic"[10] or "equalitarian."[11] Discerning an irreversible trend towards centralism that he saw as "an essential precondition,"[12] but not necessarily a guarantor, of socialism, he presaged the gloomy world of *Nineteen Eighty-Four*. He warned that centralized (and common) ownership has little meaning unless steps are taken to assure that the governed have some control over the government and that all people have more or less the same standard of living. Without these safeguards, he predicted, " 'the state' may come to mean no more than a self-elected political party, and oligarchy and privilege can return." If people had roughly equal incomes, privilege such as Comstock and Blair saw daily about them would not be based on money but on power.[13] The capitalists would be weakened, but the "priests of power" would grow stronger and exploitation would continue. Only the technique of exploitation would have changed; its fundamental nature would remain the same. Similar warnings have, of course, been sounded by others, but they have an overriding significance in Orwell's case because they point to a view of socialism as more a means than an end. Socialism, he claims, "is not in itself the final objective, and I think we ought to guard against assuming that as a system to live under it will be greatly preferable to democratic Capitalism."[14]

While repeatedly making this point, Orwell just as often talks of socialism as an end in terms of "justice" and "liberty." This makes for a marked inconsistency and confusion in his writings on the subject that is maintained by his failure to define concretely what he means by such terms as *justice* and *liberty*. Wherever they are used there is an implicit and naive assumption that not only are such objectives immutable, but they are the same for all people everywhere.[15] In making this assumption he ignores one of the most simply stated yet profound lessons of his wide experience in situations from being an imperial policeman to leading the life of a tramp—namely, his discovery of "what different universes different people inhabit."[16]

One of the most frequently used words to describe Orwell is "honest." This is appropriate, because he was markedly so, as evidenced by his unwillingness to bend facts to fit ideological straitjackets. Nevertheless, in the seductive repetition of so laudatory a word as "honest" in describing him, the *consistency of his honesty* often creates an assumption of a *consistency of ideas*. This is false. One's ideas, like one's life—like life itself—are, of course, inconsistent—honesty notwithstanding and indeed, often because of it. Orwell's inconsistencies in his views of socialism, largely shown in his failure to define such terms as *liberty* and *justice,* constitute a serious flaw in his "socialist" views, given that these terms are accorded such prominence and elasticity in sudden, unexplained shifts from a view of socialism as a tool to a view of it as a goal.

Despite Orwell's oscillation between viewing socialism as a means and justifying it as an end, there is his implicit and constant conviction that the real value of the socialist movement is that it constitutes a mobilization of the idea of equality. Calls for "liberty," "justice," and "decency," for all their vagueness, do signify an intent to improve the quality of life, to move away from inequality wherein privilege takes precedence over ability; and, while "Socialists don't claim to be able to make the world perfect ["certain evils cannot be remedied"],[17] they claim to be able to make it better."[18] In 1941 Orwell wrote that even if England should be defeated, the introduction of the "beginnings of Socialism," which might "turn the war into a revolutionary war," was of vital importance, for while "no political programme is ever carried out in its entirety . . . it is always the *direction* that counts." Once people are shown that direction, the "*idea*" of equality will survive, even in defeat. If such a socialist goal were not put before the nation, he argued, England's surrender—unlike that of the Republicans to Franco—would be as total and as devoid of the will to resist Nazism[19] as that of Vichy France. The idea of equality need not be preserved in a doctrinaire manifesto; it could be carried in a simple song like the "Marseillaise," from which a man who cannot be appealed to by "any learned treatise on dialectical materialism" could at least "grasp the central fact that Socialism means the overthrow of tyranny."[20] Orwell lamented the lack of such songs in England, for to him "to *preserve* is always to *extend.*"[21] This belief goes some way in explaining why at times his writings—despite their occasional cries for revolution—reveal a resilient, and at least small *c*, conservatism.

Another constant in Orwell's view of socialism is his steady conviction that changing the structure of society will not automatically improve the quality of life. In this regard, his comment on Dickens (which follows) was equally applicable to himself: "His whole 'message' is one that at first glance looks like an enormous platitude: If men would behave decently the world would be decent."[22] Orwell, though he was against certain institutions, was, like Dickens, more against "an expression on the human face." It is the face of the fanatic addressing the "West Bletchley revolutionaries" at the Left Book Club meeting in *Coming Up For Air*, a face full of hatred paired with a gramophone voice and the message that "we must all get together and have a good hate." Its vision is "a picture of . . . smashing people's faces in with a spanner. . . . The bones cave in like an eggshell and what was a face a minute ago is just a great big blob of strawberry jam . . . and it's all O.K. because the smashed faces belong to Fascists."[23] In *Nineteen Eighty-Four* this face of hatred becomes omnipotent and is kept so by the televised hate sessions that begin each day.

Concerned more with character than structure, Orwell said that what frightened him most about the modern intelligentsia was their inability to see "that human society must be based on decency, *whatever the political and economic forms may be*. . . . Dickens without the slightest understanding of Socialism etc., would have seen at a glance that there is something wrong with a régime [the "Soviet government"] that needs a pyramid of corpses every few years."[24] (The italics are mine.) It is his concern with the leftists' preoccupation with changing the structure of society—rather than the character of its members and institutions—that ranks Orwell among the most important critics of the English socialist movement. Within his passionate and often vindictive[25] attacks upon the Left, he time and again aims his best shots at what he calls the "inherently mechanistic Marxist notion" that moral advance necessarily follows technical advance, that a more decent life pants at the heels of modern "progress."[26] Even when good intentions are present, he notes, modernization may exact a high price in human terms. Talking of the modern housing development initiated by an administration in which Socialist and Conservative policy were indistinguishable, he writes, "When you walk through the smoke-dim slums of Manchester you think that nothing is needed except to tear down these abominations and build decent houses in their place. But the trouble is in destroying the slum you destroy other things as well." While a new housing estate for workers might provide better homes, the rules of the estate, from banning Yorkshire miners from keeping homing pigeons in their backyards to the prohibition of pubs on the estate, strike serious blows at the old communal, family-based life.[27]

Orwell believes that at its worst, the failure to see that moral advance ought to precede technical advance and changes in the structure of a state creates what he calls the "Theory of Catastrophic Gradualism." Prominent in its use to justify the often horrific changes of the Stalin regime, this theory harbors the belief that "nothing is ever achieved without bloodshed, lies, tyranny and injustice"; that "history necessarily proceeds by calamities" and one "must not protest against purges, deportations, secret police forces . . . because these are the price that has to be paid for progress."[28]

Orwell was always suspicious of claims of "progress." To those like the exponents of Catastrophic Gradualism who persistently claimed that one could not reach a just society—that one could not make an omelet without breaking eggs—he persistently asked, "But where is the omelette?"[29] For him, the word *progress,* as used in his time, conjured up visions not of a moral advance upon inequality, but of a mechanistic and materialist utopia that was actually hostile at root to the nonmechanistic and creative impulse.[30] It is this vision that Flory attacked so vigorously in *Burmese Days,* highlighting the tension that exists between the view of change as a sign of cultural vigor and as a symptom of breakdown, of cultural discontinuity. It is this latter view, expressed in *A Clergyman's Daughter,* that pervades the down-and-out trials of Dorothy Hare, causing her to dwell on the hymn line "Change and decay in all around I see."[31] It is the same view that accompanies George Bowling in *Coming Up For Air* when he discovers that the pastoral Lower Binfield of his youth is irretrievably lost—swallowed up by new factories, acres of bright-red–roofed housing estates and a huge cemetery, replete with "machine-made" angels.[32]

Orwell, does not, however, counsel a blanket opposition to technological advance or to any form of modernization, nor advocate a return to a "state of nature—meaning some stinking palaeolithic cave:

as though there was nothing between a flint scraper and the steel mills of Sheffield." He knew from firsthand experience as a manual laborer how welcome the machine might be: "It makes one sick to see half a dozen men sweating their guts out to dig a trench . . . when some easily devised machine would scoop the earth out in a couple of minutes." Furthermore, he argued that an "equal" standard of living for all required a state "at least as highly mechanized as the United States,"[33] recognizing that some mechanical advances, while they may be initially invented for a few, ultimately benefit all, because a millionaire can hardly leave others in darkness while lighting the streets for himself.[34]

In any event, he said, there can be no question of accepting or rejecting machine-civilization: the "beehive [mechanistic] state," whether we like it or not, is here to stay, because "every Western man has his inventive faculty to some extent developed." Orwell admits that he, too, found himself "perpetually seeing, as it were, the ghosts of possible machines that might save me the trouble of using my brain or muscles."[35]

Nevertheless, while he maintained that a blanket hostility toward the machine was "unrealistic," he believed that a suspicion of mechanization was healthy, insofar as it might act as a much-needed brake upon a blanket acceptance of technology. His own caution was based on his observation of what he called the "huge contradiction" that marked the idea of progress—that whereas those "qualities we admire in human beings can only function in opposition to some kind of disaster, pain or difficulty, . . . the tendency of mechanical progress is to eliminate disaster, pain and difficulty." But because the process of mechanization is so deeply habitual in us, we follow the apostles of "progress" with the "blind persistence of a column of ants."[36]

Orwell believed that such columns constituted a mindless army marching toward the kind of socialist vision envisaged by H.G. Wells, wherein "there will be no disorder, no poverty and no pain." The problem with such a vision, he says, is that even though Wells, for example, does entertain the possibility that "inequality" could occur in the mechanized utopia, with "one class grabbing all the wealth and power and oppressing the others," he suggests that all one has to do is to overthrow privilege—to switch from capitalism to socialism—and "all will be well. . . . The machine-civilization is to continue, but its products are to be shared out equally." Orwell charges that this sole reliance on a socialist-controlled redistribution of goods to solve the problems of inequality ignored the possibility that "the machine itself may be the enemy." It ignores the very real probability that once we have the habit of using machines, we will forever think of more machines as more progress. When this happens mechanization can be seen as the end of socialism rather than the means, and it is precisely this vision that most readily alienates the sensitive and creative minds that socialism sorely needs to humanize it. It is this vision that also harbors the belief that once "you have got this planet of ours perfectly into trim, you start upon the enormous task of reaching and colonizing another."[37]

Such Wellsian-inspired visions, Orwell argues, do not come to grips with the *dangers* of the machine. Rather, all they do is to "push the objective" of mechanization "further into the future," and "for the foolproof world you have substituted the foolproof solar system."[38] By way of contemporary illustration, Professor Carl Sagan, director of the Laboratory for Planetary Studies at Cornell University, writes, "One of the many virtues of the space-city proposal is that it may provide the first convincing argument for extensive manned space-flight." He continues:

The earth is almost fully explored and culturally homogenized. There are few places to which the discontented cutting edge of mankind can emigrate. There is no equivalent of the America of the 19th and 20th centuries. But space cities provide a kind of America in the skies, an opportunity for affinity groups to develop alternative cultural, social, political, economic and technological life-styles. Almost all the societies on the earth today have not the foggiest notion of how best to deal with our complex and unknown future. Space cities may provide the social mutations that will permit the next evolutionary advance in human society.[39]

For Orwell such plans, grand as they are, will still have to confront the human problems created by technological advance.

Quite apart from the effect that visions of more and more mechanization might have in alienating potential converts to the socialist cause, Orwell cautions that the headlong rush rowards mechanization ignores the lesson of his down-and-out days: that people "need" work as a measure of self-esteem and self-expression. He also notes that the belief that machines, in doing away with "work," will automatically provide more leisure time overlooks the simple but important fact that beyond the most odious manual tasks, what is one man's work is another man's play. In short, it is not dishwashing machines that the ex-dishwasher is against, but the *degree* of mechanization. As in the moral realm, if there are no limits, the impulse to invent and improve, which has now become "instinctive," means that if you set a pacifist working in a bomb factory he or she will very soon be inventing a new type of bomb. Soon "there are . . . millions of people to whom the blaring of a radio is . . . a more acceptable, more *normal* background to their thoughts than the low-ing of cattle or the song of birds."[40]

Orwell admits that the machine can make us economically freer; but the question that continues to posit itself in the face of unlimited mechanization is how new-found freedom from material need can be translated into freedom to act more as individuals.

The dilemma posed by humans being economically wealthier but less free is one that Orwell, like so many others, could not solve. What he does do, however, is alert us to the dangers inherent in the assumption that because science can solve people's material problems through labor-saving devices, it can solve their psychological problems as well. When neurosis, for example, comes to be thought of as no more invulnerable to the tools of science than diphtheria, it is only a matter of time before Big Brother's state seeks not simply to "cure" people with electric shock, but to dominate them. If "thought corrupts science, science can also corrupt thought," and, as with language, a "bad usage can spread by tradition and imitation, even among people who should and do know better."[41] Winston Smith, political prisoner, becomes Winston Smith, victim of science.

Orwell wrote in "What is Science?" of the danger to our very existence (let alone our political freedom) if we accept certain assumptions implicit in "the demand for more scientific education." One assumption is that scientific training improves one's approach to any subject and that therefore a scientist's views on all aspects of life will be superior to those of the layman. Rejecting this belief, Orwell argues that the fact that "scientific workers of all countries line up" and support their governments' policies much more readily than do writers and artists helps to illustrate the point that "a mere training in one or more of the exact sciences . . . is no guarantee of a humane or sceptical outlook."[42]

The danger of all classes being enslaved rather than liberated by science, says Orwell, stems once again from ignorance rather than malice, from the habit of mechanization in all classes that will quickly move them to devise new machines even if old ones are deliberately destroyed. Such a habit, through mass production, both reflects and is responsible for the "frightful debauchery of taste that has already been effected by a century of mechanization."[43]

The concern over the standardization of goods, which Orwell sees as a direct cause of the decay of taste and which worries him so much, is not confined to his theorizing in *The Road to Wigan Pier,* in which he goes beyond the indigenous condition to a world condition. Such concern has its origins in the oft-repeated fears of John Flory's vision of modern progress—seeing and hearing all the gramophones playing the same tune. It is the impact of standardization in the world of goods alone that causes Orwell to conclude that in the long run we may find that canned goods are more deadly weapons than guns,[44] and it is the presence of standardized goods, maintained by the use of cheap substitutes, that so thoroughly depresses George Bowling. The decay in taste signalled at Bowling's breakfast table by a label informing him of the existence of "neutral fruit juice" is symptomatic for Orwell (in 1939) of a decaying and endangered world—not just a world headed for a second world war but heading for the "after-war, the food queues, . . . the secret police and the loudspeakers telling you what to think."[45] It is from this vision of *Nineteen Eighty-Four* that Bowling, in one last desperate effort, attempts to flee and come up for air by returning to his boyhood home.

In a cameo of the modern decay of taste, we see Bowling, for lack of any other suitable eating places, entering a "streamlined" milk bar and asking himself, "Why am I coming here? . . . No real food at all. . . . Sort of phantom stuff that you can't taste and can hardly believe in the existence of." He places his order for coffee and frankfurters amid the shine of chrome and mirrors and against the noise of a radio, altogether "a sort of propaganda floating round." Then there is the shock of biting into the frankfurters:

Suddenly—pop! The thing burst in my mouth. . . . A sort of horrible soft stuff was oozing all over my tongue. But the taste! For a moment I just couldn't believe it. . . . I was still rolling the stuff round my tongue, wondering where I could spit it out. I remembered a bit I'd read in the paper somewhere about these food-factories in Germany where everything's made out of something else. Ersatz, they call it. I remembered reading that *they* were making sausages out of fish, and fish, no doubt, out of something different. . . . I'd bitten into the modern world and discovered what it was really made of. That's the way we're going nowadays. Everything slick, and streamlined, everything made out of something else. Celluloid, rubber, chromium-steel everywhere, arc-lamps blazing all night, glass roofs over your head, radios all playing the same tune, no vegetation left, everything cemented over, mock-turtles grazing under the neutral fruit-trees. But when you come down to brass tacks and get your teeth into something solid, a sausage for instance, that's what you get. Rotten fish in a rubber skin. Bombs of filth bursting inside your mouth.[46]

The wider implication of Bowling's concern is that the habit of mass-produced standardization made possible through substitutes not only threatens to render the distinction between natural and "filthy chemical" beer difficult to make, but more significantly, the "ersatz" habit makes such a distinction seem unimportant. The danger is that ultimately because "what applies to food applies also to . . . books, and everything else that makes up our environment,"[47] the distinction between ideas is in danger. As we are conditioned, indeed we condition ourselves, not to be concerned about the *degree* of difference between natural and artificial beer or cheese, so do we become uncaring of the degree of difference between those governments with power over us. In short, as standardization of goods dulls the critical ability to distinguish between manufactured goods, so, by osmosis, does it dull the critical ability to distinguish between regimes and ideas. As one soap seems as good or bad as the next, soon we say that "all politicians are the same." The result is that in time the decay of taste, which allows indifference to pose as tolerance, leads even sections of the intelligentsia to argue that "after all, democracy is 'just the same as' or 'just as bad as' totalitarianism. There is *not much* freedom of speech in England; therefore there is *no more* than exists in Germany. To be on the dole is a horrible experience; therefore it is *no worse* to be in the torture-chambers of the Gestapo."[48]

In addition to the decay in taste that the concentration upon mechanization has produced, Orwell argues that an equal danger to hopes of greater equality emerges from the parent and *mistaken* conviction that redistribution of goods will of itself make life better—will eliminate the uneasiness between one person and another. His concern here is that the apostles of socialism, because of their preoccupation with the "materialistic utopia," with "mechanization, rationalization, modernization" and the host of attendant "economic facts," will continue to proceed "on the assumption that man has no soul." The danger is not merely that scientific method will be thought to be the only solution to all problems, but that in ignoring the spiritual side of man, socialists will perpetuate the "spirtual recoil from socialism."[49] In *Keep the Aspidistra Flying,* when Ravelston asks, "But what *would* Socialism mean, according to your idea of it?" Comstock's recoil is evident in his reply: "Oh! Some kind of Aldous Huxley, *Brave New World;* only not so amusing. Four hours a day in a model factory, tightening up bolt number 6003. Rations served out in grease proof paper at the communal kitchen. Community-hikes from Marx Hostel to Lenin Hostel and back. Free abortion clinics on all the corners. All very well in its way, of course, only we don't want it".[50]

Marching into the vacuum of such a recoil, says Orwell, will be fascism, a movement that might well be accepted through its appeal to the spiritual side of man—to such things as tradition and religion.[51] As such, fascism addresses itself to all those like Dorothy Hare who are confronted by the central dilemma of *A Clergyman's Daughter,* that "faith vanishes, but the need for faith remains the same as before."[52]

Beyond the immediate impediments to a better life that Orwell saw posed by too heavy a reliance upon technology by the socialists *of his day,* a further impediment arises in his discussion of the class question. It is that if you place too much faith in merely changing the shape of society through mechanization, you are not only apt to believe that redistribution of goods through technology is all that is needed to achieve equality, but you are apt not to realize that the "issue of class, *as distinct from mere economic status,* has got to be faced more realistically."[53] (The italics are mine.) The question that has to be faced, insofar as technology is concerned, is why there is still so much exploitation of others, as evidenced by continuing class division, when with mechanization the machine has effectively replaced the servant.[54]

Obviously, in order to remove such exploitation, or at least reduce it, more has to be done than merely pressing for the removal of an unqualified belief in technology. What is required, and here Orwell returns to a favourite theme, is radical and "uncomfortable change" in the "habits and 'ideology' " of *individuals* in the upper and middle classes. If this prerequisite for abolishing class distinctions does not happen, then technology will not only belong only to the upper class, but will actually *strengthen* class division; for while technological advance tends to "some form of collectivism," this form, as we have seen, need not be egalitarian. Presaging *Nineteen Eighty-Four,* Orwell

finds it all too easy "to imagine a world-society economically collectivist . . . but with all the political, military and educational power in
the hands of a small caste of rulers and their bravos [*sic*]; . . . the
slave state, . . . the slave world." This world, he claims, may very well
be a stable society and, given the existence of enormous natural
resources, one could expect the slaves to be reasonably well off; but,
he says, it is precisely against this kind of world that we must fight.[55]
The idea that technology may well end up serving as the guarantor
of totalitarianism is also reflected in his observation that past despo-
tisms have fallen short of being totalitarian only because their
"repressive apparatus" was simply inefficient.[56] In the modern world,
however, just as the telegraph in *Burmese Days* brought scattered
district officers under more direct control of the bureaucrats in Whitehall, so technology brings the Winston Smiths under the increasing
control of Big Brother's ever-watchful telescreens.

It is true that technological advance can occasionally erode the
more visible signs of class structure and friction. This helps us to
understand the inconsistency in Orwell's views about whether or not
class distinctions and differences were decreasing in England. In 1941
he wrote that one of the most important developments in modern
England had been interclass mobility—to such an extent, in his opinion, that the old classifications of capitalists, workers, and middle
class were all but useless. An example of this was the way in which
the sudden requirements of a large and modern air force had dealt a
serious blow to the class structure in England by cutting across class
lines in the urgency of its recruitment drive.[57] As late as 1946, in *The
English People,* Orwell talked of how mass production of consumer
goods, especially clothes, makes it more difficult to determine class
by appearance, and noted that though class distinctions do remain,
the "real differences between man and man are obviously diminishing." Thus, despite the striking contrasts that he says still existed
between wealth and poverty in England, he believed that English
society was at least moving closer to a state of social equality.[58]

The appearance of *Animal Farm* in 1945 and *Nineteen Eighty-Four*
in 1949, however, constitutes a pessimistic and drastic reassessment
of Orwell's earlier hopes for the disappearance of class distinctions.
A year after *Animal Farm* was published, he was claiming that the
old class distinctions seemed to be reemerging—albeit in new guises—
and that "individual liberty is on the down-grade."[59] True, the Air
Force's urgent recruitment, necessitated by Hitler's modern techno-

logical war, might have ridden roughshod over class lines, and modern clothing techniques had removed the outward signs of class; yet as early as 1944, with victory over the Axis in sight, Orwell had to admit there was a swing back toward the old divisions. Evening dress, for example, was reappearing, as were the old distinctions between first and third class on the railways, and advertisements based on snob appeal were being enthusiastically resurrected.[60]

In any event, however much his opinions may have changed and been inconsistent on the degree to which technological advances had lowered class barriers, Orwell's fundamental attitude to the class question remained unchanged. Always and everywhere he was consistent in his belief that whatever alterations might occur in the degree of class snobbery, the real evil was that such snobbery should exist at all.

CHAPTER 5

AS WE HAVE SEEN, IN HIS EFFORTS TO COMBAT CLASS DIFFER-
ence, Orwell tried to convince the stage rebels of socialism that
it was necessary for them first to make a determined effort to change
themselves in order that they might change society. He did so not
only because he thought that everyone should make such a commitment, but because he believed that as with Christianity, the worst
advertisements for socialism—for equality—were its adherents.[1] This
was so, he argued, because, paradoxically, "Socialism in its developed form is a theory confined entirely to the middle classes," who
are educated to be snobbish and so are unprepared at heart to change
themselves.[2] Instead, they seek to realize their good intentions by
talking about a classless society while remaining at a safe distance
from the working classes with whom Orwell says they should be
acting out their good intentions. It is in Ravelston, the socialist editor of *Antichrist* in *Keep the Aspidistra Flying,* that we see the gap
between leftist intellectualism and right-wing temperament that Orwell considered the plague of so many parlor socialists—particularly
writers.[3]

Ravelston [felt] . . . uncomfortable. In a way of course, he knew—it was
precisely this that *Antichrist* existed to point out—that life under a decaying
capitalism is deathly and meaningless. But this knowledge was only theoretical. You can't really *feel* that kind of thing when your income is eight hundred
a year. Most of the time, when he wasn't thinking of coal-miners, Chinese
junk-coolies, and the unemployed in Middlesborough, he felt that life was
pretty good fun.[4]

While Orwell admitted that it was "silly," "childish," and "even
contemptible" to be dissuaded from the good purpose of a movement because of the hypocrisy of the adherents, he said that because

"*it happens*"[5] it had to be dealt with if socialism was to advance. It was against such hypocrisy, unconscious or not, that he turned with full force in *The Road to Wigan Pier*. Throughout his life his attacks upon what can be called the hypocritical Left alternated between broadsides against the middle-class Left and the intellectual Left—which were not always one and the same. The middle-class Left sometimes included writers but refers here mainly to middle-class members and supporters of the Socialist party. The intellectual Left, on the other hand, often included the middle-class members and supporters of the Socialist party but referred, at least in Orwell's view, much more to left-wing writers.[6] Here I will be mainly discussing his criticism of the middle-class socialist. Later, in the Spanish section, I will discuss the attack upon the intellectuals in general, for it was largely the result of his experience in Spain that Orwell was to view the intellectuals with a deep and permanent suspicion.

Although Orwell wanted the middle-class socialist leadership to rid themselves of the habits and ideology that make a hypocrisy of their protestations of brotherhood with the less privileged, he warned against the "summer school" approach, in which the "proletarian and repentant bourgeois are supposed to fall upon one another's necks and be brothers for ever." Such attempts succeed only, he believed, in spotlighting and intensifying differences. Just as the summer school method failed, so did the doctrinaire approach, with its outpouring of socialist cant. Orwell was not against propaganda—that is, the propagation of a belief. At the B.B.C. (*Nineteen Eighty-Four's* Ministry of Truth), during the war, he would be a propagandist himself but he was against deliberately dishonest and in this case, ineffective, propaganda. He was against bourgeois socialists who, in their baiting of the bourgeois, showed that they knew more about what they were against than what they were for and succeeded in alienating and antagonizing potential middle-class recruits by telling them that they were inferior because they didn't work with their hands. What the socialist movement needs instead, Orwell writes, is "less about 'class consciousness', 'expropriation of the expropriators,' 'bourgeois ideology,' and proletarian solidarity" and "the sacred sisters, thesis, antithesis, and synthesis; and more about justice, liberty, and the plight of the unemployed."[7]

The danger in the use of such jargon for Orwell—quite apart from making socialism's aims unintelligible to the working-class—is that by soothing the conscience of the speaker, it draws his or her attention away from the underlying problem, that while "we all rail against class distinctions . . . few people seriously want to abolish them,"[8] including socialists. The antiimperialists, he wrote—like the British Labour Party, with its socialist slogans—railed against imperialism while depending upon sweating coolies for the very standard of living that antiimperialists enjoyed and clearly didn't want to give up.[9] Similarly, he said, most of the middle class "cling like glue" to their class while vociferously advocating the classless society.

Furthermore, many would-be socialists were drawn to the socialist vision not from any love of their fellow human beings, because class distinction and unemployment bothered them, but because of what Orwell called their "hypertrophied sense of order." For such people (of whom Shaw is a noted example), he said, poverty and its habits are not only more disgusting than wrong, but are to be abolished *"from above."* Revolution is not seen as a movement of the masses below, but as rules imposed by " 'we,' the clever ones . . . upon 'them.' "[10] This, charges Orwell, explains Shaw's worship of powerful men like Stalin and Mussolini.

Such a view, he claimed, despite its good intentions, did not mean that the clever socialists were willing to rid themselves of their antagonism against the bourgeoisie. Indeed, because of their often more literary natures, they were capable of the most impassioned outrage. The "bourgeois-baiting" literature was to the point. Here, one could see the proclivity of socialist writers toward whipping themselves into "frenzies of rage" against the class to which they belonged. This great outpouring of hatred left no doubt that its authors were theoretically against exploitation but were devoid of constructive suggestions on how to improve the lot of the exploited. The result, according to Orwell, was that such diatribes convinced potential recruits to socialism that socialism was little more than the voice of hatred.[11]

It is this nexus of thought, order, and unqualified hatred of exploiters, says Orwell, that repelled so many people—especially artists and writers, whose creative talents are sorely needed to counter the dullness of the socialist vision. The vision of the socialist world, being "above all things an *ordered,* . . . *efficient* world," relies so heavily upon the vision of a superorganized and thoroughly mechanized world that belief in mechanical progress as the guarantor of order and efficiency becomes an article of faith—"almost a . . . religion." Consequently, any attempt to check the machine's advance is considered as "blasphemy." Orwell points to the power of orthodoxy in his frequent analogies between educated communists and Roman Catholics, who can regard even the "liquids you drink" as "orthodox or heretical."

By way of example of the power of socialist orthodoxy, Orwell recalls how a "prominent I.L.P.'er confessed" to him, with "a sort of wistful shame, . . . that he was fond of horses." The existence of such orthodoxy, in the grip of which a person could actually feel guilty because he harbored any sentiment for the un-socialist "agricultural past," says Orwell, is enough in itself to explain why so many "decent minds" had been alienated from the socialist cause.[12] The wider and darker implications of the power of such orthodoxy would become evident to him in Spain.

In addition to his complaints against middle-class socialists, Orwell deplored, in markedly bitter attacks, the "horrible—really disquieting—prevalence of cranks" among socialists and the population in general. With "magnetic force," he said the very word *socialism,* along with *communism,* seemed to attract "every fruit-juice drinker, nudist, sandal-wearer, sex-maniac, Quaker, 'Nature Cure' quack, pacifist, and feminist in England."[13] George Bowling's disgust with one such "crank" could well be mistaken for Orwell's in *The Road to Wigan Pier.* As Bowling comes across the Upper Binfield Estate, he meets one of the "cranks":

I began to wonder whether he was someone who'd escaped from Binfield House. But no, he was sane enough, after a fashion. I knew the type. Vegetarianism, simple life, poetry, nature-worship, roll in the dew before breakfast. . . . He began to show me round the estate. There was nothing left of the woods. It was all houses, houses—and what houses! . . . You could see in your mind's eye the awful gang of food-cranks and spook-hunters and simple-lifers with £1000 a year that lived there. Even the pavements were crazy. . . . I got rid of him, went back to the car and drove down to Lower Binfield. . . . God rot them and bust them! Say what you like—call it silly, childish, anything—but doesn't it make you puke sometimes to see what they're doing to England, with their bird-baths and their plaster gnomes, and their pixies and tin cans, where the beechwoods used to be?[14]

Because such people are so often associated with socialism, says Orwell, the ordinary man is driven away from the socialist cause in his belief that socialism is little more than a synonym for eccentricity.[15]

At first sight it would seem unlikely that such "eccentrics" and the proponents of order could tolerate each other, let alone combine in the socialist quest for equality; but what emerges from Orwell's discussions of both types is that both the bourgeois sandal-wearer and the bourgeois white-collar worker are attracted not simply by the vision of a better life in the future, but by a life cut off from the past—*from tradition*. This is what makes the socialist order the *new* order, and it is from this vision that nonsocialists flee (pursued by the charge of "bourgeois sentimentality"), not because they believe that socialism "would not work," but because they believe that "it would 'work' too well." When they flee, Orwell is afraid, they will end up in the waiting arms of fascism. Fascism offers more than discipline and order; it offers respite from the hedonistic vision of the materialist utopia by *posing* as the keeper of tradition. It offers people security gained through their link with the past. After a "bellyful of the more tactless kind of Socialist propaganda," writes Orwell, "even the Fascist bully" probably feels less like a bully and more like "Roland in the pass at Roncevaux, defending Christendom against the barbarian."[16]

In light of his harsh attacks upon socialists in the indigenous period, particularly in *The Road to Wigan Pier*, Orwell gives the impression that the socialist movement of his time was composed almost entirely of ineffectual cranks and machine-worshippers; but he was, after all, more concerned with diagnosing what he felt was wrong with socialism than with praising what he felt was right with it.[17] This is often forgotten by critics who point out, correctly, that he did not pay enough attention to "good and self-forgetful action which many middle class socialists have shown."[18]

Despite the pessimism of his novels, however, and his fear that fascism might win—that George Bowling's vision of "the after-war, . . . the barbed wire! The slogans! The enormous faces! The cork-lined cellars where the executioner plugs you from behind!"[19] might come true, Orwell did not spend all his time brooding about those things that created class divisions.[20] Writing in the dark dusk of the Thirties, he believed that the only hope of establishing socialism lay in winning the coming war against Hitler, and for Orwell this necessitated the declaration, "My country, Right or Left."[21] In short, the hope of socialism lay in an appeal to the most traditional of values—patriotism.

Not only would the call to patriotism be essential for the defeat of Hitler but, Orwell hoped, it would bring the middle and working classes close enough together so that even if a firm alliance between the two against the upper class was not effected, at least the technocratic middle class, "indispensable" to any modern industrial nation, would not be hostile to revolution.[22] At the very least, if socialism, through revolution, was to come to England, then that revolution must be supported and defended by the British fleet. And if the British fleet was to be utilized for such a revolution, the support of its officer class was essential—which meant that the middle class had to be won over through an appeal to middle-class patriotism, which Orwell believed was stronger than that of the upper classes.[23]

Despite his sudden resurgence of patriotism, Orwell did not claim that his feeling was shared by everyone: after all, this was the decade of the Oxford Union's declaration of its determination not to fight for king and country, and of the Peace Pledge Union. He did claim, however, that beneath the natural and healthy reluctance to be involved in war, which he had earlier shared, there was a deep current of loyalty that would quickly draw men to the defense of England and her empire. This is the belief expressed by George Bowling (in *Coming Up For Air*) as he recalls Lower Binfield's attitude toward the Boer War:

"Well now! Listed for a soldier! Just think of it! A fine young fellow like that!" It just shocked them. Listing for a soldier, in their eyes, was the exact equivalent of a girl's going on the streets. Their attitude to the war, and to the Army, was very curious. They had the good old English notions that the red-coats are the scum of the earth and anyone who joins the Army will die of drink and go straight to hell, but at the same time they were good patriots, stuck Union Jacks in their windows. . . . Even the Nonconformists used to sing sentimental songs about the thin red line.[24]

Orwell believed that this attitude was unchanged in 1941. Englishmen, he said, were as contemptuous of military bombast as ever but just as patriotic. It was one of those constancies behind his statement, "What can the England of 1940 have in common with the England of 1840? . . . What have you in common with the child of five whose photograph your mother keeps on the mantelpiece? Nothing, except that you happen to be the same person."[25]

Patriotism was the "invisible chain" that transcended class lines, drawing together the latent sense of brotherhood that was heightened by the threat of invasion and was essential for the establishment of socialism. It is this common emotion amid all the patent injustice and inequality, to which Orwell said socialism should appeal. Although he probably regarded such an appeal as a strategic move, his was not an appeal of cynicism. He believed that patriotism was a virtuous thing, declaring that despite the flirtations of the British ruling class with fascism, the thing that showed their moral soundness was that they were "ready enough" to die in England's defense. In one of the most moving passages he ever wrote, he talks of how the emotional bond to country, stirred by the threat of aggressive nationalism from without, can transcend class barriers, can be transmuted to a sense of family even if it is "a family with the wrong members in control."

Beneath Mr. Muggeridge's seeming acceptance of disaster there lies the unconfessed fact that he does after all believe in something—in England. . . . I am told that some months back he left the Ministry of Information to join the army. . . . And I know very well what underlies these closing chapters. It is the emotion of the middle-class man, brought up in the military tradition, who finds in the moment of crisis that he is a patriot after all. It is all very well to be "advanced" and "enlightened," to snigger at Colonel Blimp and proclaim your emancipation from all traditional loyalties, but a time comes when the sand of the desert is sodden red and what have I done for thee, England, my England? As I was brought up in this tradition myself I can recognize it under strange disguises, and also sympathize with it, for even at its stupidest and most sentimental it is a comelier thing than the shallow self-righteousness of the left-wing intelligentsia.[26]

The appeal to patriotism as a rallying point for the implementation of socialist ideas was, of course, made strictly with the view of establishing socialism in *England,* of reducing injustice in "the most class-ridden country under the sun." The appeal was not meant to promote international socialism, as is evident from Orwell's comments about the famed insularity and xenophobia of Englishmen (particularly that of the working class) and his belief that while patriotism overcomes class hatred, it just as easily overcomes any call to internationalism.[27]

In 1944 Orwell freely admitted that he had been wrong in viewing the victory over Hitler and the victory of socialism in England as mutually dependent. His appeal to patriotism nevertheless demands attention, for it demonstrates his awareness of qualities that hold men together as well as those which drive them apart and reveals his understanding of the importance of tradition. For Orwell, patriotism, as part of the observance of tradition, does not automatically imply reverence for the past, but is more a "devotion to something that is changing but is felt to be mystically the same." Above all, it fills a "spiritual need . . . for which no substitute has been found."[28] Despite his suggestion to the contrary, his own patriotism, his readiness to declare, "My country, Right or Left," reveals a conservatism that is itself a "connecting thread" through his work; for just as one cannot simply be rid of the old religious needs in the presence of mechanistic visions of the future, one cannot be rid of the old need for loyalty in the presence of new causes. Such needs may change their dress, but as Orwell knew, they will not easily disappear—despite the urging of the intellect to do so. As in *Keep the Aspidistra Flying* the old need of loyalty stays with Ravelston, the rich young editor of *Antichrist,* after he has transferred his allegiance "from God to Marx,"[29] so, says Orwell, the need stays with any member of the middle-class intelligentsia who, having lost affection for his or her native country, transfers that loyalty to another country because of nostalgia, "the need of patriotism."[30]

Drawing on personal experience, Orwell explains how such patriotism is largely an emotional reaction to long training—no matter that one's later intellectual choices may endorse its utility. In the late Thirties, during the bitter despondency among leftists over the Republican defeat in Spain, Orwell became extremely cynical about the coming "imperialist war" with Hitler.[31] He doubted whether it could do any good and seriously wondered whether it made any difference who won,[32] but after he dreamt of war the night before the Russo-German Pact was announced, he declared that Freudian analysis aside, he had become conscious of two things: "First, that I should be simply relieved when the long-dreaded war started, secondly, that I was patriotic at heart, would not sabotage or act against my own side. . . . What I knew in my dream that night was that the long drilling in patriotism which the middle classes go through had done its work." Orwell's socialist intellect had been usurped by Blair's bourgeois patriotism.[33]

Even so, large bodies of men do not determine to fight solely from patriotism, and they certainly do not do it from coercion. They determine to fight, said Orwell, from a semiconscious awareness that they are part of "some organism greater than themselves, stretching into the future and the past, within which they feel themselves to be immortal."[34] Full awareness of this fact, he says, comes only in battle. Thus, he had hoped in *The Road to Wigan Pier* that "when the widely separate classes who, necessarily, would form any real Socialist party have fought side by side, they may feel differently about one another. And then perhaps this misery of class-prejudice will fade away."[35]

Of course, there is an enormous paradox in this position—namely, that to realize brotherhood fully one needs to fight. Orwell does not address himself to this contradiction, other than making a distinction between patriotism and nationalism. Patriotism, he says, means loyalty to one's country without wishing to force its ways on other people. Nationalism, on the other hand, while it draws its power from the individual's sense of being a part of a larger organism and also moves men to fight, does wish to force one country's view onto another. Unlike patriotism, then, nationalism is not defensive but is essentially *aggressive and competitive* and is "inseparable from the drive for power."[36] Consequently, while a fully moral sense of brotherhood may be gained from patriotism, it cannot be gained from nationalism.

Although Orwell suggested in 1937 that a strong sense of brotherhood between classes might be realized by men who were under fire together, he had no experience to confirm him in this. His suggestion was nothing more than an extension of his belief that once men of different classes had worked together—acted together rather than merely mingling at forced social gatherings—they would realize that they had more in common than they thought. Confirmation of this belief came within the year. After he had joined the Independent Labour Party (rather than the Labour Party, which, he believed, had compromised itself over socialist principles–for example, in its implicit support of imperialism) he would go to Spain and fight with the Republicans. There, he witnessed the classlessness of the P.O.U.M. (a leftist militia unit). In June 1937 he wrote enthusiastically from Barcelona to his old schoolmate Cyril Connolly, "I have seen wonderful things and at last really believe in Socialism."[37]

Julian Symons, commenting on the search in the Thirties for the brotherhood among classes that might paradoxically come from war, could well have been speaking for his friend Orwell when he wrote:

What were they looking for, those members of the intelligentsia who went out and fought beside these men? One unconscious motive behind their action was the wish to obtain that contact with the working class which was denied to them in their ordinary lives. The practical difficulties of association with what was, in the Thirties mythology, a great source of good, were great. What meeting point was there between poets like John Cornford and Julian Bell, scientists like Lorimer Birch, writers like Hugh Slater, and miners from Durham, cotton-workers from Lancashire? War melts away the barriers between classes and also creates shared interests, bonds of knowledge and affection.[38]

So for Orwell, too, war, for all its unwanted horror, was an opportunity, "the greatest of all agents of change. It speeds up all processes, wipes out minor distinctions, brings realities to the surface. Above all, war brings it home to the individual that he is *not* altogether an individual. . . . People who at any other time would cling like glue to their miserable scraps of privilege will surrender them fast enough when their country is in danger."[39] Orwell did not want war, but if it was to happen, he saw in it an opportunity to galvanize inter-class unity into the basis for a socialist state. This hope, first stated in *The Road to Wigan Pier,* became a conviction after his experience in Spain.

Before Spain, Orwell's penchant for writing more from the point of view of a guilt-ridden observer than from that of an analyst of social conditions with any sharp political focus, his hatred of himself and his class, and his resulting desire to identify closely with the lower classes all combined in the absence of any theoretical base[40] to produce what can only be called a romanticization of the working class. We are left with the impression that he believed that "justice" and "liberty" are so endemic to the working class that all the rest of society has to do is to imitate the inherent goodness of laborers (but not the poor), and all will be well. Of course, Orwell's guilt-bred, sentimental view of the proletariat was something that he shared with many of his contemporaries, and like them he would take it to silly and extraordinary lengths. Just as in Germany Stephen Spender had tried to expiate his guilt of belonging to the privileged classes by allowing himself to be "cheated and exploited by the unemployed" and Christopher Isherwood consumed "vile tea" and "enormous quantities of chocolates to ruin his teeth, a malady he identified with the working classes,"[41] so Orwell would slurp his tea from a saucer in order to feel at one with the workers—although he also took childish delight in shocking his companions.[42] So strong was his desire, like that of all his fictional characters, to break free of his class and his past—which neither he nor they ever did—that his affection for the proletariat approached a sophomoric idealization that spills over even into the more remedial and analytical approach of *The Road to Wigan Pier.* In what can only be called a celebration of ignorance, he applauded the working-class disdain for education, noting how the working-class youth could not wait to leave school and to start doing "real work" instead of "wasting his time on ridiculous rubbish like history and geography."[43] He also wrote:

I have often been struck by the peculiar easy completeness, the perfect symmetry as it were, of a working-class interior at its best. Especially on winter evenings after tea, when the fire glows in the open range and dances mirrored in the steel fender, when Father, in shirt-sleeves sits in the rocking chair at one side of the fire reading the racing finals, and Mother sits on the other with her sewing,. . . the children are happy with a pennworth of mint humbugs, and the dog lolls roasting himself on the rag mat—it is a good place to be in.[44]

While Orwell constantly attacked the middle and upper classes for their prejudices, he seems to have thought that working-class people had none. Orwell's writings in this period indicate that he was incapable of seeing that the working class could be as self-interested as any other, that its members might gladly have embraced the privileges of the middle classes, given half the chance. Similarly, after he had overcome his own apprehensions of "the mob," he often saw the intellectual limitations of the working-class world as evidence of a virtuous choice to stay close to the reality of manual labor, which he believed prevented the growth of illusions of power over others. He did not see that such a decision by a member of the working class would involve a sophisticated view of the world or that the reason so many of the working class remained uninterested in upward mobility could have been the result of the very apathy of undernourishment and overwork that he described so well. It is this apathy that he saw at a meeting in his visit to Wigan. He recorded it in his diary but did not do so in his book: "I suppose these people represented a fair cross-section of the more revolutionary element in Wigan. If so, God help us. Exactly the same sheeplike crowd—gaping girls and shapeless middle-aged women dozing over their knitting—that you see everywhere else."[45]

Such statements are in blatant contradiction to his usual view of the working class, the view that makes the reader wonder why, if belonging to the working class is not such a bad thing, Orwell presses so hard for social reform. If the working class boy is wiser than the educated middle-class youth, why talk of sweeping educational reform, let alone revolution? The answer lies in Orwell's vision of social change, in which revolution would guarantee full employment and the preservation of present working-class values. It is, as one commentator suggests, a peculiarly conservative vision for a socialist,[46] but one that accommodates Orwell's belief that the fully employed working man "has a better chance of being happy than an 'educated' man.

His home life seems to fall more naturally into a sane and comely shape" and that the middle class may hopefully soon "sink without further struggles into the working class where we belong. . . . After all, we have nothing to lose but our aitches."[47]

Therefore, although Orwell shared his affection for the proletariat with his contemporaries, he stood apart from them in that he did not advocate, as did the Marxist and other socialist writers, that the workers had to be changed, had to be radicalized out of their passivity. Instead he argued that the middle and upper classes had to descend to embrace working-class values.[48] It is true that Orwell argued for class cooperation more than for class merger[49] but even in this he continued to believe that the rest of society should descend from the pedestals of privilege, and this runs directly counter to his persistent call for revolution "from below." Unfortunately, the contradiction between Orwell's sentimentalization of the working class and his call for revolution "from below" cannot be resolved, because Orwell's early writings are vague about the means whereby a socialist society is to be created.

Much of Orwell's vagueness about the *methods* to be used in creating a socialist society out of a capitalist one stems from the vagueness of socialism's *aims*—or, at least, those aims expressed by him. After all, a political platform based on a demand for "liberty and justice" is hardly new, as it could accommodate any number of movements along the political spectrum. Finally, his inattention to methods of transition from one political system to another reflects his most serious failure as a political commentator, because while he was sure of what the state should *not* be, he never clearly defined what the role of the state *should* be in people's affairs, beyond saying that on occasion it has to use violence to protect them from violence.[50] His failure to bother about the role of the state derives from his belief that structural change by itself will not bring moral improvement in society. What he fails to face up to is that just as people need to be protected from violence, so do they need administration. To have acknowledged this, however, would have meant also admitting to the possibility of inequality—at the very least, to a need for managerial "classes" in the classless society—and Orwell was not yet fully equipped to do this, despite his insistence upon the necessity of winning over the technocratic middle class to the cause of revolution. It is true that he already had suspicions about the Russian myth of equality, but hard evidence was slow in coming.

Even when it did come ("By 1940 no doubt remained"),[51] he continued to write more of state irresponsibility than responsibility.

Despite the failings of his early work, however, his "Gissingesque genius for finding the dingiest house in the most sunless street"[52] and his old habit of taking his experience, with the miners in Wigan this time, as typical of the experience of a whole class, the thing that Orwell got right, from *Down and Out in Paris and London* to *The Road to Wigan Pier,* was the atmosphere of poverty and unemployment—what has been called the "spirit of misery."[53] You can almost smell it. It is difficult today to understand the importance of *The Road to Wigan Pier,* especially because the detailed tables and figures of its first part are now so outdated. What is not fully appreciated by the contemporary reader is the gap that existed between the classes of Orwell's day and how difficult it was to cross that gap, as Orwell did, however temporarily. As Arnold Toynbee points out, "To most middle-class people the industrial working-classes were as remote as the pygmies, and the unemployment figures meant nothing at all in human terms. Today the situation has changed at least in this—that there is no longer any excuse for ignorance."[54] One of the reasons that there is no longer any excuse for such ignorance is due to Orwell's writing about the industrial working class. Although the mathematical tables may soon be forgotten or ignored, the human situations he describes, with their vivid details of lower-class squalor, are unforgettable. George Woodcock writes:

Orwell's enterprise in going among the tramps of London seemed almost as daring as that of Tom Harrison, who had lived among the head-hunters of the Solomon Islands. . . . Today most of those documentaries, which seemed so absorbingly interesting thirty years ago, are completely forgotten. . . . Orwell was in fact the only writer who gave permanence to what is normally the most ephemeral of literary crafts. Literate Englishmen of the 1960s gain their impressions of the almost extinct tramp from *Down and Out in Paris and London,* and of the conditions of the unemployed of the 1930s from *The Road to Wigan Pier.*[55]

And despite the deficiencies of Orwell's writings on poverty and unemployment, his descriptions still make it impossible for anyone who reads them to "retreat," as Alex Zwerdling notes, "into pseudo-stupidity, the innocence of ignorance." Readers of Orwell's day (and the Left Book Club, which selected *The Road to Wigan Pier,* alone had forty thousand members) had to "make a choice—either to support oppression once it had been exposed, or to begin to transform the unjust world."[56]

But even though Orwell stands out from all other middle-class writers of the Thirties in this regard, he was unquestionably unfair in much of his attack upon the middle-class socialists. A lot of this takes place in the second part of *Wigan Pier,* in which he moves from the concrete details of life among the miners to his thoughts about socialism and in which, the characters he describes (like those in *Burmese Days* and *Down and Out in Paris and London)* "represent types of their class . . . and not individuals."[57] Eccentric himself in voluntarily sojourning among the poor, he proceeds to attack the eccentricity of others, ridiculing assorted "cranks," including those who favor birth control, less oppression of women, and vegetarianism. To add further contradiction, while Orwell the eccentric is attacking the right to eccentricity, he just as strongly assails the power of socialist orthodoxy to make members ashamed of liking horses—that is, of being unorthodox by having affection for the past. The inconsistency here betrays the constant tension in Orwell's work created by his simultaneous recognition of the need for some group activity— "solidarity with the working class"—on the one hand, and the need of individualism, on the other. It lies at the heart of his most serious inconsistencies of thought.

These inconsistencies notwithstanding, Orwell had a special impact on the Left, because he decided to do without reservation what most other socialists would not risk at the time—to attack the soft spots of leftist ideology, not simply within the party structure, but also in public. Orwell's belief that if socialism was to be strengthened it had to be examined publicly led to his socialist publisher's mild charge of his being indiscreet and to more serious charges of "public betrayal."[58] The importance of Orwell's criticism is most evident when we recall the absence of what might have been a "buffer" generation in England between the young and old after World War I. The absence of this generation, which could have provided experienced guides in the political arena for the younger generation, explains Stuart Samuels's observation that the "English Left Intelligentsia of the 1930's emerged from a definite political and economic situation and not from any previously existing left-wing literary or philosophical tradition."[59] Orwell's generation, in the absence of trained guides, was fuelled more by political feelings than by political ideas, more by anger than by ideology, at the beginning of the Thirties and was therefore more prone to political illusions—from Wellsian utopias to the myths of Russian communism. It was in his role as critic of this "new boy" socialism of the Thirties that Orwell, *in the Thirties,* was so embarrassingly influential in the Left. This occurred well before his wide public acclaim for *Animal Farm* and *Nineteen Eighty-Four.*

It should be remembered that in attacking middle-class socialists Orwell was, in large part, attacking himself "as sufficiently typical of my class."[60] Yet in *Down and Out in Paris and London,* he often failed to recognize his own snobbery while complaining bitterly about that of others. Recalling his days as a dishwasher in Paris, he writes contemptuously of the American guests, "They would stuff themselves with disgusting American 'cereals' and eat marmalade at tea, and drink vermouth after dinner, and order *poulet à la reine* at a hundred francs and then souse it in Worcester sauce. One customer from Pittsburg dined every night in his bedroom on grape-nuts, scrambled eggs and cocoa. Perhaps it hardly matters whether such people are swindled or not."[61]

Also, because he was at the start of his career and therefore had not really thought through social problems of his time, such as unemployment, he could charge that "no one cared" about the kind of exploitation that he recorded in *Down and Out in Paris and London.* As Hollis suggests,[62] it seems never to have occurred to him that a lot of people cared very much about the exploited, but, more importantly, that they sincerely believed (rightly or wrongly) that the state should keep its nose out of such problems, lest its interference with the tramp's right to be tramp or beggar would set a precedent for all manner of official invasions of any individual's private life. They held that such incursion upon a beggar's free choice, however desirable in itself, might well mark an irretrievable step on the road to a kind of total state interference such as Orwell was later to abhor.

Later, however, in *The Road to Wigan Pier,* he shows that he is aware not only of the dangers of the state, but of his own snobbery. While at times he lapses into the old naivety of *Down and Out,* we see the observer beginning to analyze. Such increased awareness, particularly of the *causes* of his own attitudes toward others rather than of the attitudes themselves, was, of course, simply part of the maturing process of a young writer; but there was something else, a growing mood of urgency that had more to do with the social and political scene in England than with Orwell growing older and pushed him to search for a remedy for those ills that previously he had merely recorded. He remarks, "It hardly needs pointing out that at this moment we [in England] are in a very serious mess, so serious that even the dullest-witted people find it difficult to remain unaware of it. We are living in a world in which nobody is free, in which hardly anybody is secure, in which it is almost impossible to be honest and to remain alive."[63]

Such was the mood created by the crisis of the Thirties and felt by society at large just prior to the Spanish Civil War. Grown weary with the government's inability to deal effectively with unemployment and the dictators, much of the population felt a growing impatience with the "tactics of gradualism" at home and a growing fear of fascism. Beatrice Webb wrote in her diary, "What I am beginning to doubt is the 'inevitability of gradualness,' or even the practicability of gradualness, in the transition from a capitalist to an equalitarian civilisation,"[64] and in the same vein Orwell warns, "The tempo of events is quickening; the dangers which once seemed a generation distant are staring us in the face. One has got to be actively a Socialist, not merely sympathetic to Socialism, or one plays into the hands of our always-active enemies".[65]

The result from the Left was an unequivocal "demand for more radical thought and action."[66] In this way, what had begun for Blair as a pilgrimage of expiation took on a political purpose for Orwell as self-hatred became galvanized into political action through a sense of shared crisis. The observer becomes the doer; a commitment to change himself becomes a commitment to change society. In the latter commitment Orwell was like so many of his contemporaries, but in the commitment to change himself first, he stood apart.

Thus, in his English period, Orwell's concern with the exploited had expanded beyond the relatively closed structure of the local-level imperialists. Having done "the dirty work of Empire at close quarters," he had seen the distance between institutions and individuals. In England he had observed more the distance between human beings—between classes of the same race. Had Orwell resigned himself to remaining in Burma, where he had found that "there was no obvious class-friction,"[67] he might well have retained the simplistic rich–poor, exploiters–exploited dichotomy of *Burmese Days*, but his writing about England in the Thirties, whatever its shortcomings, reflects a definite shift away from the black–white delineation of his first novel to the grey, complex issues of the industrialized populations of the lower and middle classes. This shift is marked, in part, by his recognition of a non-malicious, unintentional, unconscious kind of exploitation. Orwell's case against leftists who vehemently denouncing imperialism while happily but unconsciously enjoying the products of imperialism's cheap labor is to the point. He also discovers that in a machine age exploitation often seems to have a life of its own that is all but independent of human will and impelled by little more than the amoral neutrality of technological change. Orwell's emphasis on unconscious exploitation more than anything else signals the maturation of the ardent antiimperialist of *Burmese Days*. In the earlier book he portrayed exploitation of others as being always willfully, if not arrogantly, imposed; once back in England it was not so simple to do this. He could even sympathize with the middle class sending their children to snobbish private schools. The narrow master–slave world of *Burmese Days*, of a few *exploiters* in an outpost of the old order, has expanded into novels about the *exploited* at large. In *Burmese Days*, Flory's self-indulgent pessimism about the world can be ended only by a bullet. In the later novels, pessimism persists but there is also hope. Imperialism has been rejected, but socialism is about to be welcomed.

To be sure, there is a common motivation in the two kinds of exploitation Orwell has written about to this date, in the cruder imperialist type and that of the middle and upper classes. This motivation does not stem simply from resistance to incommodious change threatening status and income, but is a fundamental belief in the rightness of class distinctions as a reflection of the "natural" order of things. Such an attitude is evident, from Veraswami admonishing his friend, "How can you pretend, Mr. Flory, that you are not the natural superior of such creatures [the natives]?"[68] through Comstock's and Bowling's lack of pity for the proles, to the humiliation visited upon the nearly blind miner collecting his dole in Wigan.

In examining the constancy and persistence of the belief that there are people whose proper function in life is serving others without respite or adequate recompense, Orwell takes us well beyond the evils of imperialism, for he is also showing us the cause of the remarkable resilience of the class structure in England—and beyond. Indeed the belief in the necessity of class distinctions is so strong that it lasts all the way to *Nineteen Eighty-Four*, in which Winston

Smith, in Airstrip One (London), tells us that "the Party taught that the proles were natural inferiors who must be kept in subjection like animals."[69] It is the tenaciousness of this belief that periodically curdles Orwell's optimism into pessimism and causes him to choose cooperation within class differences, rather than removal of them, as the best path to social reform.

As we have seen, while Orwell could talk of "three" Englands,[70] he could also refer to one "family," debunking the fear of the "mob," which he believed was based on an erroneous belief that there was "some mysterious fundamental difference between rich and poor, as though they were two different races."[71] It was a "family" "in which the young are generally thwarted and most of the power is in the hands of irresponsible uncles and bedridden aunts. Still it is a family, . . . with the wrong members in control—that, perhaps, is as near as one can come to describing England in a phrase."[72] As 1936 nears its end, he attacks "cranks" with the same vehemence as Ellis attacked Flory, because in his mood of urgency he sees the need for "family" solidarity, a united front against the looming threat of fascism. It now becomes necessary, for example, "for left-wingers of all complexions to drop their differences and hang together."[73] Still, the tension between group and individual is not resolved. This tension, a manifestation of the ancient freedom-versus-authority theme in political thought, would continue to haunt Orwell. It would never disappear for him but at times it would be eased. Such a time was during the early part of the Spanish Civil War. Here, for a brief time, it seemed to Orwell as if one's sense of individuality could be properly and safely surrendered to a united front that was ostensibly fighting against fascism and for the exploited at large.

III

SPAIN

CHAPTER 6

> At 6 P.M. that same day, just before the attack, [General] Miláns del Bosch imposed martial law through his Valencia region. Shortly afterward, a triumphant Tejero telephoned the general from inside the Cortes [Parliament] and declared his objective achieved *"sin novedad"* (no news). Tanks and troops moved into the streets, . . . armored units briefly occupied the state radio and television studios in Madrid.[1]

THIS IS A REPORT OF THE ATTEMPTED COUP TO OVERTHROW the elected government of Spain. The attempt took place on February 23, 1981, a near-miss rerun of Franco's uprising of July 17, 1936—the uprising that drew Orwell to Spain in the belief that if Franco won, totalitarianism was that much closer. By the time Orwell was fighting on the Aragon front in early 1937, the Spanish Civil War had already been underway for six months and in Catalonia he was seeing only part of it. However, because the lessons of Orwell's experience in Spain are best understood in the context of the complex forces behind the war that operated throughout the entire country, it seems advisable to give a brief historical background to the conflict and the way in which it galvanized "Left" against "Right," not only in Spain but in England.[2] Those readers who are familiar with the historical background are invited to ignore this section and turn to page 129.

Despite the promulgation in 1876 of a constitution (which was much abused by bitterly opposed liberals and conservatives alike) and the nominal introduction of universal male franchise in 1890, elections in Spain were decided by local *caciques,* or political bosses. In consequence, most Spaniards viewed the parliamentary system as a vehicle for their exclusion from, rather than for their participation in the government of their monarchist country.[3] To compensate for their lack of electoral power, the workers—particularly those of Catalonia—sought representation through general trade unions. Predominant among these were the Anarchist and the U.G.T. (socialist) trade unions. The U.G.T. (Unión General de Trabajadores—the Socialist Trade Union) was more Fabian than Marxist and not infused by the ideas of Bakunin, unlike the C.N.T. (Confederación Nacional del Trabajo), an anarcho-syndicalist trade union whose predecessors in the short-lived First Republic of the 1870s had played their part in the chaotically violent demands for local rights. These early demands had moved the army to reinstate the monarchy in 1874. Later, the anarchists were particularly active in Barcelona, the most industrialized city in Spain and capital of Catalonia, a region noted for its own language and customs and for a determination to gain recognition of its separate identity. In 1909 Catalan-led protests against the regime of King Alfonso XIII reached a climax when strike leaders were shot by the army. Earlier in the disturbances the rioters' ferocity had observed no bounds, as drunken workers danced through Barcelona, swinging about the "disinterred bodies of nuns," so vehement was their opposition to the *institution* of the Church and the central government in Madrid.[4] This kind of lawlessness and violence would become all too evident in the Civil War.

By 1923 the parliament was unable to cope with the problem of Catalan anarchism and problems resulting from the defeat of Spanish forces at Anual by Abd-el-Krim, the Moroccan rebel leader. Thereafter, General Miguel Primo de Rivera took control of the country, although King Alfonso XIII was still nominally its ruler. The eccentric Primo de Rivera's dictatorship was politically oppressive, but it was cushioned by the economic boom of the late Twenties, during which it won support from Spanish capital. The dictatorship ended in 1930, through a coupling of the effects of economic collapse in 1929 and the dictator's disregard for the Spanish middle class. No longer convinced that he had the support of fellow officers, the general resigned, and he died alone in Paris shortly thereafter.[5]

King Alfonso's subsequent attempt to govern did not enjoy the support of those army officers angered by his acceptance of Primo de Rivera's resignation. Amid general disaffection from the monarchy and hopes for a democratic, or at least less oppressive Spain, a group of Republican politicians, intellectuals (including José Ortega y Gasset), and Socialists met in San Sebastian (the summer capital) in 1930, with the result that by year's end revolution seemed imminent. The plans failed, however, and the conspirators were arrested. The latter claimed in their defense that the king had violated the constitution in accepting Primo de Rivera's dictatorship. The brief terms of imprisonment that the authorities meted out to the anti-monarchist conspirators reflected a growing sympathy with anti-monarchist feeling in general—particularly among the leftist parties, who, as a measure of their dissatisfaction, initially refused to participate in any parliamentary elections "under the monarchy."[6] Finally, however, as the king, "given the prevailing mood of opinion, . . . found it impossible to refuse elections" to the people, the Left agreed to "compromise" and take part in municipal elections. These were held on April 12, 1931.

Although many parts of the countryside were still ruled by local political bosses and the monarchists gained a majority nationwide in these elections, the large towns and cities voted overwhelmingly Republican; and in some places, such as Eibar in Basque country (where the people were religious rather than anarchistic but as fiercely independence-minded as the Catalans), a republic was proclaimed. With huge crowds gathering in Madrid the day after the election and impending violence in the air, the king's advisers urged him to leave Spain. The Bourbon king drove into exile, after having solemnly announced that "Sunday's elections have shown me that I no longer enjoy the love of my people. I could very easily find means to support my royal powers against all-comers, but I am determined to have nothing to do with setting one of my countrymen against another in a fratricidal civil war."[7]

Following national elections in June 1931, Socialist-Centrist parties had 318 members in the Cortes as against 60 for the Right. At its outset the Second Republic, with its nominally "socialist" government set upon democratic reform, was plagued by severe tensions and provocations from both Left and Right. On the extreme left were the anarchists who gained much support from landless peasant laborers, the victims of the gross inequalities of agrarian conditions ("the central sore" of Spain).[8] The anarchists, however, refused to recognize the legitimacy of any state. On the far right were the monarchists, seeking a return to control through the army and the state. In-between a whole spectrum of political voices clamored for a share in governing the new Spain.

In the surge of victory the government failed to give priority of treatment to the agrarian problems[9] and was led first to imprudence, then to sheer folly, attacking the Church through harsh anticlerical legislation and thereby alienating the middle classes. It decreed, for example, that there was to be an end to all religious education and that every "public manifestation of religion" would have to be given prior approval from the government. As Hugh Thomas has pointed out, "All Spanish Catholics were forced into the position of having to oppose the very Constitution of the Republic if they wished to criticize its educational or religious policy."[10]

Although on the right the middle class and landowners were respectively hostile to the government's anticlerical stance and to its limited agrarian reform (of 1932), the army was particularly upset by the passing of a statute of Catalan autonomy. A successful move for autonomy by the equally independence-minded Basques gave impetus elsewhere to like-minded separatist movements, which the army saw as a direct threat to Spain's unity—the maintenance of which provided them with their very livelihood. Such dissatisfaction led in August 1932 to an unsuccessful attempt led by Spain's most celebrated soldier, General José Sanjurjo, to overthrow the government with the help of a young fascist group (the Nationalist Party of Burgos). A prostitute revealed the details of the plan to the opposition, and it was crushed by Prime Minister Manuel Azaña's government.[11]

The remainder of 1932 was marked by an unprecedented building of an educational program that—more than tripling the number of secondary school students from that of pre-Republican days—formed an important part of a great "flood" of reform legislation: "It was as if all the reforms of Sir Robert Peel, Gladstone and Asquith had been crowded into two years' debate."[12] These reforms included a new divorce law; the legalization of civil marriage; and laws concerning forced labor, collective rents, mixed arbitration, minimum wages, labour contracts, women's rights, and recruitment in the civil service. Despite this, Prime Minister Azaña's popularity plummeted. This was due to the government's harsh repression of Anarchist uprisings—mostly in Catalonia, where, under the red-and-black flag, villages were taken over amid proclamations of libertarian communism.

National elections were held in November 1933, with the result that the Left–Right split in the Cortes was, broadly speaking, 99 to 207, with a large center-party coalition of 167 seats. The Anarchists, by and large, had refused to vote. The largest party on the right was the C.E.D.A. (Confederación Española de Derechas Autónomas), or Catholic Party. The C.E.D.A. was led by Gil Robles, who imitated Hitler (whom he had met) in allowing himself to be addressed as "Jefe" ("Chief," as in "Führer"). The loss by the Left to the electoral alliances of the right and center parties was due largely to Socialist leader Largo Caballero, who had pushed his party far to the left in an attempt to attract anarchist supporters. Meanwhile, new members were being sought for a religiously based fascist party, J.O.N.S. (Juntas de Ofensiva Nacional-Sindicalista), founded by rightists for whom Roman Catholicism (insofar as they saw it as "embodying the 'racial' tradition" of the Spaniards) played the same role as Aryan blood did for the Nazis. In 1934 J.O.N.S. amalgamated with the Falange Española under the leadership of José Antonio Primo de Rivera.[13] The potential of the Falangist Party, which was still small, lay in its appeal to a wide range of Spaniards, from students to laborers to military officers. Indeed, the antagonism of the relatively small Communist party was reserved for the Anarchists and Socialists until 1935, when the Soviet Comintern's policy was to close ranks with leftist as well as bourgeois elements in a common front against the threat of Hitler.

Following the rise of the C.E.D.A. and the monarchists in the 1933 elections, the centrist coalition–dominated governments of 1933–36 were plagued by Anarchist-led strikes. An amnesty for all political prisoners in 1934 exacerbated conditions by simply encouraging more plots: "From 1933 onwards, the villages of Navarre (like the cities of the south and center of Spain, where the Falange, the Anarchists, the Socialist and Communist youth trained in arms) rang again with the noise of drilling."[14]

The spirit of compromise, never strong, was fast evaporating as battle lines were drawn, almost daily it seemed, between the multifarious elements of Right and Left—each side convinced that the promise of the Second Republic properly belonged to them. In March 1934 Mussolini promised arms to the Monarchist leader of the Cortes in the event of an uprising against the Republic, and in June both the Catalan and the Basque separatist movements pressed for greater autonomy from the central government. The C.E.D.A. objected strongly. In answer, the Anarchists (C.N.T.) and Socialists (U.G.T.) combined in Asturias, in their first alliance for years, and declared a general strike. José Gil Robles, "Jefe" of the C.E.D.A., threatened to withdraw his right-wing party's support for the government, a threat that was taken by the U.G.T. as the prelude to a C.E.D.A. takeover—a Spanish version of Dolfuss's subjection of the Socialists in Austria.[15]

In October, carrying out his threat, Robles withdrew C.E.D.A. support of the government of Prime Minister Samper Ibáñez, which then resigned. Lerroux García (leader of the center's so-called "Radicals") took over power. His inclusion of three C.E.D.A. members in his cabinet immediately triggered off violent anti-"Fascist" strikes by the Socialists (U.G.T.) and a rebellion in Catalonia, which was promptly put down. Further disturbances throughout Spain in October 1934 were crushed, except for those in Asturias, where, unlike the rest of Spain, a broad spectrum of workers—Socialists, Anarchists, Communists (thirty thousand strong)—allied in establishing "a revolutionary Soviet" throughout the mining province. This alliance was the precursor of what would become known as the "Popular Front." Several priests were shot, churches burned, and middle-class women raped and murdered while insufficient government forces tried unsuccessfully to restore order. This was no less than civil war, and the centrist Lerroux government sent for General Manuel Goded and the forty-year-old General Francisco Franco Bahamonde to quiet the rebellion. Franco was known to be a first-rate organizer, unquestionably brave, and an extraordinarily cautious commander who had consistently declined to ally himself with any side in the political arena and, perhaps more importantly, had diligently refused to let his preferences be known. He quickly crushed the Asturias rebellion, immediately becoming a hero in Madrid. His retribution upon the defeated miners, however, was so ruthless that for many of the working class (6 to 7 million, including agricultural workers),[16] the Asturias rebellion—in which thousands were made political prisoners—became a rallying cry for a wider confrontation with the Right. For the middle classes (approximately 4 million out of the total population of 11 million), the rebellion was a clear and disturbing sign that, Franco and Goded's victory notwithstanding, the government of the Second Republic was incapable of maintaining order.

Prime Minister Lerroux's commutation of further death sentences of the rebels of Asturias caused C.E.D.A. resignations of protest and the formation of a new cabinet. Financial scandal involving Lerroux followed, and he and his party resigned in disgrace. Within weeks the new prime minister, Joaquín Chapaprieta, was involved in arguments with the C.E.D.A. over the budget, and this led to the resignations of the C.E.D.A. cabinet members. This governmental crisis in 1935, the latest in a long series of crises that had plagued the Second Republic, led to new national elections in February 1936. These were marked, among other things, by huge billboard photographs of the "Jefe," Gil Robles, accompanied by demands that he be given "the Ministry of War and all the power." The C.E.D.A., determined to gain power, formed an alliance with other right-wing groups such as the monarchists. This alliance was called the "National Front." Between the "National" and "Popular" Fronts, between cries to elect the "Jefe" and calls to remember "Asturias," there were the parties of the center.[17] Also supporting the Popular Front was the semi-Trotskyist Workers and Peasants Alliance (P.O.U.M.—Partido Obrero de Unificación Marxista), which Orwell would join in December. The elections in February 1936 resulted in 278 seats for the Popular Front, 134 for the National Front, and 55 for the center parties, whose heavy losses augured badly for compromise in the Cortes and made for even sharper Right–Left divisions. The actual votes cast for the various alliances of over *fifteen* parties showed that if the centerist and rightist parties had combined, they would have had a small numerical majority. This fact would later (and quite wrongly) be used as a claim that the Popular Front's government was illegal.[18]

Now Franco took a firm stance against the Popular Front, recommending to the caretaker prime minister that a state of war be declared so that the leftist alliance could not assume power. The prime minister refused, although urged to similar action by José Calvo Sotelo, leader of the monarchists. The Popular Front assumed office under Azaña, who again extended amnesty to all political prisoners and allowed the Catalan members to elect a government of their own. Generals Goded and Franco were transferred for their part in the ruthless suppression of the Asturias rebellion—in effect, exiled from the War Ministry to commands in the Balearics and Canary Islands, respectively.[19]

In the euphoric climate of the Popular Front's victory, murder, violence, and arson, the dark trio of Spain's political arena, spread across the country as the Left settled old scores and the Right (particularly the Falangists) sought to create chaos so that their cry for order might catapult them into power. While the Falangists rode about with their machine guns, Socialist leader Largo Caballero, intoxicated by his power and by Communist praise (at a time when "the votes of his party kept the Government of Azaña in power"), rode about declaring that "revolution" was at hand—creating dissension within the Left as well as spreading terror, no doubt, among the middle classes. In March 1936, at the same time as internal squabbling once again beset the Left, the Right, fearing leftist-inspired chaos, consolidated their forces as never before. The monarchist leader Calvo Sotelo, replacing C.E.D.A.'s Gil Robles, became leader of the Right. Part of the Right's action involved a generals' plot master-minded by General Emilio Mola, military governor of Pampalona and including General Franco. In March, acting independently in Lisbon, General Sanjurjo had approached the German Admiral Wilhelm Canaris to ask for arms in the event of an uprising.[20] By April General Mola had drawn up plans for simultaneous local, civil, and military takeovers in all provinces and Spanish-held territory, including Spanish Morocco.

Political assassinations and general violence continued, including that carried out by landless peasants, who considered the rate of agrarian reform too slow. Rumors of impending revolution were rife throughout the spring. On May 1 the Labor Day parades were held, dominated in Madrid by giant posters of Caballero (now prime minister), Stalin, and Lenin, further terrifying the well-to-do who looked down upon the leftist crowd from their balconies.

The state of tension was hardly alleviated by Caballero talking on May 24 about the impending "dictatorship of the proletariat" and the repression of "capitalist and bourgeois classes." The liberal-led Spanish workers, had been "maddened by years of insult, misery, and neglect" and were now "intoxicated by the knowledge of the better conditions enjoyed by their class comrades in France and Britain"—and *supposedly* "in Russia." If any spirit of compromise had ever truly existed after the dictatorship of Primo de Rivera between the liberal-led workers, on the one hand, and the power of the Church and the army, on the other, it was now exhausted.[21]

Political murders were daily occurrences throughout July 1936, and in the army officers were already choosing sides. Following the murder of a government *Asalto* (Assault Guard) by Falangists on July 12, members of the civil guard who were sympathetic to the Left took revenge by murdering the rightist leader Calvo Sotelo in Madrid, early in the morning of July 13. The bourgeoisie were further convinced that the government was incapable of keeping order. General Mola set the uprising for July 17, and any tentative alliances among rightist elements were now solidified. Mola would rise against the government in the north, Goded in the northeast, and Franco in the south—all of them heading toward Madrid. Calvo Sotelo's funeral and that of the slain *Asalto* lieutenant were held in the same cemetery on July 14. The lieutenant's body, covered by a red flag, was surrounded by crowds of *Asaltos,* Republicans, Socialists, and Communists giving the clenched-fist salute. Within hours, Sotelo's casket, draped in monarchist colours, was lowered, accompanied by a mass of Fascist salutes. Middle-class crowds "attacked" the vice president and permanent secretary of the Cortes. In addition, four people were killed and shots were exchanged between Falangists and *Asaltos.*[22]

The tension was so high that a meeting of the Cortes scheduled for July 21 was accompanied by a request that all members leave their firearms in the cloak room. This proposed meeting never took place. Meanwhile, although the liberal government, led by Santiago Cesares Quiroga, definitely saw the Right as its enemy, it did not regard the Left as an ally.

At 12:30 A.M. on July 17, General Franco, as part of the generals' plot, left Tenerife in the Canary Islands for Las Palmas, the islands' capital, where he would declare martial law and whence he would move to Morocco to take over command of the Army of Africa. The latter was by far the most experienced fighting force in Spain. Late in the afternoon of July 17, in accordance with General Mola's plan,[23] certain officers in Melilla (Spanish Morocco) rebelled against the garrison commander, General Quintero Romerales and shot him, together with fellow officers who had refused to rise against the government. The form of this uprising, wherein commanding officers of strategic garrisons who were not fully trusted to rebel against the government were given the quick choice of joining the rebels or being shot, would soon be repeated throughout Spain.

In a chaos of vacillation and poor communications ("there were now not two Spains but two thousand"), workers demanded arms to resist the rightist uprising that had spread from Morocco, where it was first proclaimed, to the mainland. The government knew, however, that to acquiesce in this demand not only meant giving the Left arms for self-defense but would constitute the liberal government's acceptance of a leftist revolution. Finally, the government (now under José Giral) relented and the people were armed. Early on July 19 trucks from the Ministry of War delivered rifles to U.G.T. and C.N.T. headquarters, where they were distributed to the "waiting masses."[24]

As Hugh Thomas points out, it would be a mistake to think that Spaniards generally were appalled at the coming struggle. Indeed, they "leapt into the war" with the same exuberance as did their European neighbors in 1914, and "within a month nearly a hundred thousand people" would perish "arbitrarily and without trial. Bishops would be torn to pieces and churches profaned. Educated Christians would spend their evenings murdering illiterate peasants and professional men of sensitivity." All this and more would be done because each side believed that it was right—"not only right, but noble."[25]

The lack of unanimity among the army officers explains why, dotted throughout Republican and Nationalist Spain alike, there were islands of resistance within what was otherwise an enemy sea. Even so, in July, 1936 Spain was essentially divided into a north and a south, with the northeast and the Basque provinces of the far north in Republican hands. The Republican territory, however, was progressively eaten into as the war progressed; by October 1937 most of western Spain and nearly all of the north had fallen to the rebel, or Nationalist, forces, which were much better equipped (largely by Mussolini and Hitler). By July 1938 the Nationalists had driven a hundred-mile-wide wedge into the Republican territory that reached all the way to the Mediterranean and cut off Catalonia, in the north, from Madrid in the center and from southeast Spain. Catalonia, where Orwell had fought with the P.O.U.M. in 1936–37, finally fell on January 26, 1939. Amid the chaos of impending defeat, the supreme irony of the Civil War was played out by a Republican commander, Colonel Segismundo Casado, who, resentful of the Communists' influence within what remained of the government (now led by Dr. Juan Negrín) and determined to end the war on the best terms possible, revolted against the Republican government, just as the rebel generals had done in 1936.

The result was more chaos, a civil war within a civil war in Madrid, where Casado, having objected to the Communists' call for "continued resistance" against the Nationalists, was now busy fighting his former allies. Franco, who, even before the death of Mola, had become leader of all the Nationalist forces, noted that now he would be spared "the trouble of crushing the Communists." Apart from gaining time for some Republicans to escape, Colonel Casado's attempts to reach an agreement with Franco on something less than unconditional surrender failed, and on March 27, with the Republicans in full retreat, Madrid fell to the Nationalists. The Left—mainly the working classes—had literally been overrun, and for them all that was to follow after a conflict that had claimed half a million lives[26] was a retribution as ferocious as the spirit with which the war had been fought.

In England, despite the initial mood of neutrality that greeted its outbreak, the Spanish Civil War quickly became a focus for and culmination of the feelings of political and social commitment that had been growing in the Thirties. With the failure of the League of Nations now painfully evident, Mussolini's conquest of Abyssinia, the Japanese entrenchment in Manchuria, Hitler's march into the Rhineland, and what seemed to be Dollfuss's consolidation of power in Austria, the threat of fascism loomed larger than ever.

In *Keep the Aspidistra Flying*, Gordon Comstock felt, "Our civilization is dying. . . . Presently the aeroplanes are coming. Zoom—whizz—crash! The whole western world going up in a roar of high explosives."[27] In *The Road to Wigan Pier*, which he finished a few days before leaving for Spain in December 1936, Orwell notes, "Events are moving with terrible speed. As I write this the Spanish Fascist forces are bombarding Madrid, and it is quite likely that before this book is printed we shall have another Fascist country to add to the list."[28]

Although the Spanish issues that created the civil war were extraordinarily complex, the war itself was quickly viewed by the rest of the world as a struggle between Left and Right, between good and evil. Depending on which side you supported, the war was seen either as a struggle against fascism—which, supported as it was by Hitler and Mussolini, would destroy democracy—or as a war against Communist-inspired anarchy—which, supported by the Soviet Union, would destroy Christian civilization.[29]

Despite some agreement between leftist and rightist supporters of nonintervention, the Spanish Civil War widened the gap between the Left and the Right in England and injected an air of class-consciousness into foreign and domestic policy, marking it with unprecedented "bitterness."[30] In the literary world the climate for such division between Left and Right had already been set by such distorted statements of supposed impartiality as that of John Lehmann, printed in the 1936 spring edition of *New Writing*: "*New Writing* is first and foremost interested in literature, and though it does not intend to open its pages to writers of reactionary or Fascist sentiments, it is independent of any political party."[31]

Given widespread ignorance of the complex causes of the Spanish Civil War, the most intriguing aspect of the way in which it aroused public opinion in England and abroad was that it was also seized upon as a crucible in which new and old rival political theories would be tested. In addition, competing military and sociological theories, from *blitzkrieg* to collectivization that had been gestating and spreading during the Thirties were thrown into the furnace. For many of those who went to fight in support of either Franco or the Republic in the voluntary International Brigades and similar organizations, the war was, no doubt, largely a matter of conscience in what was viewed as a decisive struggle between Left and Right. There were, of course, other motives mixed in: because its military activity was "comparatively restrained," compared to the huge areas and numbers of men in World War I, the war also provided individuals with an opportunity to test—and possibly even to distinguish—themselves;[32] and for some of those who had missed World War I this war was an opportunity to catch up. Orwell writes:

As the war [of 1914–18] fell back into the past, my particular generation, those who had been "just too young," became conscious of the vastness of the experience they had missed. You felt yourself a little less than a man, because you had missed it. . . . I am convinced that part of the reason for the fascination that the Spanish Civil War had for people of about my age was that it was so like the Great War. At certain moments Franco was able to scrape together enough aeroplanes to raise the war to a modern level, and these were the turning-points. But for the rest it was a bad copy of 1914–18, a positional war of trenches, . . . mud, barbed wire . . . and stagnation. . . . I know that what I felt when I first heard artillery fired "in anger," as they say, was at least partly disappointment. It was so different from the tremendous, unbroken roar that my senses had been waiting for for twenty years.[33]

Like many others, he found that the untried patriotism that he had experienced at Eton had circuitously fuelled a need that—once given vent in action in Spain—finally ended the old guilt of not having proven oneself.

Beyond such feelings, however, the Civil War became a rallying point, particularly for the left, and a symbol of its opposition not only to fascism, but also to economic exploitation of Spanish workers and of all workers. In Britain in particular, the war offered intellectuals committed to social and political improvement not only a chance to battle the forces of reaction in Spain, but an opportunity to fight against Hitler and Mussolini for civilization at large.[34]

That it was not just the intellectuals who were actively involved, however, is evident in the fact that of the two to three thousand British volunteers who fought on the Republican side, both in the International Brigades and outside (as Orwell did in the P.O.U.M.), the overwhelming majority were members of the working class.[35]

> They came from all over the country. . . . Some had been unemployed; some threw up jobs to join. There were miners, engineers, building workers, and indeed all trades were represented, . . . so that many of the local Aid Spain Committees had their own local lad at the front, and felt thereby a close involvement. His letters home to his family would be read out at meetings; his dependents, if he had any, visited and helped. . . . Pride in the British volunteers was great throughout the labour movement and C. R. Attlee, the leader of the Parliamentary Labour Party, visited them at the front, and lent his name to what became known as the Attlee Company of the British Battalion.[36]

Still, it was the writers—very few of whom were working class—who would articulate the intent and frustrations of the cause against Franco. Through such organizations as the Association of Writers for Intellectual Liberty and F.I.L. (For Intellectual Liberty), which included the surprising (political) mix of figures like Leonard Woolf, E. M. Forster, C. P. Snow, and Aldous Huxley, attempts, ostensibly devoid of any clear political ideology, were made to influence public opinion, and ultimately official policy, in favor of a more just society.[37]

Among intellectuals, the *Left Review*'s 1937 poll, "Authors Take Sides on the Spanish Civil War," reveals that 127 supported the Republic, five supported Franco, and seventeen were neutral. Similarly, public polls conducted throughout the war show that support ranged between 7 and 14 percent for Franco and between 57 and 72 percent for the Republic.[38] With such generally overwhelming support for the Republic—including the backing of many Liberals and Conservatives—a popular political front, especially among the working class, or at least, a "united front" of all supporters of the Republic, would have seemed assured. However, dissension within the parties over nonintervention (the rift, for example, between the more radical left wing of the Labour Party led by Aneurin Bevan and the more moderate wing), made the gaining of any party's endorsement of popular- or united-front programs difficult at best.

In this atmosphere many looked beyond the parties[39] for leadership in either their support for or opposition to the Republican (and generally leftist) causes. This mobilization of public opinion beyond normal party channels (which might mean having to form one's own local Aid Spain Committee, for example) had the effect of increasing the public's political consciousness, and indeed, for many it constituted the very *awakening* of political consciousness.[40]

Leadership on the Left or, at very least, a sense of political fraternity was provided informally by the Left Book Club (L.B.C.), which, as part of the current political concern of the literary world,[41] was founded by socialist editor Victor Gollancz, Harold Laski, and John Strachey just before the Civil War broke out. The Club (which would choose *The Road to Wigan Pier* as its March 1937 "selection") soon formed part of what was, in effect, an intellectual Popular Front that had sprung up under the impetus of the Spanish Civil War.[42] Here, the "scattered efforts of intellectual activity in the theatre, films, literature, art and music"[43] were mobilized for the leftist anti-fascist cause. However, in inviting active commitment to the leftist cause, the Left Book Club (which increased Communist membership from 1,400 in 1930 to over 15,000 in 1938), posed a great danger to the writer while providing him or her with an opportunity to become widely known—as Orwell did after having written *The Road to Wigan Pier*. The danger was that whether or not an organization is a party in the formal sense, any decision to write for it poses the danger of corrupting one's honesty. Again, it was the perennial tension between the need to act collectively in the interests of solidarity against a common enemy and the need of the individual to maintain his or her integrity as a measure of self-respect. Indeed, for writers in the Thirties, it was *the* central dilemma. W. H. Auden, Stephen Spender, Louis MacNeice, and other literary figures had argued for the independence of the artist, and by the mid-1930s, after it was seen that "political commitment had produced no art of any importance,"[44] there was the beginning of a return to the earlier ideas of the individual aesthetic. This return was suddenly arrested, however, by the demands on conscience made by the grim realities of the Spanish Civil War. The metaphors of the time became those of advance, not retreat, of Edward Upward's *Journey to the Border* and W. H. Auden's and Christopher Isherwood's *On the Frontier*. Now the young men who had missed the Great War of 1914–18 were confronted by the challenge to act out their words.

In recognizing the danger posed between political commitment and individual integrity, Orwell was hardly alone, but he stood out because he was clearer than most on the subject. With the weight of his Spanish experience behind him, he never tired of insisting that although as a citizen you can fight for an organization—for a party if you like—you should not write for it.

There is, at first reading, a blatant contradiction in Orwell's position—if one recalls that he wrote *The Road to Wigan Pier* on commission from Gollancz, a leftist editor—but it is only a seeming contradiction. Anyone who has read the book realizes immediately that although its author, like so many other writers, had turned his pen to the service of the Left, he stood apart in his fierce refusal to become captive to its orthodoxy. Indeed, at the very time that Orwell was in Spain, editor Gollancz was writing an unprecedented disclaimer of Orwell's attacks against the Left in the very book Gollancz had commissioned him to write.[45] In his independence of the party line, Orwell would soon show in *Homage to Catalonia* that he stood apart from most political writers of his day—not simply from those of the Left. For Orwell the intellectual surrender of a writer to a cause was more threatening to freedom, liberty, and justice than all of Franco's troops. This lesson of the Spanish Civil War, together with his experience of equality in the early days of the revolution within the Civil War, would be used by him repeatedly in his ongoing analysis of conditions in England.

Whether Orwell went to Spain to *write*, and then stayed to fight, or went primarily to *fight* is an open question. Bernard Crick, who believes Orwell went out to fight, points out the difficulty posed by Orwell's penchant for sometimes altering the sequence of events. Apart from having to evaluate the proffered evidence on both sides of the question, the problem of deciding who is right about Orwell's motivation remains, I think, difficult at best. This is evidenced when we compare, for example, the following statements, which are not from secondary sources, but from Orwell himself. In "Notes on the Spanish Militias" Orwell writes, "I had intended going to Spain to gather materials for newspaper articles etc., and had also some vague idea of fighting if it seemed worth while, but was doubtful about this owing to my poor health and comparatively small military experience." Yet later he writes in the introduction to a Ukrainian edition of *Animal Farm*, "In 1936 I got married. In almost the same week the civil war broke out in Spain. My wife and I both wanted to go to Spain and fight for the Spanish Government."[46]

If Orwell's primary motivation for going to Spain is not crystal clear, what is clear is that ironically, the summer of 1936, when the civil war erupted, was one of Orwell's happiest times. His friend Geoffrey Gorer remembers, "I think the only year that I ever knew him really happy was that first year with Eileen [O'Shaughnessy]." Recently married, he was still working on *Wigan Pier* at his new home in "The Stores," an old, small, and somewhat spartan cottage in Wallington, a village in Hertfordshire just north of London.[47]

If there was, on Orwell's part, any prior and urgent political commitment to political action in Spain, it was still in the process of maturation during that summer and in any case, was not to be fully realized until 1937, after his experience in Aragon (which we will examine later) and after which he wrote the letter to Cyril Connolly from the Maurin Sanatorium (where he was recovering from a near-fatal wound), declaring that "at last" he really believed in socialism, "which I never did before."[48]

After acquiring the sponsorship of the Independent Labour Party (which he did not join till 1938), he went to Spain. Having sent the completed manuscript of *The Road to Wigan Pier* to his agent on December 15, he left England just before the Christmas of 1936. What caused him to join the Republicans "almost immediately" upon arriving in Spain was the "overwhelming . . . and moving"[49] experience of being in Barcelona in the early days of the war (which will be discussed later).

In January 1937, as part of the I.L.P. contingent of the P.O.U.M., a semi-Trotskyist group that had started out as members of the Workers and Peasants Alliance,[50] Orwell was sent to the mountainous part of the Aragon Front near Alcubierre in northeastern Spain. After a relatively inactive period, he returned to Barcelona on leave in late April 1937 with the intention of seeking action in Madrid, which, he was told, would be possible if he could get the Communists to recommend him for the International Brigade. During the first week in May, however, while he was resting and waiting for a cobbler to outdo the "entire Spanish army" in providing him with big-enough boots ("the kind of detail that is always deciding one's destiny"),[51] fighting broke out in Barcelona between various elements on the Republican side.

On May 10, having refused to seek Communist endorsement for the Madrid Front after what he had seen in Barcelona, Orwell returned to the Aragon Front, where he found himself promoted from corporal to second lieutenant. Early in the morning of May 20, near Huesca, he was shot through the throat by a Fascist sniper—a near-fatal wound. After convalescing till mid-June, he returned to Barcelona to join his wife, who had only recently arrived in Spain.

By now the P.O.U.M. had been outlawed by the government, and though he had never actually been a card-carrying member of P.O.U.M., Orwell's service with them as part of the I.L.P. contingent placed him in immediate danger. After being pursued by secret police, he and Eileen crossed the French border on June 23 and shortly thereafter returned to England. By mid-July of 1937 he began *Homage to Catalonia;* but in an England of "Right" and "Left" ("terms hardly used in the political sense" before Spain), wherein the political climate was marked by ever-increasing[52] class divisions and wherein any criticism of the Left was quickly construed as affording aid and comfort to Franco, Victor Gollancz refused to consider publication of the projected book on Spain even before Orwell had put pen to paper.[53] Nevertheless, Orwell began writing and barely six months later, by mid-January 1938, had completed the book, setting down the themes that would obsess him till the end of his life.

CHAPTER 7

I N BURMA THE IMPERIALISTS HAD RULED; IN ENGLAND, IT WAS
the rich. In Spain, in the Barcelona of December 1936, Orwell saw
something he had never seen before, and it excited him. He not only
saw how the fascists were being resisted in a civil war the whole
world knew about, but he discovered a revolution—the workers in
control. Suddenly, it seemed that the exploited might yet reduce the
old social and economic imbalance and injustices that—even if they
were not consciously imposed by the thousands of absentee landlords—had spread like an untended weed, choking off whatever
remained of the Catholic Church's early moves in Spain toward
equality.[1] In a poem dedicated to the memory of an Italian militiaman, Orwell reveals part of the "thrill of hope,"[2] he felt in his first
days in the Catalan capital, an experience that he assumed he had
shared with every anti-appeasement antifascist soul in Europe when
on July 18 the generals' plot had been met with such fierce opposition
by the workers:

> But the thing that I saw in your face
> No power can disinherit:
> No bomb that ever burst
> Shatters the crystal spirit.[3]

The crystal spirit for Orwell, "the thing" that he had seen in the
face of an Italian militiaman on the day before he joined the P.O.U.M.,
was the expression, born in new hope, of an incorruptible determination to fight for a better, more decent life—a life that more than
ever before, was technologically possible.[4] For Orwell, joining a
workers' militia at the age of thirty-three, the air seemed filled with
fearless resolve.

When one came straight from England the aspect of Barcelona was something startling and overwhelming. It was the first time that I had ever been
in a town where the working class was in the saddle. Practically every building of any size had been seized by the workers and was draped with red flags
or with the red and black flag of the Anarchists. . . . Every shop and café
had an inscription saying that it had been collectivized, . . . their boxes painted
red and black [Anarchist colours]. Waiters and shop-walkers looked you in
the face and treated you as an equal; . . . revolutionary posters were everywhere. . . . It was the aspect of the crowds that was the queerest thing of all.
In outward appearance it was a town in which the wealthy classes had practically ceased to exist; . . . practically everyone wore rough working-class
clothes, or blue overalls, or some variant of the militia uniform. All this was
queer and moving.[5]

Reflecting his ignorance of some of the historical factors behind
the revolution, Orwell admitted that he did not understand much of
what was going on, nor did he like everything he saw. Nevertheless,
"I recognized it immediately as a state of affairs worth fighting for.
. . . There was no unemployment; . . . above all there was a belief in
the revolution and the future, a feeling of having suddenly emerged
into an era of equality and freedom."[6] If, as Orwell had said, there
was "no *turbulence* left in England"[7] because of the acceptance of
"them" over "us," there was spirit enough for him in Barcelona.
"Nobody said '*Señor*' or '*Don.*' . . . Everyone called everyone else
'Comrade' and 'Thou.' " Here, there was none of the cap-touching
subservience he had seen in Wigan. Here, a miner's status was equal
to anyone else's.[8]

Of course, status and the wealthy classes had not ceased to exist;
they had, as Orwell later discovered, simply donned workers' garb
and gone psychologically, if not actually, underground, awaiting their
chance to resurface. This they did after Franco's immediate threat
had been met by the initial worker–bourgeois alliance, and the alliance began to fall apart as the Communists, giving priority to the
concept of the Popular Front against fascism, sided with the more
moderate leftists and bourgeois elements of the Republic.[9] When the
wealthy classes did reappear, dotting the militia's sea of blue overalls
with their "smart summer suits," Orwell, dirty and tired from the
front, would sense the first signs that the revolution, born in working-class resistance to Franco, was dying.[10] When the secret police
of the side he had fought for hunted him in June, he would know it
was dead. But for a moment in Barcelona in late 1936, in the heady
draught of temporary victory, in spite of the city's shabbiness and its

shortages, the idea of equality seemed alive and well.

At this time the Catalan workers' militias, hastily formed by the trade unions and political parties to whom they gave as much allegiance as they did the central government, were holding Franco's Nationalists at bay until a more regular army could be trained. The militias, Orwell shows, were imbued with a chaotic optimism that was apt to dismay even the most ardent foreign supporter unused to Spanish ways. Along with the Lenin Barracks smelling of "horsepiss and rotten oats" and the "smashed furniture," greasy pannikins, and piecemeal issuance of a semi-uniform, there was the daily "instruction." For the ex–imperial policeman and Etonian O.T.C. member, this early instruction was more like comic opera. "Frightful scenes of chaos" confronted him as instructors struggled with working-class recruits who were keen to make revolution but for whom a "pull-through"* seemed as great a mystery as the Blessed Trinity.[11]

Even for a man like Orwell, who was suspicious of passionate quests for order, the lack of discipline amid the "extraordinary-looking rabble" was as disconcerting in the face of coming combat with Franco's forces as were the habitual assurances that all would be well *mañana*. Moreover, the literalness with which the Spaniards took the revolutionary phrases was astounding, if not somewhat "pathetic." "Discipline did not exist; if a man disliked an order he would step out of the ranks and argue fiercely with the Officer," who seemed just as likely to accept this without complaint—even to the point of insisting upon further abolition of the pre-revolutionary deference. Orwell remembered the "pained surprise" of one ex–regular army officer when he was addressed by a rough recruit as "Señor." The officer, still in the immaculate uniform of the regular army, replied, "What! Señor? Who is calling me Señor? Are we not all comrades?" At first, Orwell doubted that it would make for greater efficiency.[12]

These early observations are significant not just because they reveal Orwell's eye for the telling detail, which in this case meant capturing the early chaos of war, but because they testify to his early doubt that the ideal of social and economic equality could practically survive under fire. This doubt makes his later observations that equality could, and did, survive all the more convincing.

After some days of "instruction," which was little more than drilling, the P.O.U.M. column, almost unbelievably ill-equipped but full

*A cord with which a cleaning rag is drawn through a rifle barrel—in the British army.

of urgent revolutionary fervor, left Barcelona. From the torchlit railway station, amid a scene of red banners, bands, and the sound of an address by the political commissar, the column was sent to the Alcubierre on Aragon's Zaragoza[13] Front. Here, along with Buenaventura Durruti's Anarchist forces, they would see how well or badly the equalitarian forces would fare against the more traditionally trained fascist armies.

After a comic start—the Republican company's truck got lost in the fog—and after the first smells of war, "excrement and decaying food," after passing through the dismal, muddy filth of the Aragonese villages, Orwell, upon seeing his first fascists, made the soldier's sober discovery that often, except for wearing different uniforms, the enemy was "indistinguishable from ourselves." Issued with a badly rusted Mauser rifle dated 1896, and secretly afraid Orwell made his way with the rest of the "rabble" company up into the mist-shrouded hills around Alcubierre (140 miles west of Barcelona), the cold often more dreadful than the enemy. When they arrived at "the front," Orwell, seeing that they were not anywhere near the fascists (who were across a ravine, seven hundred meters away), was bitterly disappointed.

The front line here was not a continuous line of trenches, which would have been impossible in such mountainous country; it was simply a chain of fortified posts, always known as "positions," perched on each hill-top. In the distance you could see our "position" at the crown of the horseshoe; a ragged barricade of sand-bags, a red flag fluttering, the smoke of dug-out fires A little nearer, and you could smell a sickening sweetish stink that lived in my nostrils for weeks afterwards. Into the cleft immediately behind the position all the refuse of months had been tipped—a deep festering bed of bread crusts, excrement, and rusty tins.[14]

In such circumstances (though they were not typical of all the Spanish fronts), where the acquisition of food, tobacco, and firewood more often than not was of more concern than the enemy, it is not surprising that to Orwell, who had joined the P.O.U.M. to fight fascism, this period at the front (from January to May 1937) seemed among the most futile of his life: "I was chiefly conscious of boredom, heat, cold, dirt, lice, privation, and occasional danger." Yet even before the war was over, he recognized that these months on the Aragon front were of "great importance" to him and very different from anything he had experienced before.[15]

In his habitual homage to concrete experience, Orwell wrote that his time in the low sierra with the P.O.U.M. had "taught me things that I could not have learned in any other way." The essential lesson of this time was that despite chaotic birth pains, the children of equality, for all their naivety, could survive even in a world of inequality. Like the sudden spring of Alpine plants, they may die young and quickly in the cold and inhospitable air, but their very existence, however brief, had for many transformed a dream into a reality that would nurture the hopes of succeeding generations of the oppressed. Further, because the militia system was heavily composed of trade unionists (e.g., U.G.T., C.N.T., and P.O.U.M.) who held similar, if not always the same, political views, it "had the effect of canalizing into one place all the most revolutionary sentiment in the country." Accordingly, Orwell found that he had "dropped more or less by chance [through his membership in the P.O.U.M.] into the only community of any size in Western Europe where political consciousness and disbelief in capitalism were more normal than their opposites." Here, at last, people of mostly working-class origin were not only proclaiming equality but living it.[16]

Admittedly, there were serious deficiences, and confusion reigned among the early recruits (some of them aged eleven and twelve) who constituted little more than an "undisciplined mob." In addition, the military incompetence amid people who had never even held a gun gave the ex-policeman cause for not ranking the Spanish highly in their ability to wage successful war. Nevertheless, noting how it later became fashionable to decry the militias by arguing that their military inefficiencies were due to the failure of the equalitarian approach, Orwell pointed out that the militias were an "undisciplined mob" at first *not* because of the "essential . . . social equality between officers and men," but because raw troops of any army are likely to be an undisciplined mob. To blame military inefficiency on social equality was simply to ignore the acute lack of serviceable war materials on the Republican side, a lack that explained why the first casualty Orwell saw at the front was unintentionally, yet characteristically, a self-inflicted one.[17]

To be sure, the revolutionary approach to discipline, whereby one depended more on political consciousness than on regular army training for the execution of an order, shocked and angered Orwell at first, but he saw that it probably took no more time to adapt to this system than to instill unquestioning obedience among recruits in the British Army. He recalled that in January 1937 his job as corporal of maintaining discipline almost turned his hair gray, but by May he had no difficulty in getting men either to obey orders or to volunteer for dangerous sorties. Besides, he noted, whatever the equalitarian army's faults, it had held the line, buying valuable time for the Popular [regular] Army to be trained in the rear—a fact that he said sneering journalists often forgot. Most significant of all was the fact that despite the vastly better-equipped and trained Nationalist forces, the completely voluntary militias managed to stay in the line in the absence of "combat-police," who normally accompanied conscript troops. This, he believed, reflected the virtues of an equalitarian system wherein general and private alike partook of equal pay and food and "wore the same clothes." Orders were given and had to be obeyed, of course, but they were given "as comrade to comrade not as superior to inferior," so that whatever their faults, the militias provided "a sort of temporary working model of the classless society. Of course there was no perfect equality, but there was a *nearer approach to it than I had ever seen or than I would have thought conceivable in time of war*."[18] (The italics are mine.)

Unlike the kind of revolution that Orwell said was advocated from above by middle-class socialists who would impose their rules upon the ignorant masses, the revolution in Spain came from *below*. As Thomas shows, the importance of a detailed manifesto of May 1936, which declared, among its other aims, that workers would be free to organize their own communes, was that within two months, and within the Civil War, "the principles [of equality] there proclaimed were being enacted in several thousand Spanish towns." Revolution was spreading rapidly not only in towns where the Nationalist rebellion had been put down, but even where there had been no uprising. Popular Front administrative committees were sprouting up everywhere.[19]

As Orwell records, such revolution was evident not only in the military operations of the militias, but in the non-military[20] activities of peasants and workers, such as seizing and administering land, factories, and transport, and in the establishment of local soviets, including "workers' patrols to replace the old pro-capitalist police forces."[21] He admits candidly that "of course the process was not uniform" and that "it went further in Catalonia ["primarily Anarchist in direction"][22] than elsewhere. There were areas where the institutions of local government remained almost untouched." He also tells us of some areas where old local government institutions coexisted with the new revolutionary committees and mentions that in some areas independent Anarchist communes were established and operated up to a year later, ceasing to function only after the government forcibly removed them.[23]

The fact that the revolutionary aspect of this behind-the-lines reorganization was so carefully and consciously hidden from world view had a profound effect on Orwell and formed his view of how effective a weapon press censorhip *by the press* can be. In light of this, it will be helpful here if we look briefly at the kind of concrete change, as opposed to the mere sloganeering, that followed upon the mainly anarchist seizure of power in Catalonia early in the war.

Formed on July 23, 1936—a week after the Civil War had begun—the most effective administrative body in Barcelona—and therefore of Catalonia—was the Anti-Fascist Militias Committee. This organization, in which all parties were represented, was led by the F.A.I. (Federación Anarquista Ibérica), an Anarchist secret society, and C.N.T. (Anarcho-Syndicalist Trades Union), and though staffed by untrained workers, it acquitted itself well. As Thomas reports:

All the great industries of this great industrial area passed to the C.N.T.: the C.A.M.P.S.A., the Ford Iberia Motor Company, the public works company known as La Fomento de Obras y Construcciones. . . . The factory was run by an elected committee of 18 members—12 workers, 6 salaried staff members, half C.N.T., half U.G.T. . . . Barcelona thus became a proletarian town as Madrid never did. Expropriation was the rule—hotels, stores, banks, factories were either requisitioned or closed. Those that were requisitioned were run by managing committees of former technicians and workers. Food distribution, milk-pasteurization, even small handicrafts, were collectivized. . . . In factories committees of control grasped power, organizing shifts, production, labour and wages.[24]

The Anarchists, now that they shared power, proved to be more flexible than their long-standing passion and slogans for decentralization and non-parliamentary government would have suggested: for example, accepting centralization when the difficulties of running factories, which needed raw materials from outside sources, became evident. Further measures of their revolutionary flexibility appeared when they agreed to collaborate not only with other leftist parties, towards whom they had often been hostile, but even with banks that were controlled by the Socialist Trade Union (U.G.T.)[25] They also cooperated with the Communists, who, concerned only with defeating Franco as efficiently as possible, overwhelmingly favored greater centralization.[26]

Eventually, the limits of compromise were reached and the difference in theories drove the Communists and anarchists into headlong and bloody confrontation (as Orwell witnessed later in June of 1937); and despite early cooperation among the various factions of the Left, there were, of course, failures as well as successes in their attempts to change society. Nevertheless, their accomplishments in putting theory into detailed practice belied charges that social and political revolution within the war was confined merely to sloganeering.

Collectivization of agriculture, generally slower, also took place, and though there were no really large estates in Catalonia, the formula usually followed was that half of all expropriated land was to be run by a committee, with the remaining half parcelled out among the poorest peasants. The committee of the nearest town would receive half of all rent paid on the land, and the other half would be remitted. Whatever the method of agrarian reform, from Catalonia to Andalusia, "in almost every case," as Thomas records, "the peasants of Republican Spain were by early 1937 either owners of their own land or labouring for a collectivized farm. The tenant farmers and the landless labourers dependent upon a negligent landlord had vanished".[27]

The lesson implicit in Orwell's comments about the Republicans in general and their militias in particular is that such a revolution had been sustained in the face of overwhelming odds because suffering was common and generally shared. Of the Republican side as a whole, he points to the *lack* of gross disparities in wealth, which made the burdens of the war easier to bear. Writing of appalling shortages of arms and amenities in the militias, he concludes that "the fact that they did *not* disintegrate or show mutinous tendencies under these intolerable conditions . . . converted me (to some extent) to the notion of 'revolutionary discipline.' "[28]

Even so, the idea of revolutionary discipline during a time when winning the war seemed the most important thing to him was exasperating to Corporal (and later Lieutenant) Orwell only because it was different from what he as a member of the British middle class was used to. The fact that such discipline turned out to be far better in the end than he ever expected revealed to him yet another important difference between workers' revolutionary armies and bourgeois armies—namely, that discipline in the first type is based more on a sense of loyalty to fellow workers than on fear of punishment (from *above*).[29] This does not mean that Orwell underrated the power of fear—If he had, it is doubtful that *Nineteen Eighty-Four* would ever have been written—but his observation testifies to a spirit of cooperation among the revolutionary militias that, allied with necessity, sparked what he called "astonishing feats of improvisation," from using cold cream or bacon fat as a substitute for gun oil to organizing regular meals for thousands of troops in the height of battle. To Orwell such achievements were the material symptoms of a much more significant advancement among the workers—namely, a new "spirit of utterance, a freedom of speech and the press, which no one would have thought possible in time of war."[30] To argue that this new-found (if later curtailed) spirit of freedom was absolute would be as untrue as claiming that there was perfect equality in the militias. Once again, it was the *increased* sense of freedom, the *increased* sense of equality that mattered to Orwell; again, it was the sense of "direction," despite the failures, that was important and that, measured against the old state of affairs, marked the revolution as an advance.

The embarrassingly "hackneyed phrases" of the revolutionary songs being sold on the streets for a few centimos might disappear like the illiterate militiamen who eagerly purchased them in the early days of democratic hopes, but their disappearance would signify only the exile of revolutionary hopes, not their death. Of course, Orwell did not think that the experience of revolution would guarantee democracy as it was known elsewhere. It would be "childish," he wrote before the Republican surrender in 1939, to expect that democracy in the Western European sense could follow quickly upon a Republican victory, and there would, he warned, be tremendous reconstruction problems in Spain itself even if the Republicans won; but better this than if Franco won, for then even the approximation of a democratic government would disappear into the bowels of the corporative state. He believed that if the Republic won, its early experience would be invaluable, because the spirit of voluntarism and the concomitant discipline that had been gained through making common cause against Franco would better dispose the people towards democratic procedure in the future and would foil future attempts to overthrow the government. Certainly, they would be better prepared for and more disposed to the democratic process than the conscripts of Franco's army, who, like conscripts in any army, "have only a very dim idea as to what they are fighting about"[31] and to whom hierarchy, not equalitarianism, is the norm. In the volunteer

Republican armies "men were suffering" but "they were also learn-ing."[32]

Even as the possibility of socialism receded in the wake of Franco's victories and the bitter internecine fighting on the Republican side that came later, even when a Republican victory might have meant something less than socialism—possibly a "capitalist republic"—Orwell believed that "the people have seen and learned too much" to make them willing subjects of an authoritarian regime or to let themselves be pushed back into the semifeudalism of the years before 1931.[33]

The sense of making history—indeed, the importance of history as a guide to improving one's condition—had been absent among the working-class pupils of *A Clergyman's Daughter*. In Spain the sight of possibilities realized through the revolution would not be lost on the children of the poor. Here in Catalonia "they" had been challenged by "us." Furthermore, Orwell believed, the lessons of the revolutionary experience had raised the consciousness of the Spanish workers out of the apathetic condition of their English cousins, who (although they were relatively better off) might well have envisaged a better future but did not have models for realizing it. Now, as a result of the detailed collectivization of the kind already mentioned, there was in Spain a model for a better way of life, and it would encourage future generations to "preserve" and so "extend" the spirit of hope until it would be strong enough to penetrate the totalitarian armor. "The symbol of military despotism is the tank, . . . yet nearly any calibre of tank can be blown into the air by a grenade weighing only a few pounds, . . . providing that there is someone brave enough to throw it." This depends on "the mass of the people feeling that they have something to fight for."[34] The apathy and ignorance upon which regimes depend, he wrote, no longer existed in Spain after the upheaval of 1936, and the desire for feedom and a decent standard of life had spread too far to be extinguished by the deliberate obfusca-tion and persecution of a dictatorship.[35] Thus, even set against the carnage of the civil war, the revolutionary experience would be con-sidered by Orwell as a signal victory; for in the long run, just as the militiamen, despite their illiteracy, had learned the songs of revolu-tionary hope, so would the proles in *Nineteen Eighty-Four* remember the songs of yesterday. Within the collective memory of a better past—however brief it had been—there would stir the hope of a better future. The victory of political consciousness, then, was a victory not simply for the exploited of Spain but for the exploited everywhere.[36]

Scores of thousands of ordinary people had been forced into positions of responsibility and command which a few months earlier they would never have dreamed of. Hundreds of thousands of people found themselves thinking, with an intensity which would hardly have been possible in normal times, about economic theories and political principles, Words like fascism, communism, democracy, socialism, Trotskyism, anarchism, which for the vast mass of human beings are nothing but words, were being eagerly discussed and thought about by men who only yesterday had been illiterate peasants or overworked machine hands. There was a huge intellectual ferment, a sudden expansion of consciousness.[37]

For Orwell the militias exemplified the best in the ferment. In *Homage to Catalonia* he writes that insofar as "many of the normal motives of civilized life—snobbishness, money grubbing, fear of the boss, etc. [the themes of his English novels]—had simply ceased to exist" along with normal class divisions, he regards the experience as a "foretaste of Socialism." He concedes that this Spanish experience was only a "temporary and local phase" in the "enormous" worldwide struggle between exploited and exploiter but adds, "It lasted long enough to have its effect upon anyone who had experienced it."[38]

Although life in the militias may not be perfect equality, Orwell found it equalitarian to a degree that he said was all but unthinkable in the "money-tainted air" of the England of Gordon Comstock and Dorothy Hare. Above all, there was none of the dull acceptance of exploitation that he had seen in the faces of the down-and-out. Despite the incontrovertible savagery of the Civil War, Orwell noted that the "expression on the human face" of the common soldier was not that of the coal miner's subservience, the waiter's obsequiousness, or the coolie's servility, but one of hope. For Orwell this hope was especially "strange and valuable," quite apart from any political implications he drew from it. Not only did he find himself in a community wherein political consciousness and rejection of capitalism were more normal than not, but in a community where the use of the word *comrade* was evidence of genuine friendship rather than "humbug." Most of all, he found himself invigorated by an atmosphere "where hope was more normal than apathy or cynicism. . . . One had breathed the air of equality."[39]

From numerous passages like this, which record his discovery that equality was practical, one gains a sense of excitement, nearly euphoric in its tone, that is not to be found anywhere else in Orwell's writings. It is this "magic quality" of his time in Aragon, which was "so different from the rest of my life", that gives *Homage to Catalonia* its underlying almost youthful optimism. Even though he was writing the book ten years after Burma, the Orwell of Spain seems younger than the Blair of *Burmese Days*.[40]

Quite apart from the absence of privileges between officers and men and the sense of men acting voluntarily, which he enjoyed so much during his time in the militias, Orwell was, no doubt, simply experiencing the sense of camaraderie that is so commonly felt among soldiers which often forms the core of the appeal of military life. Moreover, although he had known fear, his enthusiasm—like that of many a soldier before him—was fired by the action about him, from overrunning a fascist trench near Torre Fabián to watching "like an allegorical picture of war; the trainload of fresh men gliding proudly up the line, the maimed men sliding slowly down, and all the while the guns on the open trucks making one's heart leap as guns always do, and reviving that pernicious feeling, so difficult to get rid of, that war *is* glorious after all."[41]

While this passage evidences Orwell's honest admission that he could share the "pernicious," albeit common, attraction of war, he also stresses the unattractive side of the soldier's life. He shows how heroic visions of war fade alongside the knowledge that "a louse is a louse and a bomb is a bomb," no matter whether or not you believe you are in the right, and that just as "those who take the sword perish by the sword . . . those who don't take the sword perish by smelly diseases."[42] In short, as the author of *Burmese Days*, "A Hanging," and "Shooting an Elephant" had learned, the costs of doing the "dirty work of Empire at close quarters,"[43] so the author of *Homage to Catalonia* and "Looking Back on the Spanish War" had learned the costs of *war*. Consequently, in yet another instance of how the Spanish experience would heavily influence Orwell's later conclusions about England and the world rather than about Spain, he was able to talk about the English intellectual left's ignorance of the dirty details, which made it possible for them to "swing" wildly over from " 'War is hell' to 'War is glorious' . . . with no sense of incongruity."[44] This is but one example of how Orwell's nearly euphoric reaction, although it may have been naively founded in Barcelona ("There was much of it that I did not understand")[45] and was undoubtedly spurred on by the common camaraderie of any front, nevertheless generated much that was insightful in his later work. The flash of excitement that he experienced in the militia would be tempered, however, by a much harsher reality *later* in Barcelona during the internecine fighting in the Republicans' summer of discontent in 1937, and such experiences shaped his concern that when we lack firsthand knowledge of terror, we find it easier to endorse the formation and administration of a totalitarian state. The exploitation of others, including torture, can be tolerated and advocated more easily by those who have never been subjected to it. Still, the disillusionment of 1937 was not to destroy Orwell's *new-found* hope and belief in socialism. What it did do was sharpen his own political awareness, which had been unwittingly growing through his observation of the raising of political consciousness in those about him. This alerted him, more than ever before, to the existence of "degrees," or different types, of socialism.

Before Spain Orwell had often spoken blithely about the need for socialism to improve the distribution of necessities on this "raft" in space. After the purges and witch hunting (which were simultaneously underway in Russia) that he witnessed in Barcelona when the Stalinists, and not the workers, were in control,[46] his vision of socialism would encompass more than simply a system of redistribution with a human face—it would be socialism with a "moral nose." It was because of his Spanish experience that Orwell concluded in 1940 that "Socialism *in itself*" is not necessarily an advance. In particular, the development in Spain of his awareness about political realities explains his subsequent use of the phrase "*democratic* Socialism [the italics are mine]." In "Why I Write" (1946) he recalls how "the Spanish war and other events in 1936–7 turned the scale" and that thereafter every word he wrote was "*for* democratic Socialism."[47]

This vision, inspired by "the *democratic* spirit of the militias [italics mine]" that he had experienced in Aragon in 1936–37, would (especially in his later fiction) increasingly focus Orwell's attention on instincts such as the greed for power that ran counter to a belief in equality. If socialism does not mean a classless society, it means nothing, he writes, and the militia society, for all its nascent inefficiency, was one wherein he had seen decisions made through free discussion among equals. For him this constitutes a "microcosm of a classless society." This "crude forecast of what the opening stages of Socialism might be like," he writes, "deeply attracted me" and "was to make my desire to see Socialism established much more actual than it had been before."[48]

Quite apart from the effect it had on him, Orwell's insider's account of the militias did two things. First, it challenged the Communists' charge that what the militias had achieved in the way of agricultural and industrial collectivization was of "no political significance." Secondly, as we shall see, it also revealed that the revolutionary promise of the militias was destroyed not because of their inherent weaknesses or inefficiencies (which he readily admitted to), but because of vigorous attacks on them—not so much by Franco, but by other, ostensibly anti-fascist forces. In short, the "breaking up of the old workers' militias which were organized on a genuinely democratic system" was the direct result of a "blow at equalitarianism" delivered from within the Republic.[49]

The unravelling of this paradox is one of the major achievements of *Homage to Catalonia* and is clearly a precursor of the mood of terror in *Nineteen Eighty-Four*. The extent of the attack against the militias was not fully appreciated by Orwell himself until the night of June 20, 1937, when he arrived in Barcelona with his discharge papers, after having convalesced from his wound.

When I got to the hotel my wife was sitting in the lounge. She got up and came towards me in what struck me as a very unconcerned manner; then she put an arm round my neck and, with a sweet smile for the benefit of the other people in the lounge, hissed in my ear: *"Get out!"*
. . . "What the devil is all this about?" I said as soon as we were on the pavement.
"Haven't you *heard?"*
"No. Heard what? I've heard nothing."
"The P.O.U.M.'s been suppressed. They've seized all the buildings. Practically everyone's in prison. And they say they're shooting people already."[50]

Orwell had walked into a Spanish version of the Stalinist purges. The strategy of the communists in the Civil War had always been to leave revolutionary changes of society until victory (through centralized command and control) against Franco was assured. The Anarchists, who were traditionally opposed to any idea of centralized control for anything, disagreed violently with the Communist strategy, as did the ex-Communist Workers and Peasant Bloc Party known as the P.O.U.M. Also, the P.O.U.M., whose ex-Communist leaders had attacked Stalin's show trials and called Russia the " 'bureaucratic régime of a poisoned dictator,' "[51] saw little point in simply waging war against Franco unless long-awaited social reform could be effected at the same time. Also, as Orwell described it, "The Communists hold that Fascism can be beaten by alliance with sections of the capitalist class (the Popular Front), their opponents hold that this

manoeuvre simply gives Fascism new breeding-grounds." Whatever
the merits of each sides' position, the argument over strategy periodically flared up during the war, particularly in Catalonia, and finally,
hostilities broke out between the two camps within the Republican
camp, leading in early May to the fights in Barcelona between the
Communists and the P.O.U.M., in which Orwell participated and
about which he wrote so vividly. His description is one of the best
demonstrations of how his political writing was never entirely divorced
from his aesthetic instinct, of how it had become an art.

The next three days and nights I spent continuously on the roof of the
Poliorama, except for brief intervals when I slipped across to the hotel for
meals. I was in no danger, I suffered from nothing worse than hunger and
boredom, yet it was one of the most unbearable periods of my whole life. I
think few experiences could be more sickening, more disillusioning, or, finally,
more nerve-wracking than those evil days of street warfare.
    I used to sit on the roof marvelling at the folly of it all. From the little
windows in the observatory you could see for miles around—vista after vista
of tall slender buildings, glass domes, and fantastic curly roofs with brilliant
green and copper tiles; over to eastward the glittering pale blue sea—the
first glimpse of the sea that I had had since coming to Spain. And the whole
huge town of a million people was locked in a sort of violent inertia, a
nightmare of noise without movement. The sunlit streets were quite empty.
Nothing was happening except the streaming of bullets from barricades and
sand-bagged windows. Not a vehicle was stirring in the streets; here and
there along the Ramblas the trams stood motionless where their drivers had
jumped out of them when the fighting started. And all the while the devilish
noise, echoing from thousands of stone buildings, went on and on and on,
like a tropical rainstorm. Crack-crack, rattle-rattle, roar—sometimes it died
away to a few shots, sometimes it quickened to a deafening fusillade, but it
never stopped while daylight lasted, and punctually next dawn it started
again.[52]

Although a cease-fire was effected on May 7, it had become clear
that there was no truce between the P.O.U.M. and the Communists
and that no compromise on war policy had been reached. The Communists bided their time until mid-June, when Orlov, the N.K.V.D.
chief in Spain, ordered the arrest of all P.O.U.M. leaders, claiming
that the P.O.U.M. was involved in a fascist spy ring. It was now that
Orwell was in danger, for in Barcelona the P.O.U.M.was declared
illegal, and its headquarters quickly became a prison. Andrés Nin, its
leader, was tortured and then murdered. In the paranoid manner of
the Stalinist purges, not only were P.O.U.M. members persecuted,
but many Russian leaders in Spain also "disappeared, . . . partly because

they had objected to Stalin's policy towards the Spaniards with whom they had worked so much."[53]

The purge in the Catalan capital, the time of " 'secret prisons,' " when old comrades walked in fear "past one another as though we had been total strangers," marked the height of Orwell's political consciousness in Spain[54]; but the purge's effect would go far beyond his experiences there, haunting the daylight hours of George Bowling, subduing the brave but temporary revolutionary light of *Animal Farm,* and finally overwhelming Winston Smith in the darkness of *Nineteen Eighty-Four.* Orwell had learned that the leftist could be shot as easily by someone from the Left as by someone from the Right. It was a turning point in his life.

CHAPTER 8

O RWELL'S INCREASING POLITICAL CONSCIOUSNESS, WHICH came from his understanding that within the Left a political war was being fought within the wider democracy-versus-fascism conflict, was not at all apparent to him when he decided to join the P.O.U.M. He writes, "If you had asked me why I had joined the militia I should have answered: 'To fight against Fascism,' and if you had asked me what I was fighting *for*, I should have answered: 'Common decency.' I had accepted the *News Chronicle–New Statesman* version of the war as the defence of civilization against a maniacal outbreak by an army of Colonel Blimps in the pay of Hitler."[1]

Though moved to join the P.O.U.M. militia by the revolutionary poor-versus-rich excitement in Barcelona, Orwell admitted that for him, the apparent hodgepodge of political parties and their initials— P.O.U.M, (Partido Socialista Unificado de Cataluña–the United Catalan Socialist-Communist Party) P.S.U.C., F.A.I., C.N.T., U.G.T., and J.C.I. (Juventud Communista Ibérica, P.O.U.M.'s Youth Party)— seemed relatively unimportant and only bored him. He was perplexed, for example, when P.O.U.M. soldiers pointed out "Socialist positions" at the front. "Aren't we all Socialists?" he asked naively, still not recognizing the differences, or more importantly, the significance of the differences, among the various parties within the Republic. His attitude at the beginning had been puzzlement as to why everyone couldn't drop all the political talk and get on with fighting Franco's fascists.[2]

That such a normally astute observer of events failed at first to grasp what was going on beyond and beneath the surface of the anti-fascist war illustrates one of the major points of his *Homage to Catalonia*—namely, that the press coverage of the war, and particularly

the revolutionary aspect of it described earlier, was woefully inade-
quate. The revolutionary aspect, as he charged, was in fact *"successfully covered up."*[3] (The italics are mine.) It was not that there were
insufficient correspondents; indeed, they flocked to Spain to see the
war (and included in their ranks were Louis Fischer, André Malraux,
Ernest Hemingway, Herbert Matthews, Arthur Koestler, and Antoine
de Saint-Exupéry, among others). Some, like Orwell, also fought in
the war.

Gradually, through 1937, Orwell became aware of the differences
in the thicket of acronyms, most of which, if not all, were unknown
to the outside world. He discovered it was impossible not to become
aware when his own destiny was involved—when the mere fact that
he had fought with the P.O.U.M. had made him a target for the
secret police's hunt in Barcelona in June. What he learned and would
later report in *Homage* and elsewhere was essentially this: the Republican resistance to Franco was accompanied by a social and political
upheaval that made the war "not merely a civil war, but the beginning of a revolution"—one that in the interests of Stalin's foreign
policy, the Communists were determined to crush. That "outside
Spain few people grasped that there was a revolution,"[4] that the
Communists were in fact vehemently *counter-revolutionary* "and were
more anxious even than the liberals to hunt down the revolutionaries
and stamp out all revolutionary ideas,"[5] was, Orwell stated, largely
due to the refusal of the left wing press, as much as that of the right
wing, to report it. In showing how the leftist press failed to report
the leftist revolution *(The Daily Worker* calling those who gave any
hint of it "downright lying scoundrels"), Orwell reveals the extent
of the Communist leaders' determination to preserve at any cost the
liberal–leftist alliance against Hitler and Mussolini. They were working hard, he pointed out, not merely to delay the revolution until
Franco was defeated, but to make sure it never got off the ground.[6]

On the other hand, the right wing press, which could normally be
expected to attack any leftist revolution, was also busy ignoring the
revolution's existence. Of course, because of their generally pro-Franco
(Nationalist Front) sympathies, they had no sympathy with the Popular Front. Their studied refusal to discuss the revolution within the
civil war, Orwell argued, was based on the premise that in order to
crush the revolution, which threatened substantial foreign capital
invested in pre-war Spain, it was best to deny the revolution's existence—thereby denying it any external encouragement or impetus.

Similarly, there were those left-wing propagandists who thought they were helping the Republican side by denying the revolution, arguing that any mention of it would only further stir up pro-Franco sentiment abroad, which might result in increased aid to the fascists.[7]

Hence, despite the sometimes brilliant and truthful reporting of the war (as acknowledged by Orwell in his praise of the *Manchester Guardian*), both the left- and right-wing presses acted upon the same belief—that since the revolution ought to be smashed, it should not be mentioned. If, contrary to the general rule, they did report it, their accounts were deliberately distorted for propagandistic purposes. Thus, Orwell recorded that "one of the dreariest effects of this war has been to teach me that the Left-wing press is every bit as spurious and dishonest as that of the Right."[8]

Orwell cites, for example, how the *New Statesman* refused his review of Borkenau's *Spanish Cockpit* because it contravened the paper's editorial policy (by showing how, on the Republican side, the Communists constituted the extreme right instead of the extreme left) and supposedly would help Franco. The implications of this kind of censorship, which Orwell described when his review of *Spanish Cockpit* was finally published (in *Time and Tide*), is that debate between different points of view is not only misinformed, as it was outside Spain, but that within a country such censorship, enforced by terror, drives debate underground—to be carried on in secret. The result is that instead of differences being aired, and perhaps dissipated, they fester in a society that becomes marked by "ceaseless arrests, . . . censored newspapers, . . . prowling hordes of armed police." In June of 1937 such an atmosphere, said Orwell, "was like a nightmare."[9]

Worried about the possibility of such a world in the future, Orwell, repeatedly evoking the image of nightmare, recalls commenting to Arthur Koestler, "History stopped in 1936." Koestler nodded his agreement, because while both "were thinking of totalitarianism in general," it was the Spanish Civil War they were thinking of in particular. What moved Orwell to make his remark was his reflection that

Early in life I have [*sic*] noticed that no event is ever correctly reported in a newspaper, but in Spain, for the first time, I saw newspaper reports which did not bear any relation to the facts, not even the relationship which is implied in an ordinary lie. I saw great battles reported where there had been no fighting, and complete silence where hundreds of men had been killed. I saw troops who had fought bravely denounced as cowards and traitors, and others who had never seen a shot fired hailed as the heroes of imaginary victories; and I saw newspapers in London retailing these lies and eager intellectuals building emotional superstructures over events that had never happened. *I saw, in fact, history being written not in terms of what happened but of what ought to have happened according to various "party lines."*[10] [The italics are mine.]

In light of Koestler's later confessions (after Orwell's death), it is not surprising that he nodded so readily at his colleague's comment about the corruption of honest reporting, for Koestler had engaged in exactly the kind of willful falsification that so disturbed Orwell. Koestler describes Muenzenberg, the Communist propaganda chief in Paris, striding into the writer's apartment: "He would pick up a few sheets of typescript, scan through them and shout at me: Too weak. Too objective. Hit them! Hit them hard! Tell the world how they run over their prisoners with tanks, how they pour petrol over them and burn them alive. Make the world gasp with horror. Hammer it into their heads."[11]

Many examples of such distortions from both Right and Left are given by Orwell in *Homage to Catalonia* as well as "Spilling the Spanish Beans" (1937) and "Looking Back on the Spanish War" (1942). A memorable example from the *New Statesman* accuses the fascists of making barricades with the bodies of living children, which, Orwell wryly points out, is "a most unhandy thing to make barricades with." To even the score, Orwell quotes the *Daily Worker*, whose reporting was so inaccurate that the Anarchists are accused of having attacked themselves at the Barcelona telephone exchange. Five days later a completely contradictory story of the same incident appeared in the same newspaper.[12]

Orwell did not deny that atrocities occurred and noted that the fact that they happened at all was, of course, far worse than the press lying about them. What struck him about such stories, after he drew up a list of atrocities since 1918, was that the Left and the Right hardly ever simultaneously believed the same stories and that, stranger still, yesterday's proven atrocity story could, like the *Daily Worker*'s reversal on the Barcelona telephone exchange story, quickly became today's unmitigated lie, simply because changing political conditions made the switch expedient.[13]

The fact that one believes only the stories of atrocities said to have been committed by the other side and that both sides would lie by omission, if not through outright falsification of facts, illustrates for

Orwell the power of a political orthodoxy to convince the individual by means of propaganda that commitment to the party line is always more important than commitment to the truth. This power made a deep and lasting impression on him.[14] The impression was negative—so negative, he said, that all his serious writing after 1936 was directed "*against* totalitarianism"—and we see that after 1936 the power of political orthodoxy through propaganda becomes a prime target in his anti-totalitarian attack. Although he usually disapproved of propaganda ("I hold the outmoded opinion that in the long run it does not pay to tell lies"),[15] Orwell understood its power very well from his own experience. At the front he saw that for a time the megaphone, not the rifle, was the weapon of attack. At first, he was "amazed and scandalized" at the idea of talking to rather than shooting at the enemy, because it seemed that the Spaniards were not taking the war seriously enough.[16] This approach was effective, however—as indicated by the trickle of fascist deserters. The power of even such simple propaganda became evident to Orwell in an otherwise minor event, which he reports with a sense of humor that is all too often ignored by many Orwell scholars. As the result of listening to a fellow militiaman who was an "artist at the job," Orwell recalls, "Sometimes, instead of shouting revolutionary slogans he simply told the Fascists how much better we were fed than they were. His account of the Government rations was apt to be a little imaginative. 'Buttered toast!'—you could hear his voice echoing across the lonely valley—'We're just sitting down to buttered toast over here! Lovely slices of buttered toast!' " He concludes that "in the icy night the news of buttered toast probably set many a Fascist mouth watering. It even made mine water, though I knew he was lying."[17] If the mouth could salivate in the face of nonexistent food and such trivial deception, how much more willingly would the brain accept lies that were more subtly disguised? The answer would emerge in *Animal Farm* and *Ninteen Eighty-Four*.

In his attack in *Homage* upon political orthodoxy and its propaganda, Orwell considered the leading perpetrators (though not necessarily its originators) to be the intellectuals in general and the British literary intelligentsia in particular.[18] Furthermore, although quite obviously not all journalists were intellectuals, or vice versa, Orwell's attack was spurred by what he believed to be the undue influence of the intellectuals in the press of the 1930s—before radio had stolen much of the literary person's "thunder."[19] One of his most telling broadsides took place in 1940, when he wrote "Inside the Whale," his review of Henry Miller's *Tropic of Capricorn*. Not only does this piece bare Orwell's growing disgust with the power of political orthodoxy, but more importantly, his understanding of its appeal, which resulted from the raising of his political consciousness in Spain. Because the role of allegiance to such orthodoxy, particularly among intellectuals, is central to his later writings about the conditions of modern exploitation, it is necessary to discuss his view of how such allegiance grew in England between the world wars. Once again, we see how his Spanish experience is used to discuss *England*, rather than Spain.

Dominant in Orwell's appraisal of Miller's novel is an appreciation of the American's fearless recording of facts, even the "inane, squalid facts of everyday life." Orwell does not agree that modern life should be simply accepted ("let's swallow it whole"), for this meant swallowing a world in which democratic hopes had all too often ended behind "barbed wire." Nevertheless, he considered Miller's novel important for two reasons: first, it was written without fear of orthodox opinion and second, in its acceptance of modern life, including the "dirty-handkerchief side," it mirrored the passivity and subservience of the ordinary person (i.e., the "average sensual" person).[20] In a world of "them" and "us," such an individual felt in control of personal destiny only within the narrow confines of home and work and was unconcerned by events beyond, which seemed as uncontrollable as the weather. In contrast to the relatively becalmed sea of the ordinary person's political consciousness, there was the active role of the English literary intelligentsia.

Orwell believed that the disproportionate influence of the intelligentsia, particularly among the Communists and near-Communists in the literary magazines,[21] rose largely because literature in the Thirties had involved itself more than ever before in politics. This did not mean that ordinary voices had been silent about great events beyond the ordinary individual's local environment, or that all ordinary people were the non-political, non-moral, and passive underlings about whom Orwell saw Miller writing. Indeed, just as Thomas tells us how most of the volunteers in Spain were from the working class, Orwell recalls how some of the most extraordinary books about World War I were written by ordinary people—by ordinary soldiers, for example. The difference between books by such men and books by the intelligentsia about Spain—the change that had taken place, said Orwell—was that whereas books like *All Quiet on the Western Front* were written from the *victim's* point of view by men who, though in the thick of action, were asking, "What the hell is all this about?"[22] the majority of the books on Spain were dull and bad because they were written by left- and right-wing propagandists.

What particularly concerned Orwell about the deepening involvement of literature in politics (which he did not disapprove of, in principle) was the increasing allegiance to orthodoxy, particularly Communist orthodoxy. His concern was heightened by his belief that such allegiance resulted more from an irrepressible need to *belong* to a group than from moral conviction. It was as if he were watching a group reenactment of Ravelston's transference of allegiance from God to Marx in *Keep the Aspidistra Flying*. In this view, Orwell, in his essay on Miller, returns to the problem that he first discussed in *A Clergyman's Daughter*—namely, that while it may be easy to rid yourself of "such primal things as patriotism and religion, . . . you have not necessarily got rid of the need for *something to believe in.*"[23]

Orwell argued that this need for group membership was as true for an intellectual as a bricklayer. By way of illustration he recalls how such writers and intellectuals as Evelyn Waugh and Christopher Hollis had earlier turned to the Roman Catholic Church after the emptiness of disillusionment. It was significant, he said, that they preferred the "power, . . . prestige" and "rigid discipline" of the Catholic Church over the more flexible Church of England.[24] Thus, he concluded that many of the young, anti-bourgeois intellectuals of the mid-1930s fled to the Communist party, instinctively recognizing it, albeit unconsciously, as a surrogate religion. It embodied all those values that they had ostensibly overturned but that had nevertheless resurfaced in disguise: "All the loyalties and superstitions that the intellect had seemingly banished could come rushing back under the thinnest of disguises. Patriotism, religion, empire, military glory— all in one word, Russia, . . . God—Stalin. The devil—Hitler. Heaven— Moscow. Hell—Berlin."[25] More broadly, his concern about the rush to the left reflected his conviction that while "group loyalties are necessary, . . . they are poisonous to literature, so long as literature is the product of individuals."[26]

The literary intelligentsia's allegiance to their respective orthodoxies explained for Orwell why writers of both the Right and the Left behaved so badly in Spain; but in the end it was the leftist writers who he felt had done the most damage. They had not only hidden the fact of the leftist revolution within the Civil War, but had failed to report the violent suppression of the revolution by the Republican government—especially by the Communists.

The Left's culpability in Orwell's eyes did not arise from any qualitative difference between the corruptibility of the Left or Right intelligentsias, but rose instead from the marked Right-to-Left swing from the "art for art's sake" mood of the 1920s to the political preoccupation of "Auden, Spender and Co." in the mid-1930s. Orwell, as we have seen, did not object to political commitment; he was part of it. After 1930 he asks,

Who now could take it for granted to go through life in the ordinary middle-class way, as a soldier [like Bowling], a clergyman [Reverend Hare], a stockbroker, an Indian Civil Servant [like Blair], or what not? And how many of the values by which our grandfathers lived could now be taken seriously? Patriotism, religion, the Empire, the family, the sanctity of marriage, the Old School Tie, birth, breeding, honour, discipline—anyone of ordinary education could turn the whole lot of them inside out in three minutes.[27]

It may have taken more than three minutes but the intellectuals, like Ravelston, did overturn such beliefs (at least in their own minds) and as it had once been fashionable amongst intellectual circles to hear that a writer had "been received" (into Mother Church), it now became fashionable to hear that "so-and-so had 'joined' " the party. What Orwell found troubling about the new and and predominant swing to the far left wasn't just the intellectual's need for a surrogate religion, but that the new, often middle-class and public-school-trained writers like Spender, who wrote with a spirit of political commitment, did so not from experience of having been either exploited or persecuted, but from a purely intellectual perspective. Because of this, these young people, writing in 1935–39 as anti-fascist feeling was on the upsurge, were easily and increasingly attracted by Russian communism. Orwell's experience with the Communist orthodoxy in the Spanish Civil War led him to call this "a form of socialism [that made] mental honesty impossible."[28] So successful was this intelligentsia's attack upon traditional bourgeois values that Orwell said there was "now no intelligentsia that is not in some sense 'left' " and that England was "perhaps the only great country whose intellectuals are ashamed of their own nationality," resulting in the "divorce between patriotism and intelligence."[29]

After he had become angered by the Left's slavish reliance upon party line rather than upon personal observation and experience in its distorted reporting of the Spanish Civil War, Orwell wrote, "Nearly all the dominant writers of the thirties belonged to the soft-boiled emancipated middle class,"[30] and for them the party line was particularly comfortable because they were people to whom war was fought on paper—without any more personal danger than was entailed in a move at chess.[31] Consequently, much left-wing thought, he charged, was like an innocent playing with fire, ignorant that fire was hot.[32] As Stansky remarks, it was in Spain that Orwell discovered that the fire was hot.[33]

The point here is not whether one agrees with Orwell's analysis of the literary Thirties (given most prominently in "Inside the Whale"). The essential point is that while he never denies the unavoidable presence of subjectivity—"any report that one makes of any event must depend on the evidence of one's own senses, because there is no way of getting outside one's own body"[34]—Orwell relentlessly draws attention to how the lack of concrete experience among many of those who wrote about Spain resulted in pieces that, even if they were not deliberately falsified, were nevertheless false or disturbingly cavalier in their justification of bloodshed at a distance.[35]

Of course, in suggesting that firsthand experience is the only basis of valuable knowledge, Orwell is being cavalier himself, but his exaggeration is simply a device to draw attention to those who persistently judged from afar. In this regard Orwell was particularly angered by certain lines in Auden's poem "Spain":

> Tomorrow for the young, the poets exploding like bombs,
> The walks by the lake, the weeks of perfect communion;
>   Tomorrow the bicycle races
> Through the suburbs on summer evenings. But today the
>   struggle.
> Today the deliberate increase in the chances of death,
> The conscious acceptance of guilt in the necessary murder;
>   Today the expending of powers
> On the flat ephemeral pamphlet and the boring meeting.[36]

Even though he regarded the poem generally as one of the best about Spanish war,[37] and no doubt knew that Auden had at least visited Spain, Orwell took exception to the phrase "necessary murder," commenting that it could have been written only by someone for whom murder is at most a *word*. Personally I would not speak so lightly of murder. . . . I have seen the bodies of numbers of murdered men—I don't mean killed in battle, I mean murdered. Therefore I have some conception of what murder means—the terror, the hatred, the howling relatives, the post-mortems, the blood, the smells. To me, murder is something to be avoided. So it is to any ordinary person. The Hitlers and Stalins find murder necessary, but they don't advertize their callousness.[38]

Auden's "brand of amoralism," he concludes, is made possible by being elsewhere when the murder is committed and is perpetuated by people who have not seen its costs.

In showing how the concept of "necessary" murder could be swallowed whole by people (and by such influential people) because they were so far removed from the act that its reality never touched them, Orwell shows how easily the Left's anti-fascism slipped into totalitarianism. It is this easy mental slide that, he argues, not only constituted the cardinal "sin of nearly all left-wingers from 1933 onward," but explains how the English intellectuals' opposition to Hitler was marked by a simultaneous and enthusiastic acceptance of Stalin, the O.G.P.U., and the purge.[39] But while remoteness from the bloody details may make for a kind of amoralism, the harvest of ignorance is not, in Orwell's view, as dangerous in contributing to the acceptance of totalitarian methods as the acceptance by a writer, be he intellectual or not, of the discipline imposed by a political party. Orwell believed that even writers' partial acceptance of an orthodoxy in their writing means that sooner or later they are forced "to toe the line, or shut up." They are forced to dance to the tune that declares Hitler a fascist monster on the day before the Russo-German Pact and an ally the next—to change their stance whenever Monday's dogma becomes Tuesday's heresy.[40] We are moved from falsification through ignorance to falsification through intent by people who were not duped but who, Orwell points out, were willing propagandists.

Such willful lying was evident in the Left's denial of the fact that in Spain Communists were busy killing people not because they were too far right but because they were too far left, and in the Right's inflated reports about a "Russian army" in Spain. For Orwell, this signalled far more than the extent of corruption in the modern press. It signalled—and I think this is the most important message of *Homage to Catalonia*—a much deeper danger, indeed *the* gravest danger of the future, namely, *"that the very concept of objective truth is fading out of this world."* (The italics are mine.) Not only did the slavish followers of political orthodoxy who wrote so many lies partake in the "abandonment ["peculiar to our age"] of the idea that history *could* be truthfully written," but they actually advocated that it *should not* be so written.[41]

An example of such abandonment of the concept of objective truth is given in a review by Orwell in *The New English Weekly* of June 1938. Having already noted Koestler's cry in *Spanish Testament* for unqualified party allegiance, he draws attention to how the editor of the book *Franco's Rule* speaks contemptuously of " 'objectivity neurosis.' " In such contempt Orwell was quick to see the danger of totalitarianism. Whereas in the past, falsehood was as consciously spread as it was in Spain, there had remained, he argued, an underlying belief among people of all races in the existence of facts that "were more or less discoverable." The denial of this "common basis of agreement" between individuals constitutes a denial of objective truth; rather than having a mutual concept of "science," we make claims about " 'German Science,' 'Jewish Science,' etc." This not only means that a false division can be created between scientists by talking of "German science" and "Jewish science" but that a false distinction between human beings is created. If the notion of a "common basis of agreement" is lost, so is the implication of a common species. Then, just as it is claimed that "Jewish science" is completely different from "German Science," it is a short step to claiming that Jews have nothing in common with Germans—that they are two different species: human and subhuman.[42]

Further, if the sense of objective truth is lost, then so is the sense of *degree* of truth. If there is no cake, how can there be part of one? If absolute truth is regarded as unobtainable, then just as moral relativism had gathered strength (as Gordon Comstock points out) through the loss of belief in absolute right and wrong, so will it gather strength in the belief that because there is no objective truth— "a big lie is no worse than a little lie"[43]—living in England is "no worse" than living in Nazi Germany.[44]

Orwell's argument is not that we have access to absolute truth[45] but that without belief in the possibility of achieving such access, without belief in the ideal of absolute right and wrong and of the existence of the neutral scientific "fact,"[46] we paradoxically deal in *absolute* fashion with partial truths and facts. In doing so we evict the notion of "degree," of at least trying to the "best" of our abilities to act morally in an imperfect world. If this importance of degree is

lost, then, as with any compass, the sense of "direction" is soon lost—
so that intellectuals and others can continue to busy themselves
" 'proving' that one régime is as bad as the other,"[47] that there is no
difference between police who must have a warrant and those who
can simply drag you off in the middle of the night without one. If a
"big lie is no worse than a little one," we might call murder—"execution," terror—"force," and might—"right."

Orwell, again at his best with the concrete details, warns us that
allegiance to orthodoxy makes the writer particularly vulnerable to
such distortions because the acceptance of just one "taboo" thought
ultimately means the exclusion of a whole range of thoughts—there
is the ever-present danger that "any thought which is freely followed
up may lead to the forbidden thought." If you are forbidden to think
of apples, you must soon evict all thoughts of fruit in order to be
safe. The single log becomes a logjam blocking the hitherto free-
flowing stream of consciousness. This ends up producing the "fog
of lies and misinformation that surrounds such subjects as the Ukraine
famine, the Spanish Civil War, Russian policy in Poland."[48] Such
self-censorship, even when done with the best of intentions, prepares
both writers and the public who rely upon them for information to
accept the schizophrenic habit of "doublethink." Not only does
Monday's dogma become Tuesday's heresy, but both can be believed
simultaneously. This does not mean that Orwell was against political
affiliations, as his service with the P.O.U.M. and his membership in
the Independent Labour Party a year later clearly show. Indeed, just
as he had written that "the things I saw in Spain brought home to
me the fatal danger of mere negative anti-Fascism,"[49] he declares in
"Writers and Leviathan" that in his age of crisis[50] any thinking person had a duty not to be politically neutral.

But he believed that while one might reasonably submit to a party's discipline, as a soldier in the line, a writer could not submit to
the party's discipline in what he was writing. In what he wrote, a
writer had either to be true to the facts or to shut up. To do otherwise, to write unreservedly *for* the party, he warned, was to risk swallowing the party's discipline whole, which ultimately meant inheriting
a body of "unresolved contradictions"[51] that it would be heresy even
to try to resolve.

In this regard Orwell's preoccupation with the intelligentsia (such
as Auden and others like him), who, he felt, dominated much of the
press,[52] was spurred on by his conviction that the general public did

not care about the matter of intellectual liberty one way or the other. Just as he had written in the essay on Miller about the passivity of the ordinary man accepting his lot, he believed that the public were interested neither in persecuting heretics nor in defending them. Rather, after Spain, where the neutral fact had so often been erased from the page by "educated" men in political versions of the old team spirit of public schools like Eton, Orwell concluded that the headlong and deliberate attack on intellectual honesty came from intellectuals themselves.[53]

Orwell's observations on this theme of writers and intellectuals in politics stems from his own experience of the temptations that confronted the journalist and the novelist alike. In the same way that we must be on guard not to attribute a consistency of ideas to Orwell merely because he was consistently honest, it should not be assumed that his integrity, despite his generally creditable performance as a reporter of the Spanish Civil War, consistently rose above the temptations he warned of. Even in *Homage to Catalonia,* he confessed in a letter to Jack Common (an old leftist friend), "I've given a more sympathetic account of the P.O.U.M. 'line' than I actually felt. . . . I had to put it as sympathetically as possible because it has had no hearing in the capitalist press."[54]

Likewise, in 1942, while he was broadcasting mild propaganda at the B.B.C., far from the front, he was embarrassed to recall (in his wartime diary) the passage in *Homage to Catalonia* in which he had written that "one of the most horrible features of war is that all war propaganda, all the screaming lies and hatred, comes invariably from people who are not fighting." He concludes his diary entry by writing, "Here I am in the B.B.C. less than 5 years after writing that. I suppose sooner or later we all write our own epitaphs."[55] Again, we are reminded that respect for Orwell's honesty has a tendency to breed assumptions of consistency—a persistent objectivity that the author's honesty does not bear out in this case.

In addition to the dangers posed by one's unqualified acceptance of the discipline of a political party, Orwell was alert to the danger of surrendering one's integrity to the warm embrace of friendship or to petty favor. Regarding the latter, he writes, from his experience of being a film critic, how one is often "expected to sell his honour for a glass of inferior sherry."[56] Of friendship he writes to Stephen Spender, whom he had attacked in print but later met and liked,

Even if when I met you I had not happened to like you, I should still have been bound to change my attitude, because when you meet anyone in the flesh you realize immediately that he is a human being and not a sort of caricature embodying certain ideas. It is partly for this reason that I don't mix much in literary circles, because I know from experience that once I have met and spoken to anyone I shall never again be able to show any intellectual brutality towards him, even when I feel that I ought to, like the Labour M.P.'s who get patted on the back by dukes and are lost forever more.[57]

In admitting such shortcomings Orwell testified to his concern with objectivity, unlike those who spoke of objectivity neurosis.

While the roots of his conclusion that the greatest danger to intellectual honesty comes from the intellectuals themselves are to be found in *Homage to Catalonia,* Orwell's fears of what it might mean for the future are more directly expressed in the long essay "Looking Back on the Spanish War" (1942). Here we learn that even history written *before* the disbelief in objective truth has taken firm hold is no guarantee that belief in objective truth will survive. The reason is terrifyingly simple. Orwell explains that those in power will simply rewrite history in "a nightmare world in which the Leader, or some ruling clique, controls not only the future but *the past.* If the Leader says of such and such an event, 'It never happened'—well, it never happened. If he says that two and two are five—well, two and two are five. This prospect frightens me much more than bombs."[58]

The prospect alarmed Orwell so much that he wrote a novel about it—about what he called in *Homage* his " visions of a totalitarian future."[59] Of course, the novel was *Nineteen Eighty-Four,* wherein Winston Smith's final, humiliating surrender to the Leader or "Big Brother" is his abject confession that "TWO AND TWO MAKE FIVE."[60] In order to make men rewrite and accept distorted versions of history, says Orwell, a totalitarian leadership is as likely to use torture as to employ the coercive effects of economic exploitation that he had recorded in his earlier and drearier novels.

The increasing attention that Orwell gave after Spain to such perversions of power marks a dividing line in his work—most noticeably in his fiction. Before the Spanish experience, in such books as *Keep the Aspidistra Flying,* he saw the basis of moral relativism as being mainly one of money, reflecting the rich-versus-poor view of Eric Blair. After Spain, the basis of moral relativism in his work shifts increasingly from money to power. Whereas Gordon Comstock angrily declares that God is money, Winston Smith despairingly concedes that "GOD IS POWER."[61] More than ever before, might *has* become right. Men like Orwell and his friend Major Georges Kopp (under whom he had served in the P.O.U.M.) were hunted, and often murdered, in a "reign of terror," so that they might not get away and tell the truth.[62] So would Big Brother's secret police hunt down Winston Smith, who, in trying to preserve the truth, had borne witness in his secret diary to the existence of the neutral fact *"that two plus two make four"*—believing that if the freedom to say this were granted then other freedoms would be assured.[63]

"Perhaps it is childish or morbid to terrify oneself with visions of a totalitarian future?" Orwell wrote in "Looking Back on the Spanish War." That he decided the visions constituted a real enough possibility becomes clear in his decision to write his last two and best novels. Once again, his decision is deeply rooted in memories of Spain. Worried about how many of the facts of the Civil War had been kept from the outside world by ardent propagandist writers on both sides, he was concerned that the English public, in particular, "nourished for hundreds of years on a literature in which Right [i.e., Good] invariably triumphs in the last chapter"—and thus believing "half-instinctively that evil always defeats itself in the long run"— would neither be conscious of, nor in any way be prepared to meet the threat of totalitarianism—of *institutional* lying. Why should evil defeat itself, he asked. "Who could have imagined twenty years ago that slavery would return to Europe? . . . The forced-labour camps all over Europe." The reason that we cannot imagine it, he claims, is that "in our mystical way we feel that a régime founded on slavery *must* collapse."[64] This fable of optimism is challenged by the pessimistic fable of *Animal Farm* and the terrible vision given in *Nineteen Eighty-Four* of the terrors of room 101.

In Spain, for the first time, he had seen large-scale terror used successfully as a political weapon, and his repetition of the word "nightmare" to describe it and the internecine party fighting in which he was involved sets the atmosphere for both *Animal Farm* and *Nineteen Eighty-Four,* where the misuse of power, rather than the use of money, to exploit others increasingly engages his attention.

Before moving on, it would be advisable to make a few remarks about *Homage to Catalonia,* the standard bearer of Orwell's writings on Spain. The book is generally recognized as one of his best and it certainly is one of the best personal accounts of the Spanish Civil War. I agree with these assessments, but as political commentary *Homage* has several serious flaws. It is clear that Orwell, with his typical English reserve, experienced something of a liberation of the spirit with his first close contact with the Latin temperament. He exclaimed, "I defy anyone to be thrown as I was among the Spanish working class . . . and not be struck by their essential decency; above all, their straightforwardness and generosity. A Spaniard's generosity . . . is at times almost embarrassing. If you ask him for a cigarette he will force the whole packet upon you. And beyond this there is a generosity in a deeper sense, a real largeness of spirit, which I have met with again and again in the most unpromising circumstances."[65]

Such experience is most memorably revealed in his recollection of the moving moment when an illiterate Italian militiaman stepped forward and grasped his hand in the early days of the war. Orwell talks of their mingling of the spirit—of how they bridged the language gap; "but," he adds, "I also knew that to retain my first impression of him I must not see him again; and needless to say I never did see him again. One was always making contacts of that kind in Spain."[66] This remark, with its implicit recognition of how unqualified perceptions are likely to be when they are formed in excitement, is as applicable (though Orwell does not apply it) to the political events he saw in Spain as to the individuals he met. Although he intuitively understood that such events were "transitional"[67]– that "of course such a state of affairs could not last. . . . It was simply a temporary and local phase,"[68] in the same way that the administration of land and police forces by the revolutionary soviets was transitional—Orwell uses such temporary experiences as the basis for envisioning a permanent future society. For example, he sees the militias as a microcosm of the classlessness toward which his socialism aims. There is nothing illogical in this (any more than one might view a hastily constructed hut as a good model for a sturdier house), but what is lacking in his transference of the temporary situation into a permanent theory of society is any evaluation of the initial structure's inherent weaknesses. For Orwell, the local revolutionary administrations were temporary only because of the war "that was being fought out between two political theories" within the civil war.[69]

What he does not consider is that the "temporary" nature of the

revolutionary administrations and their subsequent removal following Franco's victory might not only have been caused by the vicissitudes of the Spanish military situation between Franco and the
Republicans or between communists and anarchists, but also by the
vagaries of human nature—that the "air of equality" might last only
just so long before self-interest, or the need of efficient administration, reasserted social and economic inequality. It is surprising for
someone who deplored ignorance of history as much as he did not
to remember the post-Revolution histories of France and Russia,
where inequality crept back on the heels of the early rush to egalitar-
ianism.[70] In a reversal of his charge against the Communists in *The
Road to Wigan Pier*, he seems to assume that if the moral advance is
made, administrative efficiency will automatically follow—that there
is no need to worry much over details. This cannot be fairly used to
charge Orwell with having been deceived in his assessment of the
genuineness of the "air of equality" while it lasted; but his implication that the social revolution had failed solely because of the military situation, because the communes had been "forcibly suppressed
by the Government,"[71] rather than because of any inherent tension
between the collective and the individual, does open him to two
charges. First, he seems to have held an overly optimistic belief in
human nature that had been fired by his early enthusiasm in Barcelona. Secondly, he failed to take into account the complex problems
of administering an industrialized society such as that in Barcelona.

That he later became aware, as the anarchists had, that the collectivist spirit alone was not enough to overcome the problems involved
in running a complex industrialized society is obvious in his later
journalism. His insistence in "Our Opportunity" (1941) on winning
over the middle class as a necessary prerequisite to revolution in
England is to the point. In this he recognizes that without the support of the technocratic and managerial class, any revolution in a
modern industrial country is doomed to failure.

Still, of the disintegration of the Republican cause in general he
wrote that "the much-publicized disunity on the Government side
was not a main cause of defeat."[72] Here he was clearly wrong. While
the argument is one that mainly concerns military historians of the
war, its significance here is to show that just as Orwell's honesty does
not automatically imply a consistency of ideas, nor does his honesty
mean that he was always correct or that his works are distinguished
by "objectivity."[73] His later confession of overstating the P.O.U.M.

case testifies to this, the overstatement revealing an infatuation with the cause of revolution within the war that was plainly a reflection of his lifelong sympathy with the anarchist hatred of authority and centralization. He expressed his awareness of the problem when he explained, "I have tried to write objectively about the Barcelona fighting, though, obviously, no one can be completely objective on a question of this kind. One is practically obliged to take sides, and it must be clear enough which side I am on. . . . I warn everyone against my bias, and I warn everyone against my mistakes. Still, I have done my best to be honest."[74] What his honesty does mean is that his opinion was his own; and while this might be an achievement in any man's time, it was a special achievement in reporting the Spanish Civil War, which was so dominated by party passion. Orwell did see more clearly than most that totalitarianism was not the perversity of a particular political party—that in its attack upon the sense of objective truth, it is equally at home on the Left as it is on the Right.

The solid entrenchment of Communist regimes and their totalitarian mentality in the latter half of the twentieth century often prevents us from realizing the full measure of this achievement of Orwell's in the earlier days of what has correctly been called the "totalitarian epoch."[75] Lionel Trilling comments of Orwell's reporting of the internecine fighting in Barcelona, for example, that: "It would have been very difficult to learn anything of this in New York or London. Those periodicals which guided the thought of left-liberal intellectuals knew nothing of it, and had no wish to learn." Regarding the purge of the P.O.U.M. in June, he continues,

If one searches the liberal periodicals, which have made the cause of civil liberties their own, one can find no mention of this terror. They were committed not to the fact but to the abstraction. And to the abstraction they remained committed for a long time to come. . . . If only life were not so tangible, concrete, so made up of facts that are at variance with each other . . . if only politics were not a matter of power—then we should be happy to put our minds to politics, then we should consent to think![76]

Drawing on his colonial experience in Burma, Orwell wrote of exploiters; based on his experience at home in England, he wrote of the exploited. His Spanish experience provided him with the material for his account of exploiter *and* exploited at war. For him it was a class war, part of the long, hard "struggle" of the "gradually awakening common people against the lords of property." The old, simple rich-versus-poor dichotomy still reasserts itself when he says, "The Spanish bourgeoisie saw their chance of crushing the labour movement, and took it,"[77] and, as one critic has suggested, at times one would think that there were no workers on Franco's side.[78] For all this, however, Blair's master–slave view had now become much more sophisticated, as we can see from his later works, in which power overtakes money and bourgeois status as the exploiter's measure of success. Orwell had rediscovered the truth of his wanderings in *Wigan Pier* that "it is only when you meet someone of a different culture from yourself that you begin to realize what your own beliefs really are."[79] In much the same way as his Burmese experience had moved Blair to think about and investigate social conditions in England, so would the Spanish experience tell us less in the end about Spain and more about what Orwell believed were the clear and present dangers to hopes of equality in England. Later, in *Animal Farm* and *Nineteen Eighty-Four,* he would expand his vision to include the threats of freedom and equality in the world at large.

For Orwell the signal lessons of his Spanish experience were: that though we might argue as to how long it will last, equality is pratical as well as realizable; that truth in the Spanish Civil War, as in any war, was the first casualty, due largely to the intelligentsia's and the intellectuals' blind allegiance to political orthodoxy; and that such allegiance (because "group loyalties are necessary"),[80] in nurturing the totalitarian mentality, eventually threatens *everyone, everywhere,* with the totalitarian state. For Orwell, like so many others, the Civil War in Spain marked a crossroads on the road to servitude, a chance to meet and stop the march of fascism, which had already gained so much ground on the heels of Mussolini and Hitler. He had hoped that the war in Spain might be a "turning of the tide" away from fascism, which "for a year or two past had been haunting me like a nightmare."[81] Now the Republicans had lost, and for Orwell the nightmare would continue.

Paradoxically, of all his conclusions about his time in Spain, Orwell's recollection is that beyond his initial depression after the Republican defeat, his experience ended in *hope* rather than despair. He had seen hatred, not only of the enemy but within his own side, had been hunted by the secret police, and had sustained a nearly fatal wound. He had experienced the "horrible atmosphere of suspicion" that pervaded the Barcelona fighting and had watched for the "first time . . . a person [a Russian agent] whose profession was telling lies—unless one counts journalists." Yet, he wrote, "when you have had a glimpse of such a disaster as this, . . . the result is not necessarily disillusionment and cynicism. Curiously enough the whole experience has left me with not less but more belief in the decency of human beings."[82]

Unlike Flory, he had learned by now that there are different kinds of failures. Therefore, despite the initial bitterness on the Left following Franco's victory in July 1939, and the equally deep depression following the signing of the Stalin–Hitler pact in August 1939, Orwell's belief in socialism was able to survive. This is crucial to any understanding of his relationship to his contemporaries, many of whom had believed as strongly as he did in the coming of socialism, only to lose this belief completely in the psychological devastation wrought by the announcement of the Hitler–Stalin pact. This pact, together with the quickly ensuing war, meant that for many—leftist intellectuals in particular—the hopes of socialism were dead; and indeed, Orwell has been said to have written their "epitaph" in "Inside the Whale" when he concluded that the idea that "Socialism could preserve and even enlarge the atmosphere of liberalism" had been disproven. History held no comfort, the future no hope, and the only way out for the disenchanted of the left was to "Give yourself over to the world-process, stop fighting against it or pretending that you control it; simply accept it, endure it, record it. . . . Get inside the whale."[83]

The feeling of desolation that the war brought is captured by MacNeice:

I had only written a little of this book when Germany invaded Poland. On that day I was in Galway. As soon as I heard on the wireless of the outbreak of war, Galway became unreal. And Yeats and his poetry became unreal also. This was not merely because Galway and Yeats belong in a sense to a past order of things. The unreality which now overtook them was also overtaking in my mind modern London, modernist art, and Left Wing politics. . . . My friends had been writing for years about guns and frontiers and factories, about the "facts" of psychology, politics, science, economics, but the fact of war made their writing seem as remote as the pleasure dome of Xanadu.[84]

Spender, finding himself unable to write at all, lamented, "I feel so shattered," and Auden, his friend, who also had served on the *Left Review,* would say goodbye to the decade of commitment and leave for America. The word that best describes the response of writers of the Left at this time is *withdrawal*—so overwhelmed were they by the failure of their dream.

Here, once again, Orwell stands apart. His dream had been badly shaken but it was not destroyed by Franco's victory or the pact between Moscow and Berlin. Unlike so many other leftists, he had never trusted Russia, anyway, and that optimism that he had felt during the Spanish War sustained him. Along with "mostly evil" memories of Spain, the happy memories of the militias never left him. Five years later, in "Looking Back on the Spanish War," he could write, "I myself believe, perhaps on insufficient grounds, that the common man will win his fight [for "the decent, fully human life which is now technically available"] sooner or later, but I want it to be sooner and not later."[85]

Also, as Alex Zwerdling notes, unlike so many on the Left in the high enthusiasm of the late Thirties, Orwell did not expect any rapid establishment of socialism. Instead, despite his hope that it might be established sooner rather than later—and the pace of the revolution in Spain encouraged him in this—he "assumed that a worldwide socialist society might not be brought into being for decades, or even centuries." Nor did he assume, as noted earlier, that socialism could solve all of society's problems. He knew that some problems were probably unsolvable and that the best that socialism could achieve was to improve society, not make it perfect. This rendered him less impatient than his contemporaries, who, once Spain fell, threw in the socialist towel once and for all because their "impatience gave them little staying power."[86]

It was Orwell's lack of such impatience, allied with the lingering optimism of his Spanish experience, that gave him his staying power on the Left. He explains, "I have never had the slightest fear of a dictatorship of the proletariat, if it could happen, and certain things I saw in the Spanish war confirmed me in this. But I admit to having a perfect horror of a dictatorship of theorists, as in Russia and Germany,"[87] where "the two régimes having started from opposite ends, are rapidly evolving towards the same system—a form of oligarchical collectivism."[88]

That Orwell talked so easily of proletarian "dictatorship" is evidence of a blatant hypocrisy in his political thought. He was willing to extend the "air of equality" readily enough to the exploited, but not the exploiters. This double standard often mars his suggestion of social reform in England and is it is largely responsible for his recurring failure to deal with the question of how the state should conduct itself. What he did concentrate upon was how the state *ought* not to be constructed and (after Spain) the tension between the state's collectivist impulse and the individual and between the individual and the collectivist impulse of associations.

Paradoxically, just as Orwell's optimism for socialism was invigorated by the collectivist experiences of the militias, his pessimism about the power of orthodoxy was fuelled by the collectivist purges which consumed individuals merely because of their association with groups holding another point of view—in his case the P.O.U.M. As a consequence, after Spain, he would increasingly turn his attention toward the theorists of oligarchical collectivism. These were the men who Orwell believed would, through their love of power, at least delay the decent life for all (making it arrive "later" rather than "sooner") and, in all probability, actively work against it. In *Animal Farm* and *Nineteen Eighty-Four*, he would portray such theorists in action. In this final battle between his optimism and pessimism, between the collectivist and individualist impulses in people, his Spanish experience would be the arsenal from which some of the most telling shots were fired.

IV

THE GLOBAL VISION

CHAPTER 9

O RWELL NEVER LIKED BULLIES—THEY CAN BE THE STUFF OF nightmares, and in "Riding Down from Bangor" (1946), he says that "the twin nightmares that beset nearly every modern man [are] the nightmare of unemployment [and] the nightmare of state interference."[1] He fought both. Before Spain, as we have seen, Orwell had been largely concerned with the problems of unemployment. After Spain he increasingly turned his pen toward the problems surrounding state interference.

In January 1938, at age thirty-four, Orwell had completed *Homage to Catalonia*, which was published by Secker and Warburg in April— Gollancz wouldn't touch it. In March Orwell had fallen ill with tuberculosis, the disease that would plague him thereafter. It would cause his rejection by the army for service in World War II and finally, exacerbated by the cold climate of the Inner Hebrides, would kill him in January of 1950—seven months after the publication of *Nineteen Eighty-Four*.

In 1938, short of money (only nine hundred copies of *Homage to Catalonia* had been sold at the time of his death)[2] and only recently back from six months in a sanatorium in Kent, Orwell accepted a loan from an anonymous donor and went for a holiday with his wife in the warm climate of Morocco.[3] There, he began writing *Coming Up For Air*, in which the visions that he began to have in Spain of the coming world war with Fascism, the consequent "food-queues, . . . secret police and the loudspeakers telling you what to think," assailed George Bowling, the ordinary man of Ellesmere Road. Failing to find the old security of Lower Binfield, the home of his youth, Bowling concludes (before Orwell had written "Inside the Whale") that there is no way back from the abyss—no retreat into nostalgia, no possibility of putting Jonah back inside the whale. Unlike his old friend Porteous, the retired public school master who refuses even to think about Hitler ("this German person") and thinks that the modern world should simply be ignored,[4] Bowling sees that he is going to be caught up in the conflict, whether he likes it or not.

Orwell points to the growing storm beyond the whale of complacency in a letter of December 28, 1938. Writing of his progress on *Coming Up For Air,* which he finished before "Looking Back on the Spanish War" (in which his fears of a nightmare world of state interference are so pervasive), he notes that the novel is "really a mess but parts of it I like and it's suddenly revealed to me a big subject which I'd never really touched before."[5] The big subject, totalitarianism, would be dealt with more fully in *Animal Farm* and *Nineteen Eighty-Four,* but already, for Bowling in *Coming Up For Air,*

It isn't the war that matters, it's the after-war. The world we're going down into, the kind of hate-world, slogan-world, . . . the barbed wire, the rubber truncheons. The secret cells where the electric light burns night and day, and the detectives watching you while you sleep. And the processions and the posters with enormous faces, and the crowds of a million people all cheering for the Leader till they deafen themselves into thinking that they really worship him, and all the time, underneath, they hate him so that they want to puke.[6]

Envisaging a world of the "stream-lined" men "from eastern Europe . . . who think in slogans and talk in bullets," Bowling goes to bed in his flat (apartment), overcome by "the trememdous gloom that sometimes gets hold of you late at night." So powerful is the gloom that "at that moment the destiny of Europe seemed to me more important than the rent and the kids' school-bills and the work I'd have to do tomorrow."[7]

In January 1939, still in Morocco and as depressed as his character, George Bowling, by the prospect of war, Orwell again fell ill, and in late March returned to England. *Coming Up For Air* was published in June, a typical three-month feat which shames the delays of modern publishing; but even with the money he earned from his journalism, Orwell's income was so small that his wife took a job in the censorship department of the Army Medical Corps.

By June 1940 Orwell was extremely depressed—not least by his rejection as medically unfit for active service—and he complained bitterly that it was awful to feel so useless when fools and pro-fascists were being assigned important jobs in the war efforts.[8] His willingness to fight, despite his dark mood early in the war that George Bowling had foretold, signals a turning away (confirmed in "My Country Right or Left") from the fatalism of George Bowling and from the antiwar pamphlet that he had wanted published.[9] Above all, it was a rejection of the quietism of those "inside the whale," the quietism voiced by Henry Miller when he told Orwell in 1936 that he was an "idiot" to go and fight in Spain, as was anyone who got mixed up in such ventures *from a sense of obligation.*[10] It was a return to the belief that you cannot simply accept things, but that, just as Eric Blair had descended into the world of the poor, you have to drag yourself out of the soft belly of the whale when duty or necessity demands it of you. A Hitler or a Stalin gives you only two choices—to sink or to swim.

In 1938, in *Coming Up For Air,* Orwell portrayed an eager young bank clerk who, having listened to the "well-known anti-fascist (as you might call somebody 'the well-known pianist')," argues fiercely with a Trotskyist and seeks support from ex–World War I soldier Bowling:

"Mr. Bowling! Look here. If war broke out and we had the chance to smash Fascism once and for all, wouldn't you fight? . . ."
"You bet I wouldn't," I said. "I had enough to go on with last time."
"But to smash Fascism!"
"O, b--- Fascism! There's been enough smashing done already, if you ask me. . . . Listen, son," I said, "you've got it all wrong. In 1914 *we* thought it was going to be a glorious business. Well, it wasn't. It was just a bloody mess. If it comes again, you keep out of it."[11]

Two years later, in "Inside the Whale," Orwell still saw Bowling's latent pacifism under the bombers overhead, and Henry Miller's non-cooperative acceptance as having merit. Indeed, this feeling that Miller's disciples had a point would never completely leave Orwell.[12] It would form an undertow, if not an undercurrent, throughout his life—an unresolved contradiction of his stronger belief that one must sometimes fight rather than passively accept defeat. In 1938, even as he was writing about George Bowling in *Coming Up For Air,* George Orwell confided to Cyril Connolly that although everything he was writing was under the war's shadow of impending destruction and shot through by the conviction that the world was heading "towards a precipice," he still believed that one had to "put up some sort of fight."[13] His understanding, in "Inside the Whale," of the reasons behind Miller's "quietism" or the "sit on your bum" philosophy, as he calls it, was confronted by his stronger conviction in the same essay that "almost certainly we are moving into an age of totalitarian dictatorships" and that "to say 'I accept' in an age like our own is to say that you accept concentration camps, rubber truncheons, Hitler, Stalin, bombs, . . . gas masks, . . . press censorship, secret prisons . . . and political murders."[14]

For Orwell the inclination to fight against the totalitarian dictators finally took precedence over any gloomy mood of acceptance that he might understandably have felt in the wake of Franco's victory and the rout of the Spanish Republican forces in 1939; and so by May 1940 he was writing a letter to the editor of *Time and Tide* citing his Spanish experience as the basis for his suggestions on how best to combat the imminent German invasion of England. He joined a Home Guard battalion in which, as sergeant, he was in authority over Frederic Warburg, the publisher of *Homage to Catalonia* and later *Animal Farm*. The letter to *Time and Tide* was a precursor of longer pieces in 1940, most notably "The Lion and the Unicorn" (January 1941), in which Orwell put forward what he thought was the best war policy and the old P.O.U.M. militia experience and slogan that "war and revolution are inseparable" echoed in his beliefs that the establishment of socialism and war against Hitler were mutually dependent. England, he said, needed to follow the Spanish experience —a revolution "from below" marked by an "equality of sacrifice."[15]

Though still not accepted by the army, Orwell's spirit of resistance found other outlets. In addition to his volunteer work in the Home Guard, in August 1941 he found a job as Talks Assistant, and later Talks Producer (in the Indian section), at the B.B.C. where he took up the old cause of Eric Blair—Indian independence from the British Raj. Despite his overall frustration in this post-Spanish period, Orwell was (journalistically at least), surprisingly prolific. Apart from his film, theater, and book reviews, he wrote such pieces as "Inside the Whale" (1940), "The Lion and the Unicorn" (1941), "Looking Back on the Spanish War" (1942), and an imaginary interview with Jonathan Swift (a B.B.C. broadcast in 1942). The imaginary conversation with Swift contains two statements by Orwell that are particularly revealing, given the overemphasis that critics have placed upon the pessimistic moods of *Animal Farm* and *Nineteen Eighty-Four*. Orwell says to Swift, "I see now where it is that we part company, Dr. Swift.

I believe that human society, and therefore human nature, can change. You don't." Finally, when Swift has gone, Orwell laments, "He was a great man, and yet he was partially blind. He could only see one thing at a time. His vision of human society is so penetrating, and yet in the last analysis it's false. He could not see what the simplest person sees, that life if worth living; and human beings, even if they are dirty and ridiculous, are mostly decent."[16]

In the years 1942 and 1943, Orwell's work, apart from that at the B.B.C., was published in *New Statesman and Nation, Nation, Horizon, Partisan Review,* and also *Tribune.* He became literary editor for the latter in November 1943, having resigned from his propagandist's job "after two wasted years"[17] with the B.B.C. While working for *Tribune* he contributed a regular weekly column, "As I Please" (until 1945 and then sporadically until April 1947), in which he covered a wide range of topics all the way from politics to gardening. In addition to this, he wrote book reviews for the *Observer* and *Manchester Evening News* until 1946. Looking back on his days at *Tribune,* he wrote that although he did not think the paper was "perfect, . . . I do think that it is the only existing weekly paper that makes a genuine effort to be both progressive and humane—that is, to combine a radical Socialist policy with a respect for freedom of speech and a civilized attitude towards literature and the arts."[18] Despite his pessimism about the future, *Tribune*'s concern for such things as freedom of speech was, no doubt, conducive to Orwell's next venture into the world of the novel when, in November 1943, at the age of forty, he began writing *Animal Farm.*

Although the genesis of the book seems to have taken place as early as 1938, after his experience with the Communists in Spain, it was particularly excited by talk of a "popular Front" in England in World War II—an idea that not only represented for Orwell an "unholy alliance" of Left and Right, from bishops to Communists, but (far worse, in his view) was an idea that served to obscure the "huge though inscrutable changes that are occurring in the U.S.S.R." Orwell wanted to know whether Stalin was implementing socialism or a savage kind of state-capitalism,[19] and his determination to find out stemmed from his concern that as in Spain, the inheritors of a popular front's revolution against injustice might, in fact, turn out to be antirevolutionary if Russia had anything to do with it. The possibility that this could happen in England during the war comes from his observation of how in Spain not only antirevolutionary fervor but fascism had been "imposed under the pretence of resisting Fascism" and that "we shall see its relevance quickly enough if England enters into an alliance with the U.S.S.R."—which it did. At the very least, such an antirevolutionary stance as had occurred in Spain was diametrically opposed to Orwell's belief that victory over both fascism and capitalism was essential if either was to be successful. To Orwell the danger of an antirevolutionary stance—in England—no doubt seemed particularly acute when "so long as the objective, real or pretended, is war against Germany, the greater part of the Left will associate themselves with the fascizing process," including "wage reductions, suppression of free speech, brutalities in the colonies, etc."[20]

Though he was proven dead wrong about the interdependence of revolution and victory over Hitler, Orwell's determination to expose Stalin's regime remained and grew. Six years later he lamented that although "the world of secret police forces, censorship of opinion, torture and frame-up trials is, of course, known about, . . . it has made very little emotional impact." The result of this, he claimed, was that "there is almost no literature of disillusionment about the Soviet Union."[21] Orwell's answer to this deficiency was *Animal Farm*. The book, which was finished in February of 1944, was rejected by Victor Gollancz, Faber and Faber, and Jonathan Cape in England and by Dial Press in the United States, which maintained that "it was impossible to sell animal stories."[22] In June 1944, while the manuscript was doing the rounds of publishers, Orwell's flat was bombed. He and his wife, together with their adopted baby son, Richard, did not move into a flat of their own until October, the same month that *Animal Farm* was finally accepted by Frederic Warburg (although it would not be published for another ten months).

During this time Orwell was still at *Tribune*, and here it is worthwhile to recall Trilling's view (now widely accepted) that Orwell was one of those "figures . . . who *are* what they write," whose everyday behavior reflected the "ideas and attitudes" that permeate their writing.[23] This notion is seriously challenged if one looks beyond *Homage*, which was central to Trilling's assessment, and sees, for example, how during Orwell's time at *Tribune* a tension, and finally, a telling contradiction, between Orwell the man and Orwell the writer became obvious—most noticeably to Orwell himself. In the same way as he could attack the public school system in print yet acknowledge its merits when it came time to think of his son's education, in the same way as he had attacked Spender, yet liked him when he met him, and had attacked eccentrics while eccentric himself, he found himself at *Tribune* torn between intellectual honesty and sympathy for writers on the individual level, between the abstract ideal and concrete reality, between what he said an editor should do and what George Orwell did. He was *not* what he wrote. He commented, "The fact is that I am no good at editing. . . . I have a fatal tendency to accept manuscripts which I know very well are too bad to be printed. It is questionable whether anyone who has had long experience as a freelance journalist ought to become an editor. It is too like taking a convict out of his cell and making him governor of the prison."[24]

Early in 1945 Orwell left *Tribune*, feeling (quite rightly, as his friend and the subsequent editor of *Tribune*, T.R. Fyvel, points out) that he was unsuited for an office job. On February 15, in the closing stages of the war, he left for France as a war correspondent for the *Observer*. In Paris he was surprised to discover that among the supporters of *Libertés* (an anti-Gaullist and anti-Communist paper), he had become something of a celebrity through his recent editorship of *Tribune*. The latter, he said, was known among French journalists as "the one paper in England which had neither supported the Government uncritically, nor opposed the war, nor swallowed the Russian myth."[25] By late March he was reporting from Cologne. On March 29 his wife Eileen died in London, during an operation for cancer.

In April Orwell returned to Europe to continue writing about the war for both the *Observer* and the *Manchester Evening News*. The most striking thing about his writing during the entire war is his relative lack of analysis of the day-to-day military details of the huge struggle that was going on around the world, compared to the prolific war reporting of others; unless he was *directly* involved in the things he wrote about, his interest was not aroused to its full pitch.

Orwell's own experiences in World War II, whatever contribution they might have made, were not those of a soldier fighting the war, and so it is not surprising that his experiences—largely confined to Home Guard Duty and broadcasts to India—did not produce that firsthand enthusiasm we usually expect of war writers. It was not that Orwell failed to report the great military engagements or their effects upon conquered peoples and the like—his wartime diary is full of this—but because he was not directly involved in the military action, his published reports, though starting off with general war news, would quickly be conscripted as springboards for engaging essays on favorite subjects.[26] Even when the war was directly overhead, it occasioned in Orwell's writing not so much a detailed reporting of the military events abroad as an analysis of Britain and a return to old and familiar Orwellian themes. For example, "The Lion and the Unicorn," which was written in 1940, was subtitled "Socialism and the English Genius" and deals largely with the possibility of revolution and the establishment of socialism in Britain. In Part II, "Shopkeepers at War," Orwell writes,

> I began this book to the tune of German bombs, and I begin this second chapter in the added racket of the barrage. The yellow gun-flashes are lighting the sky, splinters are rattling on the housetops, and London Bridge is falling down, falling down, falling down. Anyone able to read a map knows that we are in deadly danger. I do not mean that we are beaten or need be beaten. Almost certainly the outcome depends on our own will. But at this moment we are in the soup, full fathom five, and we have been brought there by follies which we are still committing and which will drown us altogether if we do not mend our ways quickly.
> What this war has demonstrated is that private capitalism—that is, an economic system in which land, factories, mines and transport are owned privately and operated solely for profit—*does not work*. It cannot deliver the goods.[27]

That Orwell is clearly wrong in his analysis on this point is not as interesting as the fact that he begins with a description of the fighting above him only to end up pressing hard for the establishment of socialism in Britian. Again, in *The British Crisis*, one of his London letters to the American *Partisan Review* during the war (1942), he begins, "When I last wrote to you things had begun to go wrong in the Far East but nothing was happening politically," then quickly launches into an old theme in an essay subtitled "Social Equality." Here he writes, "The war has brought the class nature of their society very sharply home to the English people, in two ways. First of all there is the unmistakeable fact that all real power depends on class privilege." He adds that although this may not be noticed in a time of relative prosperity, in time of rationing it becomes very obvious that being rich automatically assures one of better treatment and that little can be done to correct the situation, so long as money and political power more or less coincide.[28]

Further, in one of his "As I Please" columns, while he was literary editor of *Tribune*, he announces that while "it is not my primary job to discuss the details of contemporary politics, . . . I want to protest against the mean and cowardly attitude adopted by the British press towards the recent rising in Warsaw." The theme, again recalling *Homage to Catalonia,* is the role of the press and the British intelligentsia in propaganda—especially the role of the left wing. Though he supports the idea of an Anglo-Russian alliance, he says that such an alliance cannot be based on the theory that "Stalin is always right." He attacks the British left wing in particular, charging that they are so corrupt that "their attitude towards Russian foreign policy is not 'Is this policy right or wrong?' but 'This is Russian policy: how can we make it appear right?' "29

After the end of the fighting in Europe, Orwell returned to London and wrote articles on the general election. His overall impression was that the election had been relatively fair and clean and had upset all the predictions of the would-be pollsters, including his own, by ending in a definite swing to the Left with the Labor party's victory over Churchill and his Conservative followers. In his opinion, the shift did not offer any hope that socialism would be established in England. For him it was no more than a sign of growing discontent and above all, a desire for more security in the face of unemployment, one of the nightmares of modern times. As in the wartime articles, he reverts to an old theme—in this case, imperialism. Charging that because the Labour leaders failed to tell their followers that England's prosperity depended on the exploitation of colored peoples, any decision to give India her independence (and so live up to leftist rhetoric that Orwell favoured) would be the most difficult problem for a Labour government.30

By the summer of 1945, Orwell had begun the first draft of *Nineteen Eighty-Four.* In August he became vice-chairman of The Freedom Defence Committee, formed some months earlier because of a growing concern with violation of civil liberties. In the same month *Animal Farm* was published. The book signals not only Orwell's return to the novel form, but his *entry* into the technique of the fable, with its ability to transcend the boundaries of the present. After the poor sales of *Homage to Catalonia,* it also marks the end of Orwell's experimentation with the documentary technique. In 1947 Orwell, discussing Gollancz's book *In Darkest Germany,* draws attention to the relative failure of the realistic approach in its effort to make people *"conscious* of what is happening outside their own small circle." He remarks, "The now-familiar photographs of skeleton-like children make very little impression. As time goes on and the horrors pile up, the mind seems to secrete a sort of self-protecting ignorance which needs a harder and harder shock to pierce it, just as the body will become immunized to a drug and require bigger and bigger doses."[31]

Orwell's point is well taken: for instance, thirty-four years later, in 1981, one was able to read in Hugh Trevor-Roper's review of Walter Laqueur's *The Terrible Secret* that not even members of the Jewish press in Jerusalem at the time of the war were able to believe the extent of the Nazi brutality. Even for a people for whom persecution had been a fact of life, "the whole scheme [of extermination] . . . was beyond human imagination."[32] In any event, it was not the present or the past that now made Orwell so pessimistic, but the *future*, our present, in which such immunization or emotional anesthesia might make us even more insensitive to the plight of others. It was this "after-war" following the Spanish Civil War that had haunted George Bowling in 1938 and that continued to trouble George Orwell in 1944, when, because of the Teheran Conference, he wanted to "discuss the implications of dividing the world up into 'zones of influence'" and the "intellectual implications of totalitarianism."[33] The first major attack against the latter in his fiction came in *Animal Farm* in 1945.

In his preface to the Ukrainian edition of the book, Orwell sets down his reasons for the attack. Recalling the "man-hunts" in Spain that had occurred simultaneously with the purges in Russia, he notes the shock that he experienced when, after seeing people jailed by Communists in Spain merely on suspicion of "unorthodoxy," he discovered that in England the Communist versions of the purge trials in Moscow were being swallowed whole. The gullibility of so many "numerous" and "sensible" people in England alerted Orwell to three things: (1) "how easily totalitarian propaganda can control the opinion of enlightened people in democratic countries," where people living in "comparative freedom . . . [have] no real understanding of things like concentration camps, mass deportations, arrests without trial, press censorship, etc. . . ."; (2) that because of "the belief that Russia is a Socialist country and that every act of its rulers must be excused if not imitated," the acceptance of totalitarian justifications of such acts had "caused great harm to the Socialist movement in England"; and (3) that in order to revive socialism, the "destruction of the Soviet myth [i.e., "the belief that Russia is a Socialist country"] was essential."[34]

Having thus decided on his return from Spain that he would embark upon an exposé of the "Soviet myth" ("I consider that willingness to criticize Russia and Stalin is *the* test of intellectual honesty"), Orwell had set his mind to thinking of a story that anyone could understand and that would be easy to translate into other languages[35]—a story like the old fables of Aesop, in which animals displayed the characteristics of people, which he and Eileen had discussed in bed together in the happy summer of 1936. But this wouldn't be a nursery tale populated by figures like their poodle, Marx.[36] It would be a cry from *outside* the whale—one voicing resistence to the totalitarian tendency and its attendant atrocities—a protest against those in the belly of the whale merely accepting things as they were.

Although it would be six years before it was written, the idea for *Animal Farm* jelled one day in a village where "I saw a little boy, perhaps ten years old, driving a huge cart-horse along a narrow path, whipping it whenever it tried to turn. It struck me that if only such animals became aware of their strength we should have no power over them, and that men exploit animals in much the same way as the rich exploit the proletariat."[37] Orwell had once again seized upon Blair's simplistic division of the world into rich and poor so that everyone could recognize the basic conflict between haves and have-nots; yet the attack upon the Stalinist mentality behind the Russian myth quickly revealed a sophistication that moved T.S. Eliot, who rejected the book on political grounds, to praise the work as one of the best of its genre "since *Gulliver*."[38] In light of Orwell's increasing concern with the power of orthodoxy to hold even highly individualistic minds captive, I give here a brief description of the story behind the publication of *Animal Farm*.

After the socialist editor Gollancz, who had wanted nothing to do with *Homage to Catalonia*, rejected *Animal Farm*, Orwell sent the manuscript to the firm of Jonathan Cape. An impressed reader gave a favorable report to Jonathan Cape, who then made Orwell the offer of a contract. However, before finalizing the proposal, Cape decided to check first with an official at the Ministry of Information. The official warned that the novel would injure Anglo–Soviet relations.[39] It was then, in June 1944, that Orwell sent the manuscript to T.S. Eliot at Faber and Faber, advising him that the novel was undoubtedly politically unfashionable and explaining how someone, either from Cape or the Ministry of Information, had "made the imbecile suggestion that some other animal than pigs might be made to represent the Bolsheviks." Orwell adds, "I could not of course make any change of that description."[40]

After Eliot, who was highly conscious of the "political situation at the present time" (the Anglo–Soviet alliance), rejected the novel, Orwell took it to Frederic Warburg. Not finding Warburg in his office, Orwell, in haste, reached him in a local pub. Warburg recalls the scene:

"What is it?" I asked.
"Read it yourself," he said nervously, "though I don't suppose you'll like it. It's about a lot of animals on a farm who rebel against the farmer, and it's very anti-Russian. Much too anti-Russian for you, I'm afraid. . . .
"What's it called?" I said.
"*Animal Farm*. . . . I think I can find you some buckshee paper to print it on." A few moments later he was gone.[41]

Warburg read it the same day, "never doubted that it was a masterpiece," and promptly told Orwell. Still, Warburg's decision to publish was not easy. The "great debate" that took place in his office mirrored the power of political orthodoxy (often born of the needs of alliance) to subjugate individual integrity. It was a theme devastatingly described in the very novel under discussion. Warburg writes,

Was it or was it not politically dangerous to publish this bitter satirical attack on our great ally, the Soviet Union, when its armies were rolling back the German Forces, while the U.K. and the U.S.A. had established a mere bridgehead on the French coast only a few weeks before? Senhouse had no doubts—I rather think he felt Stalin might have enjoyed the portrait of himself as the boar dictator. After all, Orwell had christened him with a mighty name, Napoleon. Our young sales manager, Peter Maxwell, supported him. My experienced London traveller, Charles Roth, was extremely worried. He was a lifelong socialist, and could not really bring himself to believe that Russia was not a socialist state, however flawed. Worst of all, I was under strong pressure from my wife. Whether it was the blood of her Circassian grandmother . . . or her belief that Russia had always been a kind of (feudal) tyranny, or the warmth of her feelings for the immense sufferings of the Russian people. . . or (perhaps strongest of all) her knowledge that it was the Russians who had done most of the fighting since 1941, . . . Pamela at that time regarded *Animal Farm* with a complete lack of sympathy. "If you publish that book," she said, "I'll leave you! Don't think I won't!"[42]

One thought plagued Warburg, namely, that if the Soviet Union was yet to come to terms with Hitler, both dictatorships might turn on the West. He was as aware as Orwell that just because censorship can be executed in a civilized manner, it is no less invidious—"just a nod and a wink and the thing is done,"—and he could envisage the possible repercussions of publication, the burst of outrage from the Russian ambassador, followed by two

smooth gentlemen from the Foreign Office. . . ."My dear Warburg . . . breach in the alliance . . . situation extremely grave . . . Minister feels sure . . . withdrawal essential . . . perhaps two or three years time . . . as a patriotic man surely understand. . . ." Then when it was all over, on a lighter note —"Off the record, of course . . . reds not our sort of people . . . Stalin awkward customer . . . read little book myself . . . haven't laughed so much since . . . all those pigs round the table . . . wonderful scene . . . reminded me of . . . well, never mind." And then as they prepared to leave—"funny thing . . . damned red like Orwell . . . fought in Spain, didn't he . . . could think it all up . . . well, well, what will these literary gents get up to next?"[43]

What Orwell got up to next, at least in his fiction, was *Nineteen Eighty-Four,* begun in mid-1945 before *Animal Farm* was published. Here, the lesson of *Animal Farm,* which, as Crick points out,[44] far transcends an attack upon the Soviet regime, would be more closely examined. Notes for *Nineteen Eighty-Four* had been in existence for some time. In 1944 Orwell was already convinced that there "will only be room in the world for two or three great powers."[45] Reiterating his Spanish-born nightmare, he wrote later that year, "If the sort of world that I am afraid of arrives, . . . two or three great super-states which are unable to conquer one another, two and two could become five if the fuehrer wished it." But while he argued that this, "so far as I can see, is the direction in which we are actually moving," he qualified the dire prediction by adding, *"though of course, the process is reversible."*[46] (The italics are mine.) The qualification takes us back to Orwell's imaginary conversation with Jonathan Swift in which he argues, unlike Swift, that men can be changed, that totalitarianism can possibly be averted if men are brave enough to fight it. This is important, because it reminds us that *Nineteen Eighty-Four* is meant to be a warning, *not* a prophecy.

As well as starting *Nineteen Eighty-Four* in mid-1945, Orwell continued with his journalism and essay writing. The result was that in 1946, despite a rest period, there appeared a rush of essays (along with various journalistic pieces), from "The Prevention of Literature" in *Polemic* in January 1946, and "Politics and the English Language" in *Horizon* in April 1946 to "Politics vs Literature" in the September–October 1946 issue of *Polemic.* Such titles, including "Writers and Leviathan," reflected Orwell's growing concern with totalitarianism: that if the latter could stamp out the "autonomous individual," then the writer was "sitting on a melting iceberg, . . . an anachronism, a hangover from the bourgeois age, as surely doomed as the hippopotamus."[47] The culmination of this concern would occur in *Nineteen Eighty-Four*, in which the conscious passivity of the writer, and everyone else, is assured through force and the destruction of language as we now know it.

By the time Orwell was writing the novel, he had decided to break completely with his old publisher, Victor Gollancz, who still had a first-refusal contract with him and had refused both *Homage* and *Animal Farm*. Orwell respected the publisher's reluctance to print books that went against Gollancz's political beliefs but decided that Warburg, who had published *Animal Farm*, and therefore "would risk anything," should be his publisher of all his future works. To Gollancz he wrote:

I am afraid of further differences arising, as in the past. You know what the difficulty is, i.e., Russia. For quite 15 years I have regarded that régime with plain horror, and though, of course, I would change my opinion if I saw reason, I don't think my feelings are likely to change so long as the Communist Party remains in power. . . . I don't, God knows, want a war to break out, but if one were compelled to choose between Russia and America, . . . I would always choose America.[48]

Confronted by such arguments, Gollancz released Orwell from the old contract. From that time on Secker and Warburg became Orwell's publishers, and he was to become their financial "salvation."[49]

Despite his worsening illness, Orwell continued to write and completed much of *Nineteen Eighty-Four* on the island of Jura in the Inner Hebrides—even after a boating accident in September 1947 that nearly drowned him and his son, Richard, in the frigid North Atlantic and could not have been good for his failing health. Seriously ill with tuberculosis in December 1947, he entered the hospital in Lanarkshire. Although he had all but finished the rough draft of his story about three totalitarian superstates (Eastasia, Eurasia, and Oceania) and the ordeal of Winston Smith in one of them—Oceania— Orwell had nevertheless given his friend Richard Rees instructions to destroy the manuscript, should he die before finishing it.[50]

In Orwell's completed vision, the totalitarian tendencies of the modern state are born in the drive for power—not the desire for power to improve society (as in the original motivation in *Animal Farm*), but power for power's sake.

This tendency, he believes, is nurtured by the increasing centralization of authority and industry that ironically, is "a necessary precondition of [democratic] Socialism."[51] The result of such a drive for power in the ruling authorities of *Nineteen Eighty-Four,* accelerated by increasing centralization, is revealed when we read what Goldstein, the enemy of Big Brother's state, has to say in his treatise "The Theory and Practice of Oligarchical Collectivism." We read that throughout history, despite changing names, there have been only three kinds of people: the High, Middle, and Low. Goldstein, redrawing class divisions that had earlier set the battle lines of Orwell's English period, notes, "The aims of the three groups are entirely irreconcilable. The aim of the High is to remain where they are. The aim of the Middle is to change places with the High. The aim of the Low, when they have an aim [usually they are too "crushed" by "drudgery" to think about anything beyond their daily existence]— is to abolish all distinctions and create a society in which all men shall be equal."[52] Although material progress has been made, argues Goldstein, no social or political change has changed this essential division.

Although Goldstein's view of history incorporates Orwell's earlier simplistic views of societal division, it also goes beyond them. What is new in Goldstein's theory, which is Orwell's essential theory of the totalitarian state, is that while once only the "High," with a few middle-class parasites, had clung to the idea of a hierarchically structured society, softening it for working-class people like the Pithers in *A Clergyman's Daughter* with sentimental promises of rewards in the afterlife, now "the new Middle groups . . . proclaimed their tyranny beforehand." Whereas they had earlier cried for equality in their quest for power, they became as tyrannical as the displaced High, once they acquired power, and now make no other pretence other than clinging to old names for equality, or variations of them such as "Ingsoc" (for English socialism). Apart from this pretense, they unapologetically attack any notion of human brotherhood. It had once been acceptable, and more importantly, safe, for the power-hungry members of this Middle group to clamor for equality—because technology had not reached a stage whereby inequality could be done away with. Once technology has made equality theoretically possible—when, despite necessary specialized functions, there is no need for the division of labor that had traditionally been the excuse for class distinctions—equality ceases to be a slogan for those in power.

Equality that might be realized becomes a threat to them and is even "assailed" by people, like those middle-class socialists of *The Road to Wigan Pier*, who are not in power but hope to be. Thus, we read in Goldstein's theory that because of technological advance, by the 1940s "all the main currents of political thought were authoritarian. . . . Every new political theory, by whatever name it called itself, led back to hierarchy and regimentation."[53]

Nevertheless, although the modern hunger for power seems to lead back to the old tyrannies, Goldstein wrote, there is a glaring difference between the old tyrannies and the new. Whereas the old tyrannies were at least partially seeded by some liberal ideas, Big Brother's regime is devoid of them. The Party, whose distant origins are in the "salaried middle class and the upper grades of the working class," is devoted to absolute opposition of liberal ideas because such ideas endanger the Party's pursuit of "pure power." In the time of Winston Smith, such opposition to liberal ideas presents no problem, but this was not always so. In the early days, immediately after the "Revolution," which (as in *Animal Farm*—and Stalin's Russia) had merely given way to a new tyranny, the Party, before consolidating its power, had moved to justify its control. Understanding that it was widely assumed that "Socialism must follow" the expropriation of capitalists as day follows night, those in power realized that the most effective way of remaining in power was to present the regime as essentially *collectivist*, in keeping with "old" socialist principles. Therefore, no Party member is allowed any private property beyond "petty personal belongings." In fact, ownership of the means of production is in fewer hands than ever before (hence "oligarchical collectivism"), creating the illusion that a "group" of owners is not as exploitative as individual capitalists, even though the "group" consists of *owners* nevertheless. For example, the house in which the interrogator of the novel, O'Brien, lives may be owned by the State, the collective, but it is still a mansion compared to the dismal rooms inhabited by members outside the Inner Party.[54]

Unlike the socialists, whom Orwell critized in *The Road to Wigan Pier* for losing potential converts by concentrating solely on economic factors,[55] the Party does take account of the nonmaterial aspects of life. It does this through Big Brother, who, while not existing as a real person, forms "the guise in which the Party chooses to exhibit itself to the world." Big Brother drains off potential dissatisfaction with the state by acting as "a focusing point for love, fear and reverence, emotions which are more easily felt towards an individual than towards an organization." Into the hole that Orwell believed was left by decline in religious belief, the Party image put the image of Big Brother, replacing the concept of God with that of another apparently all-knowing and all-powerful being.[56]

Big Brother's state is divided up into the Inner Party, or "brain of the State," the Outer Party, or "hands" of the state, and the "dumb" mass of "proles," who constitute about 85 percent of the population. What is new, compared with old tyrannies, is that from its start the Party has been "adoptive," not "hereditary" in nature—that is, it proclaims that merit, not family, is the basis of promotion. It is this, together with the secret Thought Police, that helps it to maintain power. The origins of Party membership may lie in the old salaried and professional middle classes, but admission into the Inner and Outer branches of the Party is through an examination at age sixteen. The Party does not do this, or prohibit racial discrimination, because it is in any sense liberal or fair-minded—the secret Thought Police hardly has its origin in liberal thought—but because it sees that the strength of a regime, and thus its longevity, resides in continuity of policy, and this comes not in the continuity of a bloodline, but in the continuity of a particular "world view."[57] Orwell, having advocated the change from "privilege to competence" in reforming the leadership of England, understood well the attraction of such recruitment among a populace still conscious of unequal opportunity in a world of class privilege. As Orwell also sees, however, it is the apparent fairness of the Party's (or any party's) merit recruitment system, which is based on competence rather than privilege, that obscures the fact that the end of class privilege need not mean the end of inequality. To replace privilege by merit is only to replace the criterion of class division—not to do away with such division. There is a shift here, then, from the earlier Orwell, who tends to confuse meritocracy with equality,[58] to a position in which we see that power may just as easily be the salary of meritocracy as the inheritance of privilege.

Although Winston Smith discovers how the regime maintains power by reading Godlstein's theory of oligarchical collectivism, he does not fully understand the underlying motivations of the totalitarian state until he is faced by the interrogator O'Brien in the cells of the Ministry of Love. OBrien demands,

"You understand well enough *how* the Party maintains itself in power. Now tell me *why* we cling to power. What is our motive? Why should we want power?" . . . Winston did not speak for another moment. . . . He knew in advance what O'Brien would say. That the Party did not seek power for its own ends, but only for the good of the majority. That it sought power because men in the mass were frail cowardly creatures who could not endure liberty or face the truth, and must be ruled over and systematically deceived by others who were stronger than themselves. That the choice for mankind lay between freedom and happiness, and that, for the great bulk of mankind, happiness was better. That the Party was the eternal guardian of the weak, a dedicated sect doing evil that good might come.

Instead, O'Brien answers savagely that the Party is totally uninterested in the good of others, in happiness, luxury, longevity, or money. "We are interested solely in power . . . only power, pure power."[59]

Nineteen Eighty-Four is thus not the record of a modern state in which the "perpetual uneasiness between man and man" is maintained largely through unintentional exploitation, as was the case when Orwell wrote *Down and Out in Paris and London* and *The Road to Wigan Pier*. Rather, it is a state in which exploitation is intentional, the realization of Orwell's old nightmare in 1939 of a state in which "the ruling caste deceive their followers without deceiving themselves."[60]

Having criticized Burnham for assuming in his world view (in which there is an "unalterable . . . division of humanity into rulers and ruled") that the power instinct, though admittedly confined to a few, is as natural an instinct as the desire for food and that therefore there is no need to explain it, Orwell makes the same assumption as Burham. He simply and unequivocally assumes such a power hunger and from that assumption proceeds the ultimate desire of Big Brother—total control of others' thoughts as well as their bodies.

Because of this it has been charged that Orwell's presentation of Big Brother's motivations—in terms of pure power—is ultimately unconvincing, that even the Nazis, for example, for all their power mania, preserved a belief in something else than power for power's sake that, as in the case of their racist theories, they sincerely, if fanatically, retained to the end of the Reich.[61] No doubt, Orwell does overstate his case, and such criticism of him is sound so far as it goes, but this is only as far as placing the Nazi Party, Nazi totalitariansim, alongside Orwell's vision for a comparison. What Orwell clearly wishes to show in his overstatement is that in the totalitarian states of the after-war, the "lust for naked power"[62] is *growing*. Such states, he claims, in comparison to older tyrannies, are less greedy for material possession but much more hungry for pure power.[63] He believes that unlike the time in which he wrote his English novels, status will no longer be measured in terms of property *and* power, but *solely* in terms of power. In doing so, he is assuming that people can change for the worse as easily as they can change for the better, that there are those for whom the wielding of power is an end in itself.

In arguing this, Orwell avoids the pitfall of what he once called the "lure of profundity"—that is, of thinking so deeply at times about a subject that multitudinous qualifications end up smothering an obvious truth. In this case, the truth is that from the harmless child who makes its pet perform for no good purpose to the man who delights in a crowd's instant response to his word, there is in human beings—for whatever reason and in varying degrees—a desire to control others. Perhaps it is, as O'Brien's later behavior suggests, because control of others' futures creates the illusion of control over one's own future, and thereby affords a sense of security—a sense of the predictable, the known in the face of the vast unknown. Whatever the reason, the desire to control others exists, and Orwell's purpose was not to investigate the origin of the germ, but to warn that as easily as the drive for virtue can expand, the hunger for such power can grow until, finally, it consumes all other hungers, including the desire to think and speak freely. This is the great and terrifying simplicity of his work on totalitarianism, which, in his opposition to Stalin, dates from the Thirties, when he wrote, "We cannot be at all certain that 'human nature' is constant. It may be just as possible to produce a breed of men who do not wish for liberty as to produce a breed of hornless cows."[64]

The Spanish Inquisition failed, for all its cruelty, to produce such a breed of men, argues Orwell, because it did not have available to it the apparatus of the modern state. The Oceania of *Nineteen Eighty-Four* is a modern state. What Orwell saw more clearly than most is that the technology of the twentieth century, especially its sophisticated ability to invade the individual's privacy, makes for a totally new type of state: "The radio, press censorship, standarized education and the secret police have altered everything."[65] Such methods, he believed, aided and abetted by high technology, would enable a state to exercise a much wider control than ever before; and together with the nontechnical kind of oppressive social conventions that drove Flory to the ultimate act of alienation in *Burmese Days*, widespread control would become total control.

The efficient use of technology under the control of relatively small sections of the population demands, of course, a high degree of centralization. Such centralization in the superstate of Oceania is oppressively evident in the complete physical and psychical domination of life in London (the "chief city of Airstrip One") by the four ministries.[66] Winston Simth's apartment in Victory Mansion is dwarfed by the massive buildings of the Ministries of Truth (responsible for news, entertainment, and the arts), Peace (responsible for matters of war), Love (responsible for law and order), and Plenty (responsible for economic affairs). These four ministries constitute "the entire apparatus of government."[67]

While centralization seems essential to the efficient use of power, it does not, however, necessarily assure efficiency in public services. Indeed, the most immediately striking thing about *Nineteen Eighty-Four* is that apart from the surveillance systems, nothing seems to work properly. As Goldstein notes, except for the Thought Police, "nothing is efficient."[68] From page 1 of the book, Airstrip One strikes us as being depressingly run down. This is not the futuristic setting marked by a Huxley-like, Wellsian vision of chromium-plated efficiency or Bowling's vision of the "streamlined men . . . from Eastern Europe."[69] Instead, it conjures up visions of ill-fitting uniforms, armies of ersatz coffee machines that neither give you coffee nor return your coins. It is a world of Victory Mansions hallways reeking of boiling cabbage and old mats, of elevators not working, of VICTORY GIN that is cheap and oily, and of VICTORY CIGARETTES that empty if held upright. We read of amateur repair jobs, as performed by Winston Smith, being "an almost daily irritation."

Victory Mansions were old flats, built in 1930 or thereabouts, and were falling to pieces. The plaster flaked constantly from ceilings and walls, the pipes burst in every hard frost, the roof leaked whenever there was snow, the heating system was usually running at half steam when it was not closed down altogether from motives of economy. Repairs, except what you could do for yourself, had to be sanctioned by remote committees which were liable to hold up even the mending of a window-pane for two years. . . .[70]

It struck him that the truly characteristic thing about modern life was not its cruelty and insecurity, but simply its bareness, its dinginess, its listlessness. Life, if you looked about you, bore no resemblance not only to the lies that streamed out of the telescreens, but even to the ideals [of enforcing obedience] that the Party was trying to achieve. Great areas of it, even for a Party member, were neutral and non-political, a matter of slogging through dreary jobs, fighting for a place on the Tube, darning a worn-out sock, cadging a saccharine tablet, saving a cigarette end.

In a description that immediately recalls *The Road to Wigan Pier*, Orwell goes on,

> The reality was decaying, dingy cities, where underfed people shuffled to and fro in leaky shoes, in patched-up nineteenth-century houses that smelt always of cabbage and bad lavatories. He seemed to see a vision of London, vast and ruinous, city of a million dustbins, and mixed up with it was a picture of Mrs. Parsons [a neighbour in Victory Mansions], a woman with lined face and wispy hair, fiddling helplessly with a blocked waste-pipe.[71]

Orwell's determination not to present the world of Airstrip One as one of glittering efficiency may seem puzzling at first sight—after all, he was ostensibly writing about the future. The explanation for his description is that he was not trying to describe a radically different physical world from the present, but a different psychological world—and even in this he sees *Nineteen Eighty-Four* as no more than an extension of present trends. It is the psychological future in the physical present. This is why such care was taken to establish the sense of post–World War II drabness and why the most depressing aspect of the novel is not that it is merely imaginable, but that in its physical setting, at least, it is immediately recognizable even by those readers who have no experience of living in an age of severe economic depression or in postwar ruin but have at least seen slums.

Certainly that marked characteristic of twentieth-century society, the increasing trend to centralization, is instantly recognizable by everyone. It is this dominant fact in *Nineteen Eighty-Four* that reflects Orwell's concern in "Literature and Totalitarianism" that centralization of economy, in restricting one's economic freedom, ultimately affects one's intellectual freedom.[72] Whether the economy is called "Socialist or state capitalism" does not matter, he argues, because in restricting one's economic liberty, intentionally or not, centralization affects a person's freedom "to choose his own work, to move to and fro across the surface of the earth."[73] The danger is that a restricted mentality is soon nurtured by the restricted body.

The danger is not simply that a totalitarian state such as that in *Nineteen Eighty-Four* frowns upon certain economic behavior, such as free-market dealing, but that in order to assure compliance with "correct" economic and social behavior, the state undertakes to limit the public's knowledge of other systems. In Goldstein's treatise we read, "The masses never revolt of their own accord, and they never revolt merely because they are oppressed. Indeed, so long as they are not permitted to have standards of comparison, they never even become aware that they are oppressed."[74]

As later happened in Berlin, one way of removing standards of comparison (both economic and social ones) is to build a wall, so that people cannot leave and see how others live. As early as 1939 Orwell was saying in a review of N. de Basily's *Russia Under Soviet Rule* that the fact that "it is next door to impossible for a Soviet citizen, unless on some kind of official mission, to visit any foreign country [was]—a silent admission that life is more comfortable elsewhere."[75]

Neither a barbed-wire wall nor the burning of old books, which also offer comparisons, blocks out *memory*. This still exists as a basis of comparison when all else is gone. The question, then, for a totalitarian state, which has decided upon the "correct" economic and social form of society, is how to maintain unquestioning obedience to its view of the world in the presence of both individual and collective memories of other ways of living. Just as important, is how such a state is to maintain unquestioning obedience when its world view must change in response to external pressures—when a solemn pact of non-aggression is violated overnight, when Monday's dogma becomes Tuesday's heresy. This problem, says Orwell, is a new one for the totalitarian régime, for while the older orthodoxies (such as the Church in medieval Europe) undoubtedly dictated to the individual, they at least provided one with a fixed framework of thought: "At least it allowed you to retain the same beliefs from birth to death" without tampering with one's emotions. In totalitarian states the opposite prevails, for while the totalitarian regime "controls thought, . . . it does not fix it." In order for a totalitarian state to maintain the appearance of infallibility in a rapidly changing world—a world in which the government of an Afghanistan, for example, changes overnight—ideological boundaries must continually shift and be redrawn. Although the medieval writer could remain relatively secure by working within set boundaries, the modern writer cannot, because he or she is never certain that writing "correctly" on Monday will not mean a jail sentence on Tuesday. Further, while verbal acquiescence involving an abrupt about-face can be given quickly to sudden changes in the regime's policy and is difficult to check up on, the written word can quickly be compared with what was written last week or last year. Therefore, Orwell could write that "the most

promising Russina writers show a marked tendency to commit suicide or disappear into prison."[76]

The problem for the ruled in the modern totalitarian state, then,
as much as for the rulers, is how to cope with rapid change of policy
dictated by ever-shifting conditions. In a world where television surveillance is no longer confined to department stores, but invades what
was once the privacy of the home, consciousness of the gap between
one's public verbal or written acquiescence to the regime's policy
and one's private view of reality is bound to produce acute anxiety.
Even if a wall removes the doubt raised by seeing how others live,
such anxiety can be created or at the very least, worsened by the
memory of other days. For most, such anxiety leads to a willingness
to conform—in this, at least, there is safety. For others, however, it
leads to constant tension. As Flory in *Burmese Days* swam against the
"stream"[77] of convention but secretly longed for the acceptance of
membership—to swim with the stream—so Winston Smith is caught
between the pressure of social convention and the cry of his individual conscience: "It was like swimming against a current that swept
you backwards however hard you struggled, and then suddenly
deciding to turn round and go with the current instead of opposing it. Nothing had changed your own attitude. . . . He hardly
knew why he had ever rebelled. Everything was easy, except—!"[78]

Capitulation to the official view can be made easy. We see how
the tension resulting from a conflict between the desire to belong to
the group and the desire to be true to one's conscience can be temporarily relieved by the tranquilizing effect of Victory Gin—as with
Flory's gin-swilling in Burma. The oily alcohol is readily doled out
by the Party in Airstrip One in both the gin shops and at the cafete-
rias in the ministries; but as with Flory, this is only subduing the
symptom. To ensure total capitulation to the official view, and because
of the danger of one thought leading to another, all thoughts must
be controlled—not so much by the Thought Police as by the individual. This is *Crimestop,* the instinctive ability whereby one's brain
deliberately and habitually blots out any potentially dangerous
thought.[79] Indeed, the most depressing aspect of Orwell's treatment
of this major theme (especially in *Animal Farm)* is that he shows
how, in their drive for security, the ruled often *willingly* surrender to
the ruler's method of deception by training themselves in self-
deception. It is in *Animal Farm* that Orwell first addresses himself

to the refinement of such techniques and the tragic consequences for those who dare to resist them.

Before he gives them the stirring song, "Beasts of England," as their anthem of revolution, Major, the pig who instigates the overthrow of Farmer Jones, tells the animals, "We must not come to resemble him [Man]. . . . Above all, no animal must ever tyrannize over his own kind. . . . We are all brothers. . . . All animals are equal." By the end of the story, however, not only do the pigs, led by Napoleon (Stalin), exile Snowball (Trotsky) and tyrannize their fellow animals, but finally, it becomes impossible for the common animals to tell their "brothers" the pigs from their human oppressors, because they all look the same.[80]

Superficially, the difficulty of distinguishing pigs from people, between one-time revolutionaries and their one-time masters, is due to the pigs' physical imitation of human beings—walking on two legs, dressing in humans' clothes, and even smoking and drinking. "Twelve voices [people and pigs] were shouting in anger, and they were all alike." The real difficulty lies, however, in a much more insidious imitation of human behavior—namely, misuse of language. The pigs' ability to corrupt language is evident throughout. We hear Snowball, before his expulsion from the farm, arguing, against all logic, that the revolutionary slogan "Four legs good, two legs bad" can now include birds as four-legged animals, because "a bird's wing, comrades, . . . is an organ of propulsion and not of manipulation" and "should therefore be regarded as a leg." Such corruption is also evident when, after violating Major's decree by walking on two legs like a person, Napoleon (Stalin) suddenly declares that while all animals are equal, some are more equal than others.[81] What we are seeing in such passages is that the pigs have intuitively recognized that language, as Orwell points out, is not "a natural growth," but "an instrument" that (even allowing for differences in sensory perceptions) people use more to *rationalize* their actions than to *interpret* the world as it is.[82] Thus, it is possible that Squealer, Napoleon's chief bully, "could turn black into white"; yet the proletarians on the farm, the work animals, who note this ability of the leadership soon forget it because of other weapons in the arsenal of deception. One such weapon is the deliberate *alteration* of history, as in the slogan, "Four legs good, two legs *better*."[83]

In this regard, I suspect that if the word "better" had not been emphasized by Orwell in the previous sentence, the only way in which the reader would recognize the phrase in question as being decidedly different from "Four legs good, two legs bad" would have been to go back and find the first slogan so as to compare the two. The importance of the use of the written word for the purpose of comparison, which is commonly, if unconsciously, recognized whenever we say things like, "Let me write it down—or I'll forget it," is repeatedly underscored in *Animal Farm* through the almost total unavailability of the animals' records.

Sometimes the older ones among them racked their dim memories and tried to determine whether in the early days of the Rebellion, when Jones' expulsion was still recent, things had been better or worse than now. They could not remember. There was nothing with which they could compare their present lives: they had nothing to go on except Squealer's lists of figures, which invariably demonstrated that everything was getting better and better. . . . There was, as Squealer was never tired of explaining, endless work in the supervision and organization of the farm. Much of this work was of a kind that the other animals were too ignorant to understand. For example, Squealer told them that the pigs had to expend enormous labours every day upon mysterious things called "files," "reports," "minutes," and "memoranda." These were large sheets of paper which had to be closely covered with writing, and as soon as they were so covered, they were burnt in the furnace.[84]

When one of the original resolutions of Major, that no animal should be allowed to trade, is violated by the pigs, who begin using the capitalist Mr. Whymper to act as agent between Animal Farm and the outside world, some of the animals, dimly recalling Major's resolution, begin to sniff a double standard. In reply to their inquiries, the pig Squealer asks, "Are you certain that this is not something that you have dreamed, comrades? Have you any record of such a resolution? Is it written down anywhere?" As there is no such record, the animals are satisfied that they must have been in error in questioning the new practice. Finally, Napoleon bans the revolutionary song "Beasts of England," for, if nothing else, it will keep alive a revolutionary spirit in what Napoleon clearly intends to be a non-revolutionary state, now that he is in power. Squealer reports to a disappointed "comrade" that the song is no longer necessary, because although the song was appropriate for the Rebellion, "the Rebellion is now completed." In its place the animals are given a new song, which begins, *"Animal Farm, Animal Farm,/Never through me shalt thou come to harm!"*

The pigs' reversal of original revolutionary intent does not, of course, take place until the animals' memories have faded sufficiently. Even though, as we know, memory fades quickly enough, the rulers are careful to pursue a policy of what could be called erosion by degree; so when yet another animal, noticing that the pigs are now sleeping in humans' beds, consults the official barn door, spurred by a dim recollection of the fiat *"No animal shall sleep in a bed,"* he discovers that what the commandment now says is, "No animal shall sleep in a bed *with sheets."* Likewise, he discovers that the commandment that he believed was *"No animal shall kill any other animal"* is really "No animal shall kill any other animal *without cause."*[85]

So it is that the pigs, who are the first to proclaim the change in structure—replacing the old sign, MANOR FARM, with that of ANIMAL FARM—give themselves privileges and daily grow to resemble Mr. Jones, against whose tyranny they rebelled. The lesson is that the structure of society may change, the faces of power may change, but the heart of power does not change. No matter that the farm had been industrialized under the pigs' merciless direction, with a windmill, threshing machine, hay elevator and new buildings being added; in essence it was still Manor Farm—the commissar without the yogi to counter the power instinct.[86] It was Goldstein's theory in practice: in order to remove standards of comparison, the Party member and proletarian alike "must be cut off from the past, just as he must be cut off from foreign countries," or, as Soviet dissident Andrei Sakharov said thirty-two years *later* of his native country (which served as the model for *Animal Farm*), "For most people there is no opportunity to compare the system here with systems outside."[87]

Beyond the subversion of the original and collective spirit of one revolution, however, a much more serious threat grows out of the erosion-by-degree method, which modifies history by tacking qualifying clauses onto the end of old commandments. When he charges that Snowball not only showed cowardice in the battle against invading humans, but "had actually been the leader of the human forces, and had charged into battle with the words 'Long live Humanity,' "[88] comrade Napoleon is no longer modifying the historical record, but *reversing* it; when, in his leap from the little lie to the big lie, he blatantly proclaims that the damage done to the windmill by a November gale is the fault of none other than Snowball, he has even gone beyond reversing history to *inventing* it—making the final descent in the loss of any sense of objective truth.

Beyond this perversion of truth, what is significant in Napoleon's act is that Napoleon (Stalin) does not denigrate Snowball (Trotsky) from sheer spite, from a rampant desire for revenge (as Stalin admittedly might have done), but because he has fallen into the trap of the totalitarian mentality—that one lie must, of necessity, be followed by others.

Of course, lying is hardly the exclusive sin of totalitarian societies, as Orwell makes clear;[89] but because the maintenance of control by a totalitarian regime rests largely upon maintaining a widespread belief in the leadership's infallibility, it is necessary for the leadership to *constantly* reinterpret past policy (history), so as to justify even the slightest deviation in present policy.[90] Normally, in justifying policy changes made gradually over a long period, there is little problem for the regime. This is especially true in a world like that of *Nineteen Eighty-Four* where, unlike the barnyard environment of *Animal Farm*, records are kept and there is a whole industry devoted to updating the lies of old newspapers, rewriting textbooks, and so forth. A problem does arise, however, when, despite the efforts of an industry devoted to falsifying records, the leadership of a totalitarian state has to justify a complete and sudden turnabout in stated policy—as, for example, happened regarding the invasion of Afghanistan in 1979–80. The problem posed is captured in Orwell's story of the Communist in New York who, having been absent from the room when the news of Hitler's massive violation of the Russo–German Pact broke on the radio, returned to discover the "party line" had changed while he'd been on the toilet.[91] In short, a totalitarian regime must always have an excuse ready, lest dramatic events overtake it and before the possibility of its fallibility can be seriously entertained by its followers. For Stalin (Napoleon) the excuse was Trotsky (Snowball), to the extent that, as Orwell recorded, in Spain the great charge of heresy became that of Trotskyism: "to call a man a Trotskyist is practically equivalent to calling him a murderer."[92]

Hence, in *Animal Farm*, after a minor rebellion by the hens against exorbitant demands by Napoleon for higher production has been ruthlessly crushed by Napoleon's trained dogs, "an alarming thing was discovered." It was suddenly announced that the banished Snowball had secretly been "frequenting the farm by night." The account continues:

The animals were so disturbed that they could hardly sleep in their stalls. Every night, it was said, he came creeping in under cover of darkness and performed all kinds of mischief. He stole the corn, he upset the milk-pails, he broke the eggs, he trampled the seed-beds, he gnawed the bark off the fruit trees. Whenever anything went wrong it became usual to attribute it to Snowball. . . . Napoleon decreed that there should be a full investigation into Snowball's activities. With his dogs in attendance he set out and made a careful tour of inspection. . . . at every few steps Napoleon stopped and snuffled the ground . . . and found traces of Snowball almost everywhere.
    The animals were thoroughly frightened. It seemed to them as though Snowball were some kind of invisible influence, pervading the air about them and menacing them with all kinds of dangers.[93]

More than a highly visible scapegoat, however, whether it be Snowball in *Animal Farm* or Goldstein in *Nineteen Eighty-Four* (who also proclaims, correctly, that the "revolution [Ingsoc] has been betrayed"),[94] the regime needs an instantly recognizable vocabulary tailored to accommodate rapid changes in policy so that such changes can be more easily presented and accepted by the general population. There may not always be enough time to reeducate the masses, as in *Animal Farm* when, after being taken away by Squealer for what is nothing less than thought reform, the sheep return bleating in unison, "Four legs good, two legs *better.*" Furthermore, the Party's unchanging slogans, such as "Comrade Napoleon is always right,"[95] may serve to erase only temporary doubt in the already committed— in Inner Party members—and such slogans, relying as they do on the cult of personality, may be acceptable only so long as Comrade Napoleon is alive. What is needed to maintain widespread belief in the *state's* infallibility is a language that will serve Comrade Napoleon or Big Brother with equal efficiency, that will enable the leader, whoever he (or she) is, to manipulate the public mind better and more quickly, without appearing to do so. This brings us to a consideration of one of Orwell's most outstanding contributions to our understanding of politics: his analysis of the extent to which language, as part of the process of power hunger denying equality, may be willfully corrupted as a tactic in an ever-expanding policy of deception.

Although party members in *Nineteen Eighty-Four* like Winston Smith continue to communicate in Oldspeak—that is, today's English—the Inner Party's aim is to abolish this and to establish a much-abbreviated language, "Newspeak," by the year 2050. In Oldspeak a message might read, "Those whose ideas were formed before the Revolution cannot have a full emotional understanding of the principles of English Socialism." In Newspeak this would read "Oldthinkers unbellyfeel Ingsoc." It is only through the establishment of this "official language," designed "to *diminish* the range of thought," that the process called "doublethink"—the ability to hold two different beliefs simultaneously and to believe in them equally—is most effective in protecting the ideological purity of Ingsoc, or English Socialism. Doublethink successfully hides the fact that Ingsoc is precisely the opposite of what the original English Socialism stood for. As doublethink would deal with present contradictions, Newspeak, together with the constant alteration of historical records, will thwart the possibility of contradiction in the future. Through Newspeak's studious elimination of undesirable words and of "unorthodox meanings," the Party hopes to ensure that "a heretical thought—that is, a thought diverging from the principles of Ingsoc—should be literally unthinkable."[96]

It is hardly surprising that elimination of words on so large a scale would allow Newspeak to reduce the range of thought, the range of consciousness, and shades of meaning. The result is that the world is seen in terms of black and white, "good" and "ungood." It would not be *at all* surprising that a population using such a language could view the world either as capitalist or socialist, with nothing in-between. Thus, the population could easily be encouraged to assume that socialism, and not anything like oligarchical collectivism, must follow the expropriation of capitalists. In encouraging this black–white vision of the world, Newspeak, with its deletion of adjective and adverb, not only expels shades of meaning, but also does away with whole concepts like political equality. The result is that a Newspeak slogan that stated, "All men are equal," would signify nothing more than all men are physically the same.[97]

In its reduction of the number of words, Newspeak at its worst is a direct attack upon metaphor, which, being the expression of conscious comparison, draws heavily on our knowledge of the past and shades of meaning. At this point, continuous alteration of the past, so that it can no longer be referred to reliably, together with fewer words with which to refer to it, combine to render the metaphor virtually useless as an agent of thought and precise explanation. Because of its destruction of nuance, of the shades of meanings and old meanings, Newspeak has to rely heavily on "euphony," the musically hypnotizing quality of word arrangements, to convey its message; but as Newspeak is not expected to be firmly implanted until 2050, Old-speak must somehow be adapted as a transition language, even if it is not as euphonious. In *Nineteen Eighty-Four,* doublethink (itself a Newspeak word) helps to provide a bridge between Oldspeak and Newspeak, because it dismisses any reference to the past that Old-speak might suggest—even when the past is only minutes old.[98]

Doublethink is not the only bridge used, however, and particu-larly for the mass of unsophisticated proles, Oldspeak is turned into a language of deception by the almost mechanical reproduction of worn-out phrases. They are so familiar that they glide over the con-sciousness in rapid-fire succession, conveying the hypnotic *tone* (as Newspeak will do even more efficiently) that the speechmakers desire to induce. This prevents the listener from really thinking about what is being said. As Orwell wrote in "Propaganda and Demotic Speech" after his B.B.C. experience, "One's impulse in speaking [particularly in dictating which "is always slightly embarrassing"] is to avoid the long pauses, and one necessarily does so by clutching at the ready-made phrases." Such phrases are nothing less than substitutes for work—for thought. The attack on the ready-made phrase, the result-ing jargon and its "remoteness from the average man," particularly in political speeches and broadcasts, can be found frequently in Orwell's writing.

In 1946, presaging the language of *Nineteen Eighty-Four,* Orwell wrote that those who are "likeliest to use simple concrete language, and to think of metaphors that really call up a visual image, are those who are in contact with physical reality. . . . It follows that language, at any rate the English language [Oldspeak], suffers when the edu-cated classes [the Inner and Outer Party] lose touch with the manual workers."[99]

Just how out of touch the Inner and Outer Party members are with manual workers, the proles, is seen when Syme, a fellow worker of Winston Smith, curtly asserts, "The proles are not human beings."[100]

Of listening to the ready-made phrases that are so often repeated by political speakers, Orwell wrote in 1946:

One often has a curious feeling that one is not watching a live human being but some kind of dummy: a feeling which suddenly becomes stronger at moments when the light catches the speaker's spectacles and turns them into blank discs which seem to have no eyes behind them. And this is not alto-gether fanciful. A speaker who uses that kind of phraseology has gone some distance towards turning himself into a machine. The appropriate noises are coming out of his larynx, but his brain is not involved as it would be if he were choosing his words for himself. If the speech he is making is one that he is accustomed to make over and over again, he may be almost unconscious of what he is saying. . . . And this reduced state of consciousness, if not indispensable, is at any rate favourable to political conformity.[101]

Three years later, in *Nineteen Eighty-Four,* Winston Smith is sitting in the cafeteria of the Ministry of Truth, listening to Syme talk of how Newspeak will so reduce the number of words that soon thought as they know it will cease to exist and orthodoxy will mean not thinking—having no need to think. In the background Winston can hear

[a man with] a strident voice . . . still talking remorselessly away. . . . His spectacles caught the light and presented to Winston two blank discs instead of eyes. What was slightly horrible, was that from the stream of sound that poured out of his mouth it was almost impossible to distinguish a single word. Just once Winston caught a phrase—"complete and final elimination of Goldsteinism"—jerked out very rapidly and, as it seemed, all in one piece, like a line of type cast solid. For the rest it was just a noise, a quack-quack-quacking. And yet, though you could not actually hear what the man was saying, you could not be in any doubt about its general nature. He might be denouncing Goldstein and demanding sterner measures against thought-criminals, . . . he might be praising Big Brother . . . it made no difference. Whatever it was, you could be certain that every word of it was pure orthodoxy, pure Ingsoc. As he watched the eyeless face with the jaw moving rapidly up and down, Winston had a curious feeling that this was not a real human being but some kind of dummy. It was not the man's brain that was speaking, it was his larynx. . . . [He was emitting] a noise uttered in unconsciousness.[102]

For Winston Smith the culmination of doublethink and mechanical language comes on the sixth day of "Hate Week." The "great orgasm" of hate "was quivering to its climax and the general hatred of Eurasia had boiled up into such delirium that if the crowd could have got their hands on the 2,000 Eurasian war-criminals, . . . they would unquestionably have torn them to pieces." Then halfway through the speech it is announced that Oceania is no longer at war with Eurasia, that Eurasia is now an ally and Oceania is at war with Eastasia. When the Party speaker, who has been exciting the crowd to a fury that often drowns his amplified voice with a beastlike roaring, is handed a piece of paper informing him of the change of enemy and ally, "nothing altered in his voice or manner or in the content of what he was saying, but suddenly the names were different."[103]

The interesting point is that once the crowd understands the switch, it does not occur to them to question the dramatic change in policy.

Instead, upon seeing that now the sea of placards and slogans are proclaiming the opposite message to what the speaker is saying, the crowd instantly assumes that it is "sabotage," that Goldstein's sabo- teurs have produced the placards. The crowd proceeds to go wild, tearing down the offending posters and banners.

But within two or three minutes it was all over. The orator, still gripping the neck of the microphone, his shoulders hunched forward, his free hand clawing at the air, had gone straight on with his speech. One minute more and the feral roars of rage were again bursting from the crowd. The Hate continued exactly as before, except that the target had been changed.

The thing that impressed Winston on looking back was that the speaker had switched from one line to the other actually in mid-sentence, not only without a pause, but without even breaking the syntax.[104]

The significance of these passages is not simply that they show how Orwell habitually infused his fiction with his own experiences, or even how often the psychological atmosphere of this "futuristic" novel is really that of the present—indeed, of Nuremberg (or of any mass rally)—but that they illustrate the extent of the divorce from external reality that has been effected by the Party. The latter has trained its members to believe that reality exists only in the collective mind of the Party, that "it is impossible to see reality except by look- ing through the eyes of the Party."[105]

One could argue that such control of ideas, of alternate views of reality, inhibits free speech. This may be true, but of course, it is equally true that free speech by itself may be no more than the license or means to babble nonsense or act libellously. What the destruction of ideas and alternate perceptions through language does do is some- thing far worse—it inhibits the habit of *debate*, which lies at the heart of the free society and is kept beating through the lively discussion of different and wide-ranging points of view. Without debate we end up with a state that quite apart from being oppressive and inhib- iting free speech, is essentially stagnant, incurious, and especially stultifying to any creative impulse. Worst of all, this is true not only of the Inner Party, but of all those outside it—especially, in the arts and the sciences.

CHAPTER 10

F OR ORWELL THE MOST PRESSING DANGER OF THE TENDENCY
toward greater centralization of government, exemplified in the
party's control of the language, was that the "autonomous individual"[1]
was threatened with extinction. The threat was particularly ominous
for writers, who help to preserve the tradition of debate; and dictatorships aside, the most invidious aspect of this danger was, as Blair
had discovered in the rich's exploitation of the poor, that it was often
unintentional.

Orwell saw that the constant and increasing assault against a writer's integrity (or, for that matter, that of any artist), while it is a
result of monopoly control over the media, is caused more by "the
general drift of society rather than by active persecution." Still, the
result of monopoly—particularly in wartime, when propagandists
were in demand—was that the writer found it necessary at least to
"earn part of his living by hack work." This meant joining institutions like the Ministry of Information and the B.B.C. that, while
helping the writer to subsist, also often dictated a writer's opinions,
turning him or her into a kind of petty bureaucrat espousing only
official policy.[2] In such cases, notes Orwell, the writer is "called a
reporter, but is treated as a megaphone."[3] It is a short step from that
position to one that would characterize a totalitarian state like Oceania,
where, because four ministries comprise the entire governmental
apparatus, people like Syme, Winston Smith, and Ampleforth who
have any literary skill or pretensions at all find themselves employed
by the Ministry of Truth. In performing his job, Winston, completely untroubled by his deliberate falsification of history and current events, is as determined as any of his coworkers to excel in the
art of deception—making it "impossible," for example, "for any human

being to prove by documentary evidence that the war with Eurasia had ever happened."[4]

Once again, Orwell draws heavily on his own experience in portraying a fictional character. It is in his wartime diary, not Winston Smith's, that we read

I have now been in the B.B.C. [where the name Stalin was "completely sacrosanct"][5] about 6 months. . . . Its atmosphere is something halfway between a girls' school and a lunatic asylum. . . . Nevertheless one rapidly becomes propaganda-minded and develops a cunning one did not previously have. E.g. I am regularly alleging in all my newsletters [broadcasts to India] that the Japanese are plotting to attack Russia. I don't believe this to be so, but the calculation is:

If the Japanese do attack Russia, we can say "I told you so."

If the Russians attack first, we can, having built up the picture of a Japanese plot beforehand, pretend that it was the Japanese who started it.

If no war breaks out after all, we can claim that it is because the Japanese are too frightened of Russia.[6]

While this is an honest moment for Orwell, it is hardly a proud one. It does show, however, that well before he wrote *Animal Farm* and *Nineteen Eighty-Four,* he had experienced not only the temptation of, but the surrender to what he later called in "The Prevention of Literature" (1946) the "dangerous proposition . . . that intellectual honesty is a form of antisocial selfishness." The most dangerous implication of the proposition is that although most people may readily agree to short-term tactical lying in time of war, if the war (or war preparation) becomes permanent—as it does in *Nineteen Eighty-Four*— then the short term becomes the long term. Lying becomes the norm, and one cannot, even by an act of will, confine it just to military matters. Lying becomes a habit in all areas of life, especially in a totalitarian state in which control of the past by deception is deemed essential to protecting the myth of infallibility. In such a state, "lying would still continue even if concentration camps and secret police forces had ceased to be necessary" because history is seen as "something to be *created* rather than learned."[7] (The italics are mine.)

Just as lying is not confined to any one sphere of activity, neither is the dominance of bureaucracy over the individual writer confined to merely instructing him or her on official political pronouncements. This state interference with the artist spreads beyond official duties more than it does in the case of a bureaucrat, because to lie about facts inevitably leads one into lying about feelings, which is the working domain more of the artist than of the bureaucrat. In any event, the integrity of the would-be artist comes under heavy attack in the Ministry of Truth (in *Nineteen Eighty-Four*), which is not only concerned with altering the past, but, primarily, with keeping the population placid by giving easy access to simple-minded entertainment, including films, plays, novels, and poems written in a nondescript style. For example, the novels designed for proletarian consumption have only half a dozen plots and are swapped about by the "Rewrite Squad."[8] This is both the logical extension of the increasing centralization of the press, which Orwell noted in his essay "Boy's Weeklies," and the result of sophisticated technology, as predicted in *The Road to Wigan Pier*. In "The Prevention of Literature," he describes how "Disney films, for instance, are produced by what is essentially a factory process, the work being done partly mechanically and partly by teams of artists who have to subordinate their individual style."[9] The danger of all this is that in its further erosion of individual integrity, the weight of orthodox opinion gains and the sense of objective truth is diminished. Even if prose is composed in solitude, beyond a production line and out of the range of telescreens, (as Orwell argues all serious prose has to be),[10] the heretical ideas it may contain are unlikely to spread because of the lack of nonofficial distribution channels and the punishment that would certainly follow underground distribution.

The fate of the prose writer in a totalitarian society is crucial, because it focuses attention on what Orwell saw as an unsolved "dilemma"— namely, that while society can hardly be run in the sole interest of artists, who may not be as necessary to society as coal miners and milk carriers, "without artists civilization perishes." This dilemma was not solved by the state employing the writer, for, as we have seen, this was ruinous in forcing the artist inevitably to toe the official line. Further, to the suggestion that writers could write what they wanted in their spare time, Orwell, doubtless drawing on his own experience at the B.B.C., correctly countered that writing lies about something that doesn't matter to you is as physically tiring as writing about something that matters a great deal.[11] In most cases such effort saps one's energy for any spare-time writing.

This left Orwell, for all his socialist vision, with the belief that despite its grave faults, capitalism (particularly laissez-faire capitalism), at least afforded writers, and artists in general, an escape. By offering your wares to the free market,[12] you could at least avoid the demeaning flatteries of patronization, on the one hand, and having to toe the official line on the other. The implications are as clear for the citizen as for the artist. Socialism might bring collectivism, even equality, but there is a constant danger that government and technology, through the centralization that, ironically, is required to enforce that equality, may deny the freedom of the individual. The danger is especially acute for the writer, because "literature as we know it is an individual thing, demanding mental honesty and a minimum of censorship." Because he believed that "this is even truer of prose than of verse," Orwell regarded "the atmosphere of orthodoxy" as being "completely ruinous to the novel, the most anarchical of all forms of literature."[13]

In 1944 Orwell was still confident that a people, in this case the English, "could centralize their economy without destroying freedom in doing so."[14] In *Nineteen Eighty-Four* he is obviously in grave doubt. In his treatment of language control, however, a curious thing happens: although prose has fallen victim to Big Brother's deadly censorship in the superstate, verse of unknown authorship is permitted. This does not mean that verse is not carefully watched (for example, Ampleforth, one of Smith's coworkers, is jailed for allowing the word *God* to remain in a poem),[15] but it does mean that verse is relatively tolerated. Why? Well, says Orwell, "even in a society where liberty and individuality had been extinguished, there would still be need . . . for patriotic songs and heroic ballads celebrating victories." This toleration of verse extends particularly to the proles in *Nineteen Eighty-Four,* because the Inner Party considers them stupid, and therefore harmless, revealing what might prove to be a grave miscalculation on the part of the totalitarian administration. We are told that the Party, by means of a "versificator," manufactures apparently meaningless rhymes, set to music, and hate songs to make the proles' lot more acceptable. What the Party does not take into account, however, is the possibility of *improvisation*—the fact, as Orwell notes in "The Prevention of Literature," that when "many primitive peoples compose verse communally, . . . someone begins to improvise, . . . somebody else chips in with a line or a rhyme when the first singer breaks down, and so the process continues until there exists a whole song or ballad which has no identifiable author."[16]

Such unidentifiable authorship would make it impossible to arrest those guilty of heresy against the regime's orthodoxy and might encourage others to join in. The originally meaningless verse could thus quickly become as potentially subversive as mime theater, which, in saying nothing, can say anything.[17] This possibility grows in proportion to the bureaucratic tendency (especially among those who are unable to grasp the subtlety of the poetic nuance and are too embarrassed to admit it) to look for form rather than content as a guide to what is permissable. It is the known "form" that gives comfort to Dorothy in *The Clergyman's Daughter* by providing her with the familiarity of a traditional hymn. Just so, it affords ease of mind to a bureaucrat who is anxious to do everything "by the book"—like a border guard who looks more for the correct size and shape of a passport rather than for what is in it.

Continuity of form is vitally important to the Inner Party, for whether it be a question of a hate rhyme or a Newspeak sentence, the continuity of form allows the Party (and, to a lesser extent, Whitehall in *Burmese Days*) to present new policy in familiar doctrinal dress—as in the case of the enemy suddenly changing from Eurasia to Eastasia. In this way the Party can make new policies appear not to contradict supposedly infallible Party precepts. This explains why when real change comes in totalitarian societies, it is so often signalled by a change in the form of a message rather than by the message itself. This has bred a brand of scholarship in the West that, under the name of Kremlinology, attempts, along with other techniques, to detect real change in the Soviet Union by concentrating upon minute change in "form." In this regard it is relevant to note how, under the dreaded eye of censorship in Oceania, the only hope that the proles have to survive the obsessively formalized world of Big Brother may ironically lie in the very verse produced for them by the Party.

The Party in Oceania allows the proles to sing such apparently silly rhymes as,

> It was only an 'opeless fancy
> It passed like an Ipril dye,
> But a look an' a word an' the dreams they stirred!
> They 'ave stolen my 'eart awye.[18]

What the Party does not see is not only that this "leniency" runs the risk that heretical thoughts will be spread through improvisation by unidentifiable authorship, but that the very form of the verse, that of the traditional English music hall song, is likely to recall older songs. Such recall is dangerous to the Party. Whether or not the words make sense, the verse *forms* remind the singer or singers of another time, of history, of an alternative way of life, and in so doing, constitute a threat to the state's supposed infallibility.

If the words do make sense, as when Winston Smith inquires about "Oranges and lemons, say the bells of St. Clement's" and discovers that what is now a "museum used for propaganda displays" was once a church, then the memory of another time, reinforced by concrete evidence, is that much stronger.

All the while that they were talking the half-remembered rhyme kept running through Winston's head. Oranges and lemons say the bells of St. Clement's, You owe me three farthings, say the bells of St. Martin's! It was curious, but when you said it to yourself you had the illusion of actually hearing bells, the bells of a lost London that still existed somewhere or other, disguised and forgotten. From one ghostly steeple after another he seemed to hear them pealing forth. . . . He had even started humming to an improvised tune.[19]

Thus, while the form of such rhymes is easy to police, the form itself can conjure up another time, a possible alternative. Indeed, the very utterance of the songs becomes an exercise in reawakening a consciousness, not only about the past, but about what it is to be fully human in the present. As simple as it may be, the very consciousness of song ("the birds sang, the proles sang, the Party did not sing")[20] keeps alive in simple form other possibilities than the present, possibilities that the stripped prose of Newspeak seeks to kill, as surely as it kills the habit of debate.

Unlike the needs of the arts, the requirements of science would seem at first sight to pose a major difficulty standing in the way of implementing a language of deception, be it Newspeak or the jargon-filled Oldspeak, which Orwell believed could affect all areas of endeavor.[21] As he points out in "The Prevention of Literature," a scientist must be guaranteed a certain amount of intellectual freedom, even in a totalitarian society. Atom bombs cannot be manufactured if the scientist is required, as Winston Smith is, to believe that two and two make five.[22] Nevertheless, in a world of superstates— Eastasia, Eurasia, and Oceania—science, insofar as it fathers increased production, must be carefully controlled, because increased production, which would raise the living standard, is not wanted by the Inner Party. So long as the people are comfortable, they will not want more consumer goods, which would raise the standard of living; "for if leisure and security were enjoyed by all alike, the great mass of human beings who are normally stupefied by poverty would become literate and would learn to think for themselves. They would then, sooner or later, realize that the privileged minority had no function, and they would sweep it away."[23] Hence, in a world where it was no longer possible to return to an agricultural past, because, as Orwell noted in *The Road to Wigan Pier,* "the tendency towards mechanization . . . had become quasi instinctive . . . , the problem was how to keep the wheels of industry turning without increasing the real wealth of the world?"[24]

It can hardly be argued that this is the "problem" of present-day governments, totalitarian regimes included, but—and herein lies the popularity of *Nineteen Eighty-Four*—the psychological climate of a totalitarian state today (and on occasion, the non-totalitarian state) strikes us as being remarkably similar to that of *Nineteen Eighty-Four*. This is because every area of endeavor is brought under control, as much to maintain governmental power as to improve the human condition—and often solely to maintain power. In any case, whatever the hidden motives for their power hunger, the Inner Party of Oceania and the rulers of Eurasia and Eastasia do not want to increase production, not even for purposes of war. Like most superpowers today, they already possess enough nuclear weapons to annihilate each other. Because of this capability, the leaders, while they have decided that the answer to the threatening problem of overproduction caused by science is war, have also decided that such conflict, though continuous, must be limited, like a never-ending Viet Nam. In this way, the war is not intended to be decisive in terms of permanently changing boundaries. It is in the main not so much a war against an external enemy as one "waged by each ruling group against its own subjects"[25]—whose consciousness the leadership does not want to raise. The slogans of war, apart from evoking images of heroic sacrifice, help to explain away the scarcity of consumer goods. They also channel existing hostilities into permanent "war-hysteria"[26] and are used to justify the continuous oppression and inequality that are needed to keep the Party in power. In this sense, for the Party, war *is* peace.[27]

Such continuous war, or at the very least such continuous war preparation, which the Party needs to divert domestic attention away from domestic failure, is more easily maintained by leaders than we think. In *Animal Farm* Napoleon appeals to the sense of common good in his followers: "Discipline, comrades, iron discipline! That is the watchword for today. One false step, and our enemies would be upon us. Surely, comrades, you do not want Jones back?"[28] In *Nineteen Eighty-Four* the common enemy is different, but the technique is the same, with Goldstein and his Eurasian hordes being kept permanently in the mind of the public by the daily hate. Both leaderships illustrate that they reject what Orwell said was the shallow, hedonist philosophy of so many leaders who wrongly believe that most people want nothing more than an easy, safe life.[29]

The rulers of *Animal Farm* and *Nineteen Eighty-Four*, Orwell makes clear, understand what Hitler, Stalin, and Churchill knew: that quite apart from nationalist appeal to the fatherland, Mother Russia, or whatever, human beings, in addition to comfort and pleasure, "at least intermittently, want struggle and self sacrifice, not to mention drums, flags and loyalty parades."[30] Orwell's view here is again an extension of something he wrote in *The Road to Wigan Pier*: namely, that it is only in the face of hardship and pain that claims of victory fulfill our need for the heroic vision. Of course, people do get tired of "Better an end with horror than a horror without end" (Hitler) or "Blood, sweat and tears" (Churchill), and for this reason the Inner Party is ever predicting that final "victory" is within sight.[31]

Continuous limited war does not mean, however, that total territorial conquest of each other in the future is not desired by the rulers of the superstates. On the contrary, while one of "the two aims of the Party" is to discover through science "against his will what another person is thinking, . . . the other [discernible in present states] is how to kill several hundred million people in a few seconds without giving warning beforehand." This will enable the state to satisfy its two basic aims: that of conquering the world and that of extinguishing "once and for all the possibility of independent thought." All scientific research in *Nineteen Eighty-Four* is dedicated to this end; and although no more A-bombs are dropped, because of the possibility of a retaliatory holocaust, all three superstates keep producing and stockpiling A-bombs for "the decisive opportunity which they all believe will come sooner or later." Because of the "decisive opportunity" theory, the search for new weapons continues unceasingly, even though in *Nineteen Eighty-Four* warfare has remained more or less conventional for the past forty years: "helicopters are more used than they were formerly, bombing planes have been largely superceded by self-propelled projectiles, . . . but otherwise there has been little development."[32]

The problem raised by the increasing search for new weaponry even within the framework of limited conventional war, however, is that the scientist must still be allowed to work on the belief that two and two make four, that there is an external reality *independent* of the Party. Thus, some independent thought, if not actually encouraged, has to be tolerated even within the boundaries set by the non-nuclear needs of limited war. Still, the Party, says Orwell, does exert control, insofar as limited war means limited science: "The scientist of to-day is either a mixture of psychologist and inquisitor, studying with real ordinary minuteness the meaning of facial expressions, gestures, and tones of voice and testing the truth-producing effects of drugs, shock therapy, hypnosis and physical torture; or he is chemist, physicist, or biologist concerned only with such branches of his special subject as are relevant to the taking of life."[33]

At first sight such limited science may not seem possible, in view of Orwell's own argument that once one free thought is allowed, others will follow or, conversely, that by removing the taboo on one thought, the logjam of taboos will burst. That a tunnel-visioned science devoted only to war is possible is evident in Orwell's essay, "What is Science?" Here we are reminded of the inability of many scientists to hold out against nationalism. He points out, for example, that while Hitler had probably destroyed the long-range promise of science in Germany, there were nevertheless large numbers of German scientists who were very willing to produce the weapons for the Nazi cause and that without these scientists Germany's rampage could not have gone as far as it did.[34]

The point is simply that although knowledge of objective truth may be allowed to humans, this is no guarantee that the broad *world* view this allows will cause them to act humanely rather than to surrender themselves to a narrow nationalist view. Of course, as Orwell pointed out in 1945, some do act humanely, taking the wider view and refusing to limit their work to nationalist purpose if their research is aimed toward the destruction of people rather than toward their preservation.[35] By their example alone, such researchers can disseminate the idea of unlimited ideas—of a world free of perverted science. The question for a totalitarian state is how to contain such individuals, how to permit a sense of objective truth to exist among scientists (who, unlike the artist, are considered essential) and yet prevent the growth of a "world view" that causes some scientists to perceive the reality beyond that of the Party.

In *Nineteen Eighty-Four* the Inner Party's answer is to blinker the vision of scientists through controlling their language, and thereby their thoughts. This, of course, means the need for a language specially designed for science—called the "C" vocabulary of Newspeak. While the "A" vocabulary consists of words that are necessary for business transactions and everyday living, from drinking to riding in the tube (subway) and the "B" vocabulary consists of words made to serve the Party's political ends, the "C" vocabulary consists "entirely of scientific and technical terms" that have been stripped of "undesirable meanings."

Very few of the C words had any currency either in everyday speech or in political speech. Any scientific worker or technician could find all the words he needed in the list devoted to his own speciality, but he seldom had more than a smattering of the words occurring in the other lists. Only a very few words were common to all lists, and there was no vocabulary expressing the function of Science as a habit of mind, or a method of thought, irrespective of its particular branches. There was, indeed, no word for "Science," any meaning that it could possibly bear being already sufficiently covered by the word *Ingsoc*.[36]

For the Party, such a vocabulary, like the other two, is an ideal way of exerting state control over the idea of objective truth. Leaks of objective truth do occur, however, even beyond the scientific community. Winston Smith, "just once in his life, . . . had possessed—*after* the event . . . concrete, unmistakable evidence of an act of falsification . . . like a fossil bone. . . . He had held it [an old newspaper clipping] between his fingers for as long as thirty seconds" before he put it in the "memory hole"[37] in the wall from which a stream of air would transport it to destruction in the great furnaces of the Ministry of Truth.

This incident demonstrates that the use of Newspeak, indeed, of any new language, is not enough in itself to alter the past, that language is merely an auxiliary technique of thought control. Above all else, one has to learn to control one's memory. "To make sure that all written records agree with the orthodoxy of the moment is merely a mechanical act. But it is also necessary to *remember* that events happened in the desired manner. And if it is necessary to rearrange one's memories or to tamper with written records then it is necessary to *forget* that one had done so."[38] If one is to succeed in this, the trick, as Smith realizes, is to apply the process of doublethink on itself —that is, to lie to yourself that you are not lying. The process finally becomes intuitive and is similar to trying to think of someone's name: the harder you try, the longer the name will be forgotten. This latter experience is unconscious, but doublethink is a conscious attempt to be unconscious, like thinking of everything at once in order to think of nothing—a case of overload destroying the fuse of memory, which would otherwise illuminate the past. Consequently, you become unconscious of the act of deception just performed.[39] It is an attempt to erase memory, never to forget the Inner Party's central tenet that the past is infinitely changeable, to believe the Party's claim that it invented airplanes, to believe its fantastic claims of overfulfilled production quotas, and thus to believe that reality exists only in the mind of the Party and "is not external."[40]

Smith, however, clinging to his individuality, being "the last man," resists the deception of the Party, even though he daily becomes part of that deception himself when he casually alters production figures as part of his job at the Ministry of Truth. In particular, he clings to the layman's belief in science—at least in a reality beyond the Party—by clinging to memories of natural laws that are not mutable. He recalls (indeed, cultivates) the memory that "stones are hard, water is wet, objects unsupported fall towards the earth's centre."[41] His determination to keep such things firmly in mind while at a desk job is a recognition of Orwell's belief, expressed in *The Road to Wigan Pier,* that once you stop using your hands, then, with the advance of science, you lose a large part of your consciousness.[42] It was, no doubt, one of the reasons he loved gardening.

Winston's spirit of resistance, his quest to assure himself of a reality that is not just beyond the Party but of another time, is captured in his visit to a small shop in the prole quarter of town. He picks up a lump of glass, at the heart of which there is "a strange, pink, convoluted object." Upon inquiry Winston discovers from the old shopkeeper that it is something called "coral." What attracts Winston to the object, more than its beauty, is its "uselessness."[43] Reminding us of Orwell's declaration that "so long as I remain alive and well I shall continue . . . to love the surface of the earth, and to take pleasure in solid objects and scraps of useless information,"[44] Winston buys the lump of glass immediately. What fascinates him most of all, like the socialist in *Wigan Pier* who shamefully confessed to Orwell that he liked horses, is "the air it seemed to possess of belonging to an age quite different from the present. . . . It was a queer thing, even a compromising thing, for a Party member to have in his possession.

Anything old, . . . anything beautiful, was always vaguely suspect." Above all, Winston's resistance to the notion that reality is what the Party says it to be is the manifestation of Smith's lingering belief that *"freedom is the freedom to say that two plus two make four. If that is granted, all else follows."*[45]

Such resistance is pitted, however, against the subtle arguments of interrogator O'Brien. To the latter's claim that the earth is only as old as the Party, Winston protests, arguing that there are bones and fossils long predating people. O'Brien asks, "Have you ever seen those bones, Winston? Of course not. Nineteenth century biologists invented them. . . . Outside man there is nothing."[46]

In presenting O'Brien's argument in terms of "who has seen the wind?" Orwell paradoxically reveals Smith's vulnerability, and our vulnerability, to unscientific argument through revealing our blind acceptance of a wide range of "scientific facts" with proofs that lie beyond our relatively narrow experience. He shows how much of what we believe, particularly in science, is accepted on faith—solely on the authority of "experts." In this sense, Orwell wrote, "Shaw is right. This *is* a credulous age."[47]

Indeed, as early as 1935 Orwell has Dorothy Hare (in *A Clergyman's Daughter*) entertaining O'Brien's thesis that reality is not external: "The truism that all real happenings are in the mind struck her more forcibly than ever before."[48] That Dorothy Hare's truism is so seriously questioned by Winston Smith in *Nineteen Eighty-Four*, fourteen years later, marks a significant maturation in Orwell. It reveals his concern with the ever-present danger that in overemphasizing the cerebral at the expense of the physical, the things we can feel, we run the risk of disbelieving the evidence of our senses—that in the full meaning of the phrase, we lose *touch* with reality. If this happens, we are already halfway to accepting O'Brien's claim that "there is nothing that we could not do. Invisibility, levitation—anything. . . . We make the laws of Nature" and that "whatever the Party holds to be truth, *is* truth."[49]

That Winston Smith is a "flaw in the pattern" and holds out against such claims (or at least, holds out longer than most) is due largely to his inability either to control his thought through doublethink or to break the old habit of thinking in Oldspeak, even though he rewrites history in Newspeak. As we have already seen, it is not that he dislikes his work of altering Oldspeak in the Ministry of Truth. On the contrary, "Winston's greatest pleasure in life was in his work." Like Orwell, who had worked in the propaganda section at the B.B.C. and who thought that had the regime been devoted to a better cause, he would have enjoyed nothing better than being one of the Gestapo specialists who track down authors through painstaking studies of style, Winston finds that regardless of the purpose of the job, there were jobs "so difficult and intricate that you could lose yourself in them."[50]

Winston's difficulty, however, is that so long as he clings to the old concept of objective truth rather than the Party's stark *"black-white"* vision of the world, he cannot willingly give himself over to Newspeak. His fellow worker, Syme, warns him of the danger: " 'You haven't a real appreciation of Newspeak, Winston,' he said almost sadly. 'Even when you write it you're still thinking in Oldspeak. I've read some of those pieces that you write in *The Times* occasionally. They're good enough, but they're translations. In your heart you'd prefer to stick to Oldspeak, with all its vagueness and its useless shades of meaning.' "[51]

Winston knows that Syme is right: unable to accept the Party's concept of reality, he cannot accept its language or Syme's vision that in another sixty years or so, no one will be living who can understand Oldspeak—language as we know it today. Still, the totalitarian state does not maintain total control over dissenting opinions by language alone. When lies fail there is always terror, and terror works. This is the lesson with which Orwell, the ex-imperialist policeman and fugitive from the Communist police, ends *Nineteen Eighty-Four*. His point is not that the instigators of terror always win, but that they win more often than is generally believed or more often than we want to admit.[52]

"REPORT YOURSELF." "Go . . . REPORT YOURSELF AGAIN!" . . . I was in a world where it was *not possible* for me to be good. . . . It was possible . . . to commit a sin without knowing that you committed it, without wanting to commit it, and without being able to avoid it," and "Whenever one had a chance to suck up, one did suck up, and at the first smile one's hatred turned into a sort of cringing love."[53] This is not the political prisoner Winston Smith, cowering before the Party's electric shock, "cured" by being made "sane" by O'Brien;[54] it is young Eric Blair being "cured" of bedwetting at St. Cyprian's. Orwell adds,

There was a boy named Beacham, with no brains to speak of, but evidently in acute need of a scholarship. Sambo was flogging him towards the goal as one might do with a foundered horse. He went up for a scholarship at Uppingham, came back with a consciousness of having done badly, and a day or two later received a severe beating for idleness. "I wish I'd had that caning before I went up for the exam," he said sadly—a remark which I felt to be contemptible, but which I perfectly well understood. . . . It is a mistake to think such methods do not work. They work very well for their special purpose. . . . The boys themselves believed in its efficacy.[55]

While at times it is risky to try to tie in an author's childhood experiences to his or her work as an adult and wrong-headed to confuse all coercion with terror, the passages cited are nevertheless important in following Orwell's concern with the subject of terror. They deserve attention—not simply because "Such Were the Joys" was written two years after *Animal Farm* and shortly before *Nineteen Eighty-Four*, thus making the connection between his childhood experience and his adult writing more tenable—but because in reflecting the schoolboy's passive acceptance of his lot, they point directly to the psychological background of *Nineteen Eighty-Four*. They testify to the fact that without a developed sense of history, one is particularly vulnerable to a reign of terror, if for no other reason than that one has no *knowledge* of anything else.[56] He wrote: "The weakness of the child [like those pupils of Dorothy Hare and the adults of *Nineteen Eighty-Four*] is that it starts with a blank sheet. It neither understands nor questions the society in which it lives; . . . other people can work upon it, infecting it with the sense of inferiority and the dread of offending against mysterious, terrible laws."[57]

We recall that Orwell also wrote of his own school days at St. Cyprians: "I did not question the prevailing standards. . . . There were no others."[58] As we saw earlier, it is precisely because of the lack of standards of comparison that the proles fail to realize that they are oppressed. In such circumstances it is hardly surprising that the men of terror win, not now and then, here and there, but everywhere and always; for a people devoid of history is a people unused to the very *idea* of change—let alone revolt.

Nevertheless, despite all the awesome evidence of perverted power about him, Winston Smith continues to resist, and this is what makes him exceptional, then finally heroic. Daily aware of the highly disciplined, *institutionalized* attack by the Party on the concept of objective truth, (which differs from the haphazard, if voluntary, attack that Orwell believed was launched by the intellectuals in the Thirties), Winston Smith, having resisted the techniques of deception, now resists the techniques of sheer terror. He does so despite his knowledge that as a member of the Party, his whole life is under the watchful gaze of Thought Police. He can resist, at least for a time, because he draws strength from the belief, held earlier by Dorothy Hare in *A Clergyman's Daughter*, that whatever happens externally— "even when you're practically starving—it doesn't *change* anything inside you."[59] Thus, he believes that "the inner heart, whose workings were mysterious even to yourself, remained impregnable."[60] Iron bars may end your political freedom, but your metaphysical freedom, the freedom to think what you will inside the cell, is indestructible. O'Brien destroys this inner freedom, however, and it is this that is the ultimate nightmare, the final tragedy of *Nineteen Eighty-Four*.

The method O'Brien uses to break Winston (because "it is intolerable to us [the Party] that an erroneous thought should exist anywhere in the world") is yet another extension of the Party's attack upon the concept of external reality beyond the Party. While there is nothing new in terror being used as a means of coercion, the new and terrifying element in Oceania is that terror is constant. It is constant because there is no distinction made between the dissenting thought and the dissenting act. "Thoughtcrime," or, in Newspeak, "crimethink," means death. The techniques of terror in Orwell's last work, such as the daily hate session, are new only insofar as they employ the latest gadgetry of a perverted science. As the following passages show, *Nineteen Eighty-Four* is merely the culmination of Orwell's concern that the power of orthodoxy, aided by increasing centralization and science, would eventually smother the individual.[61]

It was a voice that sounded as if it could go on for a fortnight without stopping. It's a ghastly thing, really, to have a sort of human barrel-organ shooting propaganda at you by the hour. The same thing over and over again. Hate, hate, hate. Let's all get together and have a good hate. Over and over. It gives you the feeling that something has got inside your skull and is hammering down on your brain. But for a moment, with my eyes shut, I managed to turn the tables on him. I got inside *his* skull. . . . I felt what he was feeling. . . . Smash! Right in the middle! The bones cave in like an eggshell and what was a face a minute ago is just a great big blob of strawberry jam. Smash! There goes another. That's what's in his mind, waking and sleeping, and the more he thinks of it the more he likes it. . . .

The world we're going down into, the kind of hate-world, slogan-world. . . . [It is the world of] the rubber truncheons. The secret cells where the electric light burns night and day, and the detectives watching you while you sleep; . . . the processions and the posters with enormous faces, and the crowds of a million people all cheering for the Leader till they deafen themselves into thinking that they really worship him, and all the time, underneath, they hate him so that they want to puke.[62]

This is not Winston Smith in *Nineteen Eighty-Four* but George Bowling speaking in England just before the Second World War. Following is Winston Smith in Oceania in the "after-war": "The next moment a hideous grinding speech, as of some monstrous machine running without oil, burst from the telescreen at the end of the room. . . . The Hate had started."

In its second minute the Hate rose to a frenzy. . . . In a lucid moment Winston found that he was shouting with the others and kicking his heel against the rung of the chair. . . . It was impossible to avoid joining in . . . a hideous ecstasy of fear and vindictiveness, a desire to kill, to torture, to smash faces in with a sledge-hammer, . . . turning one even against one's will into a grimacing, screaming lunatic. And yet the rage that one felt was an abstract, undirected emotion which could be switched from one object to another like the flame of a blowlamp. . . . At one moment Winston's hatred was not turned against Goldstein at all, but on the contrary, against Big Brother, the Party, . . . the Thought Police; . . . yet the very next instant . . . his secret loathing of Big Brother changed into adoration.[63]

Despite their similarity these passages also show that while the gadgetry of science may coerce, it is, in the final analysis, unreliable as a means of permanent conversion, for quite naturally there is the tendency of victims to turn periodically against their indoctrinators or torturers. In order for the totalitarian Party's members to feel totally secure, they must have total conversion. This, as O'Brien knows, involves near-total removal from external reality so that contrary to Winston's belief in its inviolability, the will—the inner, private self— can be broken down as much as the body. So long as the mind has some evidence of a reality beyond the Party, it has a saving point on which to focus amid the vertigo of drugs and electric shock.

In describing this process of breaking a prisoner down, which begins for Winston at the moment of arrest, Orwell once again demonstrates his grasp of the concrete details of subjugation. The moment Winston and his girlfriend, Julia, are arrested by the Thought Police in the old pawn shop, which they had thought was a hideaway from

Party surveillance, we are given an unmistakable sign that Winston—the last man, the last autonomous individual—is doomed. His end is signalled when the glass paperweight with the piece of coral embedded in it is smashed by one of the policemen. As the coral, "a tiny crinkle of pink," rolls across the floor, Winston thinks, "How small it always was!"[64] Having failed previously in a conversation with an old prole to capture a sense of a past that was so different from existence under the Party, Winston had found in the paperweight a "visible" and "solid" reminder of that past. Its very existence, *solid* evidence of an alternative way of life, had refuted the Party's claim that the only reality was theirs and that it existed only in the present.

Now the tangible representation of another reality is broken. It is the first step in breaking Winston, because it is a break with the past. The second step is for O'Brien to follow the rule of thumb for all police, isolation of the prisoner. In this case Smith, after having been taken from a large common cell, is put into a "high-ceilinged windowless" confinement chamber with glittering walls where (as Bowling predicted) the light burns constantly, quickly removing one interned there ever farther from a sense of external reality through eliminating the distinction between night and day: "He did not know where he was. Presumably he was in the Ministry of Love; but there was no way of making certain. . . . There were four telescreens, one in each wall. . . . It might be twenty-four hours since he had eaten, it might be thirty-six. He still did not know, probably never would know, whether it had been morning or evening when they arrested him."[65]

Before the final isolation some other Party members, now prisoners, pass through the common cell, but their confusion about time only adds to Winston's. Indeed, their passage further isolates him psychologically. When Ampleforth, the poet, is brought in, Winston asks him what he has done. Ampleforth answers, "There is only one offence is there not?" Likewise, when Parsons, Winston's dim-witted fellow tenant from Victory Mansions, is brought in and Winston asks what he has been arrested for, Parsons quickly replies, "Thoughtcrime!" The two most striking things about the new "political" prisoners are Ampleforth's ready acceptance of the charge, as if it were as legitimate as a nonpolitical charge such as murder, and Parsons' abject servility.

"Of course I'm guilty!" cried Parsons. . . . "You don't think the Party would arrest an innocent man, do you? . . . Thoughtcrime is a dreadful thing, old man. . . . It's insidious. . . . Do you know how it got hold of me? In my sleep! . . . There I was, working away, trying to do my bit—never knew I had any bad stuff in my mind at all. And then I started talking in my sleep. . . . Do you know what I'm going to say to them when I go up before the tribunal? 'Thank you,' I'm going to say, 'thank you for saving me before it was too late.' "

"Who denounced you?" said Winston.

"It was my little daughter. . . . Pretty smart for a nipper of seven, eh? . . . I'm proud of her. It shows I brought her up in the right spirit, anyway."[66]

The widespread acquiescence of the victims, like the subservience of the animals in *Animal Farm* who publicly confess to crimes they did not commit, demonstrates how alone Smith is and why he is "the last man in Europe," a phrase that served as *Nineteen Eighty-Four's* working title. It also shows how a totalitarian regime, through appealing to the normal need to expiate guilt, can manage to maintain a steady stream of arrests. These can then be used to justify the need for continuing surveillance and terror. In such a situation, the leader replaces God. "Everyone is washed clean," says O'Brien of those who are tortured and interrogated. He tells Winston about three prisoners in particular: "I saw them gradually worn down, whimpering, grovelling, weeping—and in the end it was not with pain or fear, only with penitence. By the time we had finished with them they were only the shells of men. There was nothing left in them except sorrow for what they had done and love of Big Brother. It was touching to see how they loved him. They begged to be shot quickly, so that they could die while their minds were still clean."[67]

That Big Brother has replaced God is obvious throughout the novel, but what O'Brien exemplifies and later reveals to Winston Smith about the new totalitarianism is that the administrators understand that "hatred" is no more exhausting than "love."[68] This is the novel's final salvo against the belief that evil men must necessarily be worn down by good. The success of terror in *Nineteen Eighty-Four* is clearly an attempt by Orwell to counter the tenacious Western, and more specifically English, belief that "it can't happen here"—to counter the "bosh about our natural genius for 'muddling through' "[69] and the almost mystical conviction that "a régime founded on slavery *must* collapse."[70] The terror is especially heightened by the fact that the victims simply vanish without trace—always at night: "The great purges [like the Stalinist purges] involving thousands of people, with public trials of traitors and thought-criminals who made abject confession of their crimes and were afterwards executed, were special show-pieces not occurring oftener than once in a couple of years. More commonly, people who had incurred the displeasure of the Party simply disappeared and were never heard of again."[71]

Though Winston Smith, unlike his fellows, resists feelings of guilt because he clings to a sense of objective truth, he does share their common fate. Like them, too, he suffers from the common and constant anxiety—the added terror—that emanates from the fact that in Oceania there is no codified set of rules to which you can refer as a guide to acceptable, or at least safe, behavior. There is "no law" in Oceania. When Smith opens a book in a hidden corner and begins his secret diary, he is only "reasonably" certain that he faces death. Because thoughts and actions "are not formally forbidden," your sense of morality is not fixed, as it was in the medieval Church, for example, or under a modern legal code. The "hole" that Orwell said was left by the failure of religion remains unfilled. The result is permanent anxiety—the condition of our age—an anxiety that becomes even worse when confronted by the Party's assumption that if a person "is naturally orthodox, . . . he will in all circumstances know, without taking thought, what is the true belief or the desirable emotion."[72]

The best possible antidote to such anxiety is close adherence to *"crimestop, blackwhite,* and *doublethink,"* to be "unable to think too deeply on any subject whatever." This is not a total cure for anxiety or total insurance against arrest, but it will at least insulate you to some extent against the lack of formal rules and the intrusion of contradictions suggested by external reality. It is in this sense that ignorance *is* strength.

In a way, the world-view of the Party imposed itself most successfully on people incapable of understanding it. They could be made to accept the most flagrant violations of reality, because they never fully grasped the enormity of what was demanded of them, and were not sufficiently interested in public events to notice what was happening. By lack of understanding they remained sane. They simply swallowed everything, and what they swallowed did them no harm, because it left no residue behind, just as a grain of corn will pass undigested through the body of a bird.[73]

Quite apart from the fact that the absence of formal rules encourages such frantic loyalty to the Party, it also makes it easier for the state to arrest you without having to justify its action by reference to

law, to any specific charge other than the catchall, "Thoughtcrime."
The absence of formal rules also protects the state from charges of
violating the rules of what had once been English socialism. If there
are no rules, no stated civil liberties, how can the state violate them?
Thus, there is no legal requirement for the Party to justify the gross
inequalities of "Ingsoc," to explain why it is that oligarchical collectivism is more oligarchical than collectivist, or why 85 percent of the
population (the proles) is in servitude to the Party, or why Big Brother
is Napoleon writ large. Consequently, Orwell shows how the absence
of written law joins corruption of language in making rapid shifts of
policy more acceptable to the general public.

Much of the reason for Winston Smith's resistance is his rejection
of this world without laws. Because of this he finds comfort, indeed
seeks comfort, in the laws of nature. In these, at least, there is a
sanity, an understandable order and purpose that can be discerned
in the hardness of a rock, the falling of the rain, the flowering of
shrubs. Even his rendezvous with Julia in the countryside becomes,
in his flight from the present, a journey back to the old reality like
the attempted escapes of George Bowling, Gordon Comstock, and
John Flory before him. Amid the colorful abandon of tree and flower,
in what he wistfully calls the "Golden Country," he undergoes a
"slow shock of recognition": "He knew it by sight. . . . On the opposite
side the boughs of elm trees swayed just perceptibly in the breeze,
and their leaves stirred faintly in dense masses like women's hair.
Surely somewhere nearby, but out of sight, there must be a stream
with green pools where dace were swimming."[74]

This, of course, is a return to the hidden pool of Bowling's youth,
the secret fishing hole behind Binfield House. As Flory had fled the
stifling atmosphere of the Club, heading into a riot of jungle to be
refreshed and cleansed by a private hidden pool, as Comstock heads
into the country with his girl to escape the city where he has had
visions of heads stuck in gas-ovens and future wars, and as Bowling
retreats to the country from the "prison" of conformity on Ellesmere
Road and his visions of the "after-war, . . . the slogans, . . . the enormous faces," so Smith flees the *reality* of Airstrip One, of what the
others had only envisioned with horror. Paradoxically, however, in
fleeing this reality he does not flee from consciousness, but seeks to
increase it in his experience of the solid, visible objects of the natural
world.

Winston feels so oppressed by the world of terror that even having sex with Julia while on the country outing takes on a meaning beyond pleasure. It is an act that is not yet fully controlled by the Party, for as Julia says, "all this marching up and down and cheering and waving flags is simply sex gone sour." Winston sees that sex is not completely dominated by the Party, despite the fact that all emotions have been so tainted by the Party's terror that even he can no longer look at Julia's nakedness with "pure lust," as one could have in the old days. In these circumstances, sexual intercourse for Julia and Winston, as well as being physically pleasing, becomes a highly conscious rebellion, a "political act" against a political orthodoxy that relies heavily on turning sexual energy into hysterical political obedience. "When you make love you're using up energy; and afterwards you feel happy and don't give a damn for anything. They [the Party] can't bear you to feel like that. ... If you're happy inside yourself, why should you get excited about Big Brother and the Three-year Plans and the Two Minutes Hate . . . ?"[75]

Sex is grudgingly permitted because of the Party's need to procreate,[76] but thereafter the family tie is essentially destroyed by the early psychic separation of child from parent through the systematic training of the Hitler Youth–like organization called the "Spies." It is through this organization, as demonstrated in the case of Parsons and his daughter, that Party surveillance as an instrument of terror is extended to the family keyhole. Again, this act of state interference is not a wildly futuristic vision, but a mere extension on a massive scale of present behaviour by some governments.

Winston Smith's private rebellion against such gross invasion of privacy is effected, among other acts, by his secret affair with Julia (also a Party member) and by the keeping of a diary through which he can constantly remind himself of what is in front of his nose, that "sanity is not statistical," that even if you are a "minority of one," still there is "truth and . . . untruth." In the final analysis, however, he is doomed because in his cell he is alone—because he has found privacy, and not in spite of it. O'Brien makes the point, "Alone—free—the human being is always defeated. It must be so, because every human being is doomed to die, which is the greatest of all failures. [O'Brien then offers escape.] "But . . . if he can make complete, utter submission, if he can escape from his identity, if he can merge himself in the Party so that he *is* the Party, then he is all-powerful and immortal."[77]

In the absence of religion, most specifically the absence of Christianity, O'Brien's invitation to partake with others of a strong sense of immortality makes a powerful appeal. Its appeal is to that latent need, which Orwell believes is in all of us, to believe in *something*— to share at least in some sense of "brotherhood." Indeed, it is Winston's suspicion that O'Brien belongs to the forbidden "brotherhood" of Oceania that first lures him into betraying his heresies to O'Brien. The fact that totalitarian regimes implicitly appeal to the subliminal desire for brotherhood explains for Orwell why the Soviet Union, with all its cruelty and terror, could win over "people like the Dean of Canterbury" who were dispirited by the waning attractiveness of their own organizations. Indeed, the appeal of seeking immortality through Party identification is the basis for Orwell's belief that "power-worship" is "the new religion of Europe."[78]

At first, Winston Smith, like John Flory before him, refuses any such invitation to submerge his individuality in exchange for the company of others. Gradually, however, through a nightmarish torture of isolation, drugs, beatings, electric shock, and incessant questioning, he is worn down to "a bowed, grey-coloured, skeleton-like thing" that screams and rolls on the floor in its own blood and vomit, whimpering for mercy. His obedience to the Party passes from that of coercion to an obedience of his own will. After a time, without O'Brien standing over him, alone in his cell, bereft of the simplest debate that might question his abject surrender, he takes up a pencil in his hand and clumsily begins to write: "FREEDOM IS SLAVERY," "TWO AND TWO MAKE FIVE," and "GOD IS POWER."[79]

Finally, the only remaining shield—personal loyalty, his feeling for Julia, his last memory of reality, of truth beyond the party—is shattered. It comes when he is dreaming about the "Golden Country," Bowling's old vision of peace and security amid a madly changing world. "He could feel the short springy turf under his feet and the gentle sunshine on his face. At the edge of the field were the elm trees, faintly stirring, and somewhere beyond that was the stream where the dace lay in the green pools under the willows."[80] He wakes up suddenly, calling out Julia's name. Immediately realizing that the telescreens will have heard him, will have recorded that while he had surrendered to the Party, he was still secretly dreaming. "He lay back on the bed and tried to compose himself. What had he done? How many years had he added to his servitude by that moment of weakness? . . . He had hoped to keep the inner heart inviolate." Immediately, the guards come for him, and the last morsels of his private self are irreversibly purged from him in Room 101. Herein lies the ultimate terror. Physically, it is not an unusual room, but psychologically, it is the most feared of all. As O'Brien explains, it is the room wherein each individual's worst fear comes alive. For some "it may be . . . death by fire, or by drowning, . . . or fifty other deaths. There are cases where it is some quite trivial thing, not even fatal."[81] For Winston Smith, as with Orwell, it is the fear of rats.[82] Strapped to a chair, he sees the cage coming nearer and nearer. "Winston heard a succession of shrill crics . . . [and] he fought furiously against his panic. . . . Suddenly the foul musty odour of the brutes struck his nostrils. There was a violent convulsion of nausea inside him. . . . Everything had gone black. For an instant he was insane, a screaming animal. Yet he came out of the blackness clutching an idea. There was one and only one way to save himself. He must interpose another human being . . . between himself and the rats." As the pink hands and whiskers of one of the rats press against the wire, Winston screams, "Do it to Julia! Do it to Julia! Not me. Julia! . . . Not me! . . . Not me!"[83]

At this moment the lingering vestiges of *individual* pride and dignity are extinguished forever in Winston Smith. O'Brien has cured him of rebellion; he has, as promised, made Winston "sane." Winston now belongs totally to the Party. Released, he is a walking zombie awaiting death—the bullet in the back of the neck that will surely come. Having satisfied the Party, having fallen subservient to the terror that the Party uses, not for the accumulation of wealth, but for the sheer "intoxication of power, constantly increasing and constantly growing subtler," Winston is left alone after his public confessions to await his end quietly. Drinking his Victory gin, his mind back in the Ministry of Love, "with everything forgiven, his soul white as snow," he gazes up at the enormous poster of the Leader. "Forty years it had taken him to learn what kind of smile was hidden beneath the dark moustache. O cruel, needless misunderstanding! O stubborn, self-willed exile from the loving breast! Two gin-scented tears trickled down the sides of his nose. But it was all right, everything was all right, the struggle was finished. He had won the victory over himself. He loved Big Brother."[84]

So Smith's destruction is the final illustration of what Orwell, in 1944, considered to be one of the most dangerous fallacies in nontotalitarian countries: the belief (like that of Dorothy Hare) that under a dictatorship "you can be free inside." It is the belief that "despite the face of the Leader, four feet wide" glaring all about you, "up in the attics the secret enemies of the régime [like Smith] can record their thoughts in perfect freedom." It is a belief, writes Orwell, that does not take into account the fundamental horror of isolation, does not understand that if Defoe had really lived on a desert island, he could not have written Robinson Crusoe, "nor would he have wanted to."[85] Winston Smith's diary did not keep him free inside—at best, it was only temporarily therapeutic. No matter who you are—Winston, as in Churchill, or Smith, as in the common man—you will break.

Finally, what Orwell tells us is that quite apart from the more efficient use of terror and totalitarian methods of deception that help to undermine the desire for intellectual liberty, there is a much more insidious power at work. Though not realized by Dorothy Hare, Winston Smith, or the painter who told Orwell in 1944 that he would be a pacifist under a German occupation "so that I can get on with my work," the fundamental enemy of intellectual freedom, says Orwell, is the attempt to isolate oneself from one's fellows. The occasional need for solitude notwithstanding, he argues that while it is possible to work without thinking, "it is almost impossible to think without talking,"[86] which implies the company of others. Of course, once you talk you expose your thoughts. In a totalitarian society this means putting your political freedom at risk, for you do not know what thoughts will follow. Moreover, because those in power do not know what will follow, they will try to forestall heresies by refusing to declare *any* subject politically "neutral," as exemplified by Stalin's and Hitler's pronouncements on "decadent" art: if there is no neutral ground, even in the state's view of art, you are either "for" or "against" the state. On the one hand, Orwell argues, the risk of communicating with your fellows must be taken if your intellectual and political freedom, and ultimately your humanity, is to have any chance of survival; yet the story of Winston Smith, who tried to live in his own world for a time but then sought the uninhibited company of Julia, though one of bravery, is ultimately one of defeat. The totality of his defeat is captured in the sentence "He loved Big Brother."

For Orwell, however, all is not lost to the totalitarian state. As the animals, unaware of their collective strength, had inspired Orwell to write *Animal Farm*, Winston Smith is inspired to write that "if there is hope, . . . it lies in the proles."[87] It is a return to Orwell's faith in the virtues of the working class, but the question for those in the servitude of the totalitarian state is, what evidence is there for such faith?

Orwell argues that the proles in *Nineteen Eighty-Four* do have weapons with which to fight the totalitarian state, whether or not they realize it. The first is their numerical superiority. Physically, they are as capable of rebellion as the whipped animals that had inspired *Animal Farm*. Constituting 85 percent of the population, "they needed only to rise up and shake themselves like a horse shaking off flies. If they chose they could blow the Party to pieces tomorrow morning." The problem, however, is that the proles fail to realize their potential for revolt. The problem is a lack of *any* kind of political consciousness, and *"until they become conscious they will never rebel, and until after they have rebelled they cannot become conscious."* Politically, they are the direct descendants of the coal miners of Wigan: "It was not desirable that the proles should have strong political feelings. All that was required of them was a primitive patriotism which could be appealed to whenever it was necessary to make them accept longer working hours or shorter rations."[88]

Unlike the members of the Party, however, the proles' consciousness is not deliberately blunted by active ideological indoctrination—at least, not by anything beyond the standard newscasts. Rather, it is blunted by the Party's perpetuation of what Orwell sees as the "ancestral" rut of the poorest British worker: "They were born, they grew up in the gutters, they went to work at twelve, they passed through a brief blossoming-period of beauty and sexual desire, they married at twenty, they were middle-aged at thirty, they died, for the most part, at sixty. Heavy physical work, the care of home and children, petty quarrels with neighbours, films, football, beer, and, above all, gambling, filled up the horizon of their minds."[89] It is as if the early sections of *The Road to Wigan Pier* have been transported to the world of Airstrip One. Even in Victory Mansions the haunting image of the haggard, old-before-her-time housewife in *Wigan* reappears as we are introduced to Mrs. Parsons, "a woman with lined face and wispy hair, fiddling helplessly with a blocked waste-pipe."[90]

Still there is hope. Just as the Party fails to realize the potential of verse as a subversive weapon, insofar as traditional rhyme forms can bring to mind alternative ways of life, it likewise fails to see the danger inherent in allowing the proles to gamble. While gambling may blunt political consciousness of inequality by offering prizes as a sop to the underprivileged and offering them hope of bettering their lot, the very presence of the concept of "luck," of "accident," runs counter to the concept of infallible planning by an infallible Party.

It may well be, of course, that until Ministries of Information in totalitarian governments perfect their methods of deception, of being able to rationalize everything that happens (including the failure of five-year plans), the government will tolerate the belief in luck as a convenient explanation of those events that contradict the state's supposed infallibility.[91] The danger to the state, however, is that though the concepts of luck and planning may reasonably coexist, the belief in luck, even if it does not erode belief in any person's supposed political infallibility, may well suggest the idea of a reality beyond the control of the state. If ever this idea were to become widely held, then the power, if not the infallibility, of the state would most likely be widely questioned. Therein lie the seeds of rebellion.

As in the case of the revolutionary potential of verse, however, the question in *Nineteen Eighty-Four* is how, if ever, the proles will become conscious enough to recognize, and organize against, the massive deceit that is being worked upon them. Indeed, they may not—the prognosis of *Nineteen Eighty-Four* is not good—but if there is hope in this matter, it lies in something that the proles have that no one else in Airstrip One possesses, and this is a strong sense of loyalty. This is not a public loyalty, not a loyalty to the Party that has to adapt to each new policy, but a "fixed" loyalty to each other. By contrast, the Party members are marked by a lack of simple friend-ship for each other and by an acceptance of cruelty that reveals the divorce between the heart and mind that George Bowling feared would mark the streamlined men from modern Europe. This differ-ence between the proletarian and Party members, between the "Low" and "Middle-High" strata of society, is demonstrated early in the novel, when Smith describes the outrage with which a prole mother objects to a particularly bloody and violent movie scene:

There was a wonderful shot of a child's arm going up up up right into the air a helicopter with a camera in its nose must have followed it up and there was a lot of applause from the party seats but a woman down in the prole part of the house suddenly started kicking up a fuss and shouting they didn't oughter of showed it in front of kids . . . until the police turned her out i don't suppose anything hap-pened to her nobody cares what the proles say typical *prole reaction.*[92]

Similarly for Winston Smith, the Party member, the song he heard ("It was only an 'opeless fancy, . . .") is nothing more than some

lines turned out from a versificator, "without any human interven-
tion whatever," but the proles quickly adopt it and the washerwoman near Winston's and Julia's hideaway infuses it with such
emotion that for Winston she turns "the dreadful rubbish into an
almost pleasant sound. . . . It struck him as a curious fact that he had
never heard a member of the Party singing alone and spontaneously.
It would even have seemed slightly unorthodox, a dangerous eccentricity, like talking to oneself."[93]

It is the recurrence of this song, the fact that it outlives the Hate
song, that makes us realize why hope lies in the proles. Unlike a
Party member, who "is expected to have no private emotions," the
prole has preserved the old emotions, such as personal loyalty and
this keeps the prole class more "human" than the Party.

> They had not become hardened inside. They had held on to the primitive
> emotions which he [Smith] himself had to re-learn by conscious effort. . . .
> Everywhere stood the same solid unconquerable figure, made monstrous
> by work and childbearing, toiling from birth to death and still singing. Out
> of those mighty loins a race of conscious beings must one day come. You
> were the dead; theirs was the future.[94]

Contrary to what Goldstein has said, that the proles will be incapable
of rebelling because "there is no way in which discontent can become
articulate," the songs for the proles incorporate the primitive emotions and do articulate, however roughly, the proles' hope, though
they do not yet know it. Describing how Winston is listening to the
washerwoman sing, Orwell tells us that there are "everywhere, all
over the world, hundreds of thousands of millions of people just like
this, people ignorant of one another's existence, held apart by walls
of hatred and lies, and yet almost exactly the same—people who had
never learned to think but who were storing up in their hearts and
bellies and muscles the power that would one day overturn the
world."[95]

The proles have made the songs their own and express through
them what little individuality they have retained. Much of this *emotional*, if not intellectual, individuality results from the proles keeping touch with the reality beyond the Party through their work. You
could share in their future, Smith believed, "if you kept alive the
mind as they kept alive the body."[96] The proles' more frequent contact with the physical world through manual labor helps them in
maintaining a grip on reality and is crucial in withstanding the
onslaught of the state's deception—most specifically, Newspeak; for

(as Orwell wrote in *The English People*) "the people likeliest to use simple concrete language, and to think of metaphors that really call up a visual image [through which the *"blackwhite"* world of Newspeak can be challenged], are those in contact with physical reality."[97] It is this concretely based imagery that must invade the Party if the feeling individual is to survive. Winston sees such hope in Julia:

A thing that astonished him about her was the coarseness of her language. Party members were supposed not to swear, and Winston himself very seldom did swear, aloud, at any rate. Julia, however, seemed unable to mention the Party, and expecially the Inner Party, without using the kind of words that you saw chalked up in dripping alley-ways. He did not dislike it. It was merely one symptom of her revolt against the Party and all its ways, and somehow it seemed natural and healthy, like the sneeze of a horse that smells bad hay.[98]

Finally, then, and this is Orwell's concluding message, the battle for the future in the totalitarian society is between those who keep both heart and mind alive through keeping touch with the reality of the physical world and those who surrender heart and mind to the reality of the Party. This theme of Orwell's is best captured in the scene in which Winston tries to explain to Julia that even the past, "if it survives anywhere," lives on "in a few solid objects with no words attached to them, like that lump of glass there," and in the scene during their escape to the country:

A thrush had alighted on a bush not five metres away, almost at the level of their faces. Perhaps it had not seen them. It was in the sun, they in the shade. It spread out its wings, fitted them carefully into place again, ducked its head for a moment, as though making a sort of obeisance to the sun, and then began to pour forth a torrent of song. In the afternoon hush the volume of sound was startling. Winston and Julia clung together, fascinated. The music went on and on, minute after minute, *with astonishing variations,* never once repeating itself, almost as though the bird were deliberately showing off its virtuosity. . . . Winston watched it with a sort of vague reverence. For whom, for what, was that bird singing? No mate, no rival was watching it. What made it sit at the edge of the lonely wood and pour its music into nothingness? . . . But by degrees the flood of music drove all speculations out of his mind. It was as though it were a kind of liquid stuff that poured all over him and got mixed up with the sunlight that filtered through the leaves. He stopped thinking and merely *felt*.[99] [The italics are mine.]

This is not an injunction to stop thinking, even though we could cynically point out that it is precisely because Winston Smith thinks so much that he ends up dead. Rather, it is a clear conviction that if our minds are to withstand the electronic world, we must periodically go back to nature and to things without utilitarian value. In them and in their profusion at the simplest level, we see that although each tree is made of wood, each rock of minerals, each bird of flesh and blood, no two are exactly alike. Winston himself realizes this when he sees "some tufts of loosestrife" growing in the cracks of a cliff. "One tuft was of two colours, magenta and brick-red, apparently growing on the same root. He had never seen anything of the kind before."[100] We see at once similarity and variation—that in nature, of which we are a part, the first does not preclude the second. Nature's myriad proofs of external reality give the lie to the daily cant of fanatics of political orthodoxy and their language, which evades concrete experience of anything outside the Party's grasp.

To escape the totalitarian mentality, then, says Orwell, we must develop the habit of participating in, or at the very least observing, the physical world. In so doing we become conscious of the tree of Man, each individual needful of the same nourishment, singularly rooted yet diverse. The knowledge of such diversity in the realm of nature breeds tolerance also of diversity in the realm of politics.

At any rate, spring is here, even in London N.1, and they can't stop you enjoying it. This is a satisfying reflection. How many a time I have stood watching the toads mating, or a pair of hares having a boxing match in the young corn, and thought of all the important persons who would stop me enjoying this if they could. But luckily they can't. So long as you are not actually ill, hungry, frightened or immured in a prison or a holiday camp, spring is still spring. The atom bombs are piling up in the factories, the police are prowling through the cities, the lies are streaming from the loudspeakers, but the earth is still going round the sun, and neither the dictators nor the bureaucrats, deeply as they disapprove of the process, are able to prevent it.[101]

CHAPTER 11

O RWELL KNEW THAT LOWER BINFIELD WAS LOST FOREVER, but this did not mean that he had lost hope. In his retreat to the isolation of Jura, he did not renounce his faith in the political system he called democratic socialism. Instead, his retreat and the book that this allowed him to work on were a restatement of his pessimism about the modern age.

He believed that centralization on top of collectivization meant that power, being far less divisible than money, tends to accumulate in the hands of fewer people. This, allied with the totalitarian outlook that truth is what the Party decrees, corrupts not simply socialism but *any* political movement. In 1941 he had written, "The movement towards collectivism goes on all the time, though it takes varying forms, some hopeful, others horrible."[1] Four years later, in his review of Cyril Connolly's *Unquiet Grave,* wherein Connolly gives a resounding "No" to the claim that "man will find fulfillment only through participation in the communal life of an organized group," Orwell writes that Connolly's "error" is "in assuming that a collectivist society would destroy human individuality. The ordinary English Communist or 'fellow-traveller' makes the same assumption. . . . It does not occur to them that the so-called collectivist systems now existing only try to wipe out the individual because they are *not* really collectivist and certainly not egalitarian—because, in fact, they are a sham covering a new form of class privilege."[2] Similarly, in reviewing two books, one an attack on capitalism and the other a defense of it, Orwell wrote, regarding their common conclusion that each other's policy would end in slavery, that "the alarming thing is that they might both be right."[3] Just as every line in *Animal Farm* was aimed in support of democratic socialism and against totalitarianism, so were they directed in *Nineteen Eighty-Four*. In showing how the "horrible forms" of collectivism were not restricted to any particular section of the political spectrum—that madness could come from any direction, left or right—the focus of Orwell's writing after *Animal Farm* changed from a *leftist* revolution gained and lost through the corruptibility of power to totalitarianism, *left or right,* entrenched through the corruptibility of power.

There have been those who, after reading of the terrors of Room 101, have advanced the theory (some vehemently, others more civilly) that Orwell lost his socialist faith by the time he'd reached *Nineteen Eighty-Four*. What they have lost sight of, or do not understand, is one of the basic tenets of any creative writer, and one that Orwell asserted as early as *The Road to Wigan Pier*—namely, that to write creatively, even of tragedy, one has to possess the spirit of hope. Even Laurence Brander, for all his criticism of Orwell, understands this. He notes that the Newspeak appendix to *Nineteen Eighty-Four* and the Goldstein quotations that speak of the corruption of a socialist ideal "are full of zest and joy" and "could only have been written by a man who was reasonably well" (though he assumes, without citing any evidence, that these sections must therefore have been "written earlier").[4] Bernard Crick challenges the point that Orwell gave up his socialist belief even further by pointing out (correctly, I believe) that "pessimism" is not necessarily "defeatism" and just as sensibly noting "how much the description of Ing-Soc depends on Fascism as well as Communism."[5]

Finally, those who assert that Orwell lost his socialist faith do not understand that to recognize the dangers that face the system in which one has faith is not necessarily to lose that faith. It is the failure of some critics to recognize this that leads them into the nonsequitur that because Orwell's faith in socialism—expressed in the hope he placed in the proles—is weakly rooted, his faith is weakly held. This surely is to confuse pessimism with defeatism. Orwell knew of the power-nourished cancer within the body politic, but he also knew that remissions *do* occur—no matter how serious the prognosis may be. We may be skeptical of the basis for his hope that the proles would serve as the advance guard of a democratic socialism; indeed, insofar as we are asked to believe that 85 percent of the population, the proles, are to be ignored by the Party, *Nineteen Eighty-Four* leaves us little choice but to be skeptical of Orwell's belief. Nevertheless, we can hardly use this as a rationale for doubting the sincerity with which his belief was held.

If one is not convinced of this sincerity by the fact that as late as 1948 Orwell was still actively advocating a "Socialist United States of Europe,"[6] perhaps the following, written to Francis A. Henson of the United Automobile Workers (a labor union in the United States) less than seven months before Orwell's death, will offer the skeptic further proof:

My recent novel is NOT intended as an attack on Socialism or on the British Labour Party (of which I am a supporter) but as a show-up of the perversions to which a centralized economy is liable and which have already been partly realized in Communism and Fascism. I do not believe that the kind of society I describe necessarily *will* arrive, but I believe (allowing of course for the fact that the book is a satire) that something resembling it *could* arrive. I believe also that totalitarian ideas have taken root in the minds of intellectuals everywhere, and I have tried to draw these ideas out to their logical consequences. The scene of the book is laid in Britain in order to emphasize that the English-speaking races are not innately better than anyone else and that totalitarianism, *if not fought against,* could triumph anywhere.[7]

In short, the voice of disappointment about socialism is not that of rejection—the voice of gloom is not the voice of doom. The careful distinction Orwell makes between warning and prophecy is highly significant, for it is the pervasive contemporary notion that *Nineteen Eighty-Four* is meant to be prophecy (contrary to what Orwell himself said) that nourishes the idea that he had given up not just his faith in socialism, but his will to live.[8] It encourages the belief that his withdrawal to the island of Jura was more a death wish than the retreat of a writer who had plans to write much more and who sought such an old, lonely place because in his heart he preferred the past to the present.[9]

Despite the debate about whether *Nineteen Eighty-Four* signals the end of Orwell's socialist faith, it is generally agreed that much of the novel's importance is due to the fact that it is the culmination of all of the major themes that inhabited Orwell's earlier and lesser-known work: Flory's subjugation by imperialism, Comstock's hatred of capitalism, Dorothy Hare's loss of faith, and Bowling's loss of the past. But if these are old themes from his journalism, essays, and novels, there are also new ideas that sound a new note of maturity in Orwell's post-Spanish political writing. There are still occasional shrill prop-

agandist passages during World War II ("Either we turn this war
into a revolutionary war . . . or we lose it"[10] and the penchant for
exaggeration ("I dare say the London gutters will have to run with
blood. All right, let them if it is necessary"),[11] but there is also an
increasing tendency to transform political feelings into critical political ideas. The twenty-two pages of Emmanuel Goldstein's THE
THEORY AND PRACTICE OF OLIGARCHICAL COLLEC-
TIVISM in *Nineteen Eighty-Four* are to the point. Here the old feelings of Blair about the exploitation of the poor, about the subservience
of the lower classes to the bureaucratically supported "they," and
about the lying of the press in Spain pass into a carefully thought-
out theory.

Animal Farm is in no way as sophisticated as *Nineteen Eighty-Four*
in its explication of the structure of the totalitarian state, but political
theory is still present. Ironically, it reaffirms Orwell's belief that a
change in society's structure alone does not of itself constitute a moral
advance. Expression of this idea in his later works reveals the perennial conflict between the revolutionary and the moralist, between the
yogi and the commissar, between the individual and the group, and
it reflects the tension between the pessimistic Orwell, who believed
that "on balance life is suffering, and only the very young or the very
foolish imagine otherwise,"[12] and the hopeful Orwell who, in his
imaginary interview with Swift, was confident that individuals and
society can change for the better and that "life is worth living."[13]
Finally, there was the uneasy balance between the "two viewpoints"
that Orwell thought were "always tenable": first, how can you change
people until you have changed the shape of their society and, second,
what is the good of altering the shape of society before you have
improved the nature of human beings?[14]

Orwell's concern is that no matter what viewpoint rulers adopt it
is no guarantee that they can solve *the* "central problem" of revolution—indeed, of life—namely, the abuse of power. So long as rulers
fail to confine violence to the least amount necessary for civilized life,
even the best intentions will be quickly corrupted into injustice. As
a consequence, a wedge is driven between rulers and ruled, separat-
ing them farther rather than uniting them in common cause for a
better society in which everyone would treat others as equals. This
problem had worried the policeman Blair into a guilt-ridden resignation from the imperial service, and finally, it obsesses Orwell the
writer. The problem, of course, remains unsolved in Orwell's works

as it does in the world, but out of this obsession came *Animal Farm* and *Nineteen Eighty-Four*, the two novels by Orwell that best examine not only evil consequences of the tyrannical abuse of power, but also the rationalization of it by those in power and the often willing acceptance of such abuse by the very people who are its victims.

On the Aragon Front in Spain, Orwell had experienced a sense of brotherhood that had filled him with optimism. Also in Spain—this time in the streets of Barcelona—he had seen and felt the "nightmare" world of "ceaseless arrests . . . and prowling hordes of police."[15] As a result, both the kind of life he wanted and the kind he feared were recorded in *Homage to Catalonia*. In *Animal Farm* and *Nineteen Eighty-Four*, the detailed abuse of power whereby the kind of life he wanted could be perverted and subverted into the kind of life he feared is investigated. For Orwell the least evil form of government is the democratic socialism of the early pages of *Animal Farm*, and that was quickly overthrown. The greatest evil is the "oligarchical collectivism" of the early pages of *Nineteen Eighty-Four*, and that might not be overthrown.

Above all, the last novel is both the culmination and the expansion of the theme first sounded in *Burmese Days*. This is the pessimism born of Orwell's realization that while there are good reasons to form associations of men in the interests of brotherhood—for example, to mitigate their physical and spiritual poverty and even to safeguard and expand their freedom—such associations are depressingly vulnerable to attack by those who crave power. Orwell's pessimism was progressively exacerbated by the recognition that in any collectivity the attempt to be rid of the individual's self-interest for the good of the group is apt to excite a call to be rid of the individual. It is the individual's right to say what he or she thinks, even when it conflicts with the views of the collectivity that Orwell consistently defends. Quite apart from the climate of the cold war, which accelerated the initial sales of *Nineteen Eighty-Four*, it is our instant recognition of Winston Smith as an individual pitted against bureaucracy that gives the novel such a strange intimacy and urgency. Though the year of the novel is 1984, we are confronted by the present.

A manifestation of this tension between the individual and the group—one that also reflects the old tug-of-war between Orwell's pessimism and optimism—is his vacillating views of the proles and Winston Smith. The proles, like Faulkner's heroes in their capacity to "endure tomorrow, tomorrow and tomorrow," symbolize the quietism of Henry Miller's "ordinary" man's acceptance, of "robbing reality of its terrors by simply submitting to it."[16] They are inside the whale and live on. Winston Smith breaks out—but dies. To choose between the proles' endurance, which stems more from acceptance of the world than from bravery, and Smith's brave determination to rebel is one of the central dilemmas of Orwell's work on totalitarianism.

That the dilemma looms so large in his final work is due to the fact that Orwell was better at diagnosing what he saw as evil than at prescribing against it. This limitation is plainly evident even in *Burmese Days,* in which, for all his hostility to the exploitation effected by the Raj, no constructive alternative is suggested. Next, for all he tells us of the symptoms of poverty and unemployment in England, the confusion between equality and equal opportunity undermines his all-too-brief formula for social reform in Britain. Then, despite his exuberance in reporting about the Spanish revolution, which he hoped would help set the pattern for ending exploitation in England (and indeed, everywhere), there is the same lack of analysis of how the details of the Spanish experience—the collectives and such—can be adapted for English use.

In his final novel, Orwell's turning away from oligarchical collectivism, while not a rejection of the ideals of the collectivist vision, is devoid of a plan for improvement, even though he believes that some kind of efficient and centralized state is necessary if the socialist vision is to be achieved.[17] There is only a watery hope that the proles, as a kind of unconscious but potential Home Guard, will someday mobilize. All across the bleak landscape of Airstrip One, there is no armory in sight, no hint of a scaffolding for future action, but only the dark certainty of the four towering ministries that form the concrete forts of Orwell's pessimism.

The notion held by some that Orwell turned away from his socialist belief, though unconvincing, is understandable when one remembers how, after Winston Smith's total defeat, there is no firm counterattack, not even a slightly theoretical equivalent of the twenty-two–page THEORY AND PRACTICE OF OLIGARCHICAL COLLECTIVISM—no THEORY AND PRACTICE FOR A DEMOCRATIC SOCIALIST COLLECTIVISM. The absence of any such counterattack from his socialist position helps us to understand how Orwell's position amid his contemporaries as the "Left's Loyal Opposition"[18] ("the left hated him")[19] is so misunderstood

outside England. It helps explain, too, I think, how in this period of
the cold war, Orwell is often hailed, especially in the United States,
as a champion of the Right and how a news vendor once "thrust a
copy of *Nineteen Eighty-Four* into the hands of Isaac Deutscher in
New York, saying 'You must read it, sir. Then you will know why
we must drop the atom bomb on the Bolshies!' "[20] This incident is
interesting, because while it exemplifies a common misconception
about Orwell, it nevertheless reveals a basic truth about all his writings—that he is a better social critic than he is a political thinker.
Although we always know unequivocally what he is *against*, we are
never as certain about what he was *for*—the very criticism he levelled
against the bourgeois baiters of the bourgeoisie.

Of course, as a novelist and journalist Orwell was under no obligation to suggest remedies for society's ills. It is enough for a novelist and journalist merely to identify and describe the ills—and Orwell
did this in incomparable fashion, from Kyauktada to Room 101. Still,
the failure to think equally deeply about possible solutions is a sin-
gular failure for a man who claimed that one of his prime purposes
was to write *"for* democratic Socialism" and listed among the "four
great motives for writing . . . [the] desire to push the world in a
certain direction, to alter other people's idea of *the kind of society that
they should strive after."*[21] Such an aim is hardly satisfied by arguing,
"It seemed to me then—it sometimes seems to me now . . . that
economic injustice will stop the moment we want it to stop, and no
sooner, and if we genuinely want it to stop the *method adopted hardly
matters."*[22] (The italics are mine.)

This attitude led Orwell into a laziness that produced his irritating
confusion over the role of the state and of modern technology and
does, indeed, rob his "social protest," at least, of any "theoretical
foundation."[23] Knowing what he was against, however, Orwell was
at his best writing about totalitarianism. It is true that he learned
much about totalitarian states from other writings on the subject—
from Koestler's *Darkness at Noon,* for example, and Souvarine's
accounts of the Stalinist purges. In view of other novelists' work,
however (such as that of Dickens, Eliot, and Hardy), the question
reamins: why is Orwell still regarded as not only probably the most
important political writer of his time, but as one of the "finest prose
writers of any English age"?[24] The answer lies in his vigorous avoid-
ance of jargon, which mirrors his overall rejection of the pressures
of orthodoxy. Although he was a man who revelled in his contradic-

tions,[25] he did not counsel nonconformity for its own sake, as his attacks on the so-called socialist "cranks" testify. What he did counsel against, especially after Spain, was the blind acceptance of "phrases invented by someone else,"[26] phrases characterized by a lack of original imagery that glided, through the force of habit, over the consciousness and embedded themselves, unchallenged, in the mind of the listener. To accept others' ideas so easily and habitually, he believed, was the first step toward accepting their domination. In this sense he had learned better than most how potent a weapon language is. He could use the language as poorly, as abstractly, and as unfairly as anyone else ("all tobacconists are fascists"),[27] but it was because he knew so well the temptations involved that he was so useful in alerting us to their dangers. Nearly forty years ago, in 1946, he wrote of how "defenceless villages are bombarded from the air, the inhabitants driven out into the countryside, the cattle machine-gunned, the huts set on fire with incendiary bullets: this is called *pacification*."[28] As "war" can be called "pacification," then "freedom" can become "slavery" and "democracy" can be used to mean just about anything you want it to mean.[29]

In his fresh choice of metaphor, all the way from waging war against the clichés of imperialism, Orwell developed in his writing an extraordinary ability to reduce the big political problems of his day—and thus, perhaps, of most days—down to concrete events. As in his description of how a police superintendent shoots an animal to death because he feels compelled by others' expectations and how a waiter's loyalty to his class becomes lost in the constant coming and going between kitchen and dining room, he presents the big problems in terms of personal, everyday experience and so could simplify complex issues without making them appear simplistic. In these ways he has not only contributed to the common language of despair—"Big Brother," "Newspeak," "Doublethink"—but has enabled us to see politics as one person to another, rather than as an abstract relationship, so that we, too, might diagnose, through the help of more vivid imagery, some of the more general problems of politics. (For Orwell "all issues are political issues.")[30]

Furthermore, although unashamedly stating his bias, he was also determined to retain an unbiased eye (by acting out his belief that "the more one is conscious of one's political bias, the more chance one has of acting politically without sacrificing one's aesthetic and intellectual integrity").[31] Thus, he reinforced, in the world of realpolitik, the equally traditional belief that we might still approach the study of politics with moral conviction rather than with amoral intellectuality. While abhorring the kind of totalitarian mentality that can be seen in self-styled moral majorities, he said, in effect, that a person who studies politics can, among other things, be angry yet truthful and even be useful in writing and putting things right (or at least in making them better than they are). Winston Smith and Julia, the lovers of *Nineteen Eighty-Four*, are condemned to search in vain for words to express whatever they are still able (or, rather, allowed) to feel, and while Orwell hoped that the decay and corruption of language might be rescued by some conscientious fellow journalists, he recognized with dismay, particularly in Spain, that many of them are the archenemies of a fresh and revitalized language.

Orwell's pessimistic vision takes us in the end to the stark horror of Room 101, where reality is defined entirely by the corrupted vocabulary of the Party. As with the stereotypes of imperialism in *Burmese Days* and the subservient animals in *Animal Farm*, Orwell attributed the longevity of such conditions—particularly, the language of Big Brother's tyranny—to the mass of "gramophone" minds whose sense of security is strengthened by the growth of monolithic order and modernization.

It is particularly the gramophone mind, listening to the same tune and the ready-made phrases that anaesthetize the brain, that Orwell warned us to guard against, lest our familiarity with the tune's rhythm and lyrics lull us into a dumb acceptance of our own brand of Newspeak. Such was the fate of those who, during the Korean War, actually started to believe, as a result of the sheer repetition of Western broadcasts, that North Koreans and South Koreans belonged to different races or, later, that the North Vietnamese were a different race from the South Vietnamese, or those who use the expression "the free world" without recognizing that the phrase embraces governments whose repressive measures against individuals are closer to totalitarianism.

Above all, Orwell shows how such surrender to words is, at root, an abject acceptance of the idea that all truth is relative. He argues that such surrender is not confined to the uneducated, but can affect those whom we would least suspect—the scientists, who do not appear overly concerned and "do not see that any attack on intellectual liberty, and on the concept of objective truth, threatens in the long run every department of thought."[32] When this happens we lose our compass bearings in a sea of orthodoxy. The orthodoxy may not always be evil, but there is always the temptation to read magnetic north as true north. Once truth is regarded as relative, so is everything else, including cruelty. Thus, Orwell shows how corrupt language becomes one of the most perverse and pervasive forms of *social,* as well as *political,* tyranny.

In spending so much of his effort on this theme, which he considered the most poisonous distillation of all that is wrong in totalitarianism, he demonstrated, especially in his last novel, how the choice of one's vocabulary may well be the most basic freedom we possess. It is the first line of defense against the madness of Room 101. It is not simply freedom of speech he is talking about, but rather the freedom—and indeed the obligation—to say what we mean. He warns us that if we are to preserve the private self within the public realm in which we must, ironically, participate to retain our individuality, then we must remember that in our choice of words we construct our own constraints and limitations, not only of thought, but ultimately of action. And so, long after the year 1984 has passed, Orwell's last work, as the culmination of all that went before, will endure—because ultimately, his attack is not directed so much toward a political system as upon a state of mind.

Able at times to work only an hour a day, Orwell finished the final draft of *Nineteen Eighty-Four* by November 1948, having returned to Jura in the summer after a period in hospital. Soon after his return to the island, he was confined for much of the time to his bed. As his publisher, Frederic Warburg, notes, only two courses were open to him: to press ahead with the novel and risk a fatal relapse or to stop writing and give his body a chance to regain the strength needed for possible recovery.[33] His decision to keep writing was surely no surprise. In a notebook kept in the last year of his life he comments:

It is now [1949] 16 years since my first book was published and abt [*sic*] 21 years since I started publishing articles in the magazines. . . . There has literally been not one day in which I did not feel that I was idling, that I was behind with the current job, and that my total output was miserably small. Even at the periods when I was working 10 hours a day on a book, or turning out 4 or 5 articles a week, I have never been able to get away from this neurotic feeling.[34]

No typist could be persuaded to make the long journey, including two sea crossings and an eight-mile walk to Orwell's rather primitive home on Jura, to type out the final draft from the rough draft, which he said would be virtually unintelligible without verbal instructions. Therefore, despite his ever-weakening condition, he typed it himself—no doubt, hastening his death. On January 6, a month after having posted the final draft, he entered the Cotswold sanatorium in Gloucestershire.[35] He felt, understandably enough, that his running battle with tuberculosis had prevented *Nineteen Eighty-Four* from being a better book, writing to Julian Symons with characteristic and pessimistic modesty that because of his lung disease he had "ballsed it up." Similarly, he informed Warburg that it wouldn't be a book that he would "gamble on for a big sale," suggesting that only ten thousand copies be run off.[36] He couldn't have been more mistaken. As it turned out, of course, Winston Smith's ordeal was to make Orwell famous. People who had never read and have not read a word of Orwell the journalist or essayist to this day, people who knew nothing and know nothing else about him were about to be stunned by his vision of the second "nightmare" that had beset modern man. Thus, Big Brother, Newspeak, and Doublethink would forever pass into the language, and throughout the world *Orwellian* has become an adjective that immediately summons up a terrifying vision of the future—and the present.

By the end of March 1949, after he had corrected the proofs of *Nineteen Eighty-Four,* Orwell's disease got worse. He had a relapse and was forbidden by the doctors to use a typewriter. Asking that his will be sent to him, he wrote a letter to his friend Richard Rees expressing concern about his young son's future and declaring his wish that Rees be empowered to have the final say in any literary question—as in the case of the American Book-of-the-Month Club, which wanted to make substantial cuts in *Nineteen Eighty-Four* with a view to making it the selection for July 1949. (The literary executorship would later be shared by Orwell's second wife, Sonia.) Eight days later, on April 8, Orwell wrote to Rees, telling him that the novel (without cuts) had been accepted by the Book-of-the-Month Club. In the same letter he expressed a wish to see his son, Richard, in the event that the treatment of his tuberculosis with streptomycin, which had awful side effects, should fail to contain the disease and "before I get too frightening in appearance."[37] Nevertheless, by mid-April, having finished a promised review of Churchill's *Their Finest Hour,* he felt well enough to write his American publisher, "I have my next novel mapped out, but I am not going to touch it until I feel stronger."[38]

In June, *Nineteen Eighty-Four* was published by Secker and Warburg in England and Harcourt Brace in the United States. For the remainder of 1949, Orwell mostly wrote letters to personal friends, although he did write a synopsis and a few pages of a projected short story. He also made notes for essays he planned to write—in particular, one on Joseph Conrad and another on Evelyn Waugh. In early September, three months after *Nineteen Eighty-Four* had appeared in print, he entered University College Hospital in London. On October 13, while he was still in hospital, he married Sonia Brownell, who was an editorial assistant for *Horizon* magazine and whom he had known since 1945. He told his friend Julian Symons that he looked forward to going to America upon his recovery to report on the Deep South.[39] On January 21, shortly before he was due to go to another sanatorium—this time in Switzerland—Orwell died. He was forty-six years old.

PREFACE TO NOTES

As my references to the four volumes of *The Collected Essays, Journalism and Letters of George Orwell*, edited by Sonia Orwell and Ian Angus, refer to the British Penguin paperback editions, I have included here a table that will allow readers of the Harcourt Brace Jovanovich (HBJ) editions (which have the same pagination as the Secker and Warburg editions) to find the approximate corresponding pages in their editions.

Wherever a citation refers to *Homage to Catalonia*, the reader should know that I have used the Penguin edition (first published in 1966) of Orwell's *Homage to Catalonia*, which includes Orwell's essay, "Looking Back on the Spanish War." *Homage to Catalonia* comprises pages 7–221, while "Looking Back on the Spanish War" comprises pages 225–46.

VOLUME I

HBJ	P	HBJ	P	HBJ	P	HBJ	P
1	23	140	164	280	312	420	460
10	32	150	173	290	323	430	471
20	42	160	183	300	334	440	482
30	52	170	194	310	344	450	493
40	62	180	205	320	354	460	504
50	72	190	216	330	365	470	514
60	84	200	227	340	376	480	525
70	95	210	238	350	388	490	537
80	103	220	249	360	397	500	548
90	113	230	259	370	408	510	559
100	124	240	270	380	418	520	570
110	134	250	281	390	429	530	581
120	143	260	292	400	440	540	591
130	154	270	302	410	449		

Volume II

HBJ	P	HBJ	P	HBJ	P	HBJ	P
10	24	130	156	250	286	370	419
20	35	140	167	260	298	380	430
30	45	150	177	270	310	390	441
40	56	160	189	280	320	400	453
50	67	170	200	290	332	410	464
60	78	180	210	300	343	420	474
70	87	190	221	310	353	430	486
80	101	200	232	320	364	440	497
90	112	210	243	330	375	450	508
100	123	220	254	340	386		
110	134	230	265	350	397		
120	145	240	276	360	408		

Volume III

HBJ	P	HBJ	P	HBJ	P	HBJ	P
10	24	120	145	230	266	340	386
20	35	130	156	240	277	350	397
30	46	140	167	250	288	360	408
40	57	150	178	260	298	370	419
50	68	160	189	270	310	380	430
60	78	170	200	280	320	390	441
70	90	180	211	290	331	400	452
80	101	190	222	300	342	406	459
90	112	200	233	310	354		
100	123	210	244	320	364		
110	134	220	255	330	375		

Volume IV

HBJ	P	HBJ	P	HBJ	P	HBJ	P
10	26	140	170	270	312	400	454
20	37	150	181	280	323	410	465
30	49	160	191	290	334	420	476
40	60	170	202	300	345	430	486
50	70	180	213	310	356	440	497
60	82	190	224	320	367	450	509
70	94	200	235	330	378	460	519
80	104	210	246	340	389	470	530
90	114	220	257	350	400	480	541
100	126	230	268	360	411	490	551
110	137	240	279	370	423	500	562
120	148	250	290	380	434	510	573
130	159	260	301	390	444		

NOTES

PREFACE TO THE SECOND EDITION

1. Gordon Bowker, in his recent book *George Orwell* (New York, London: Little, Brown, 2003), suggests that Orwell told friends he changed his name from Eric Arthur Blair to George Orwell to escape "black magic" revenge on him because of a childish wax effigy voodoo experiment he and the late Steven Runciman carried out against a bullying fellow pupil when they were at Eton. A few days after they broke the leg of the effigy, the boy broke his leg in a football match and a few months later died of leukemia. Despite Orwell having told friends this was a reason for his name change, his explanation seems unconvincing at best, insofar as the change did not occur until fifteen years after the incident.

CHAPTER 1

1. Orwell, *CEJL*, I, p. 265.

2. Laurence Brander, *George Orwell* (London: Longmans, Green and Co., 1954), p. 4.

3. Cyril Connolly, *Enemies of Promise* (New York: Macmillan, 1948), p. 160. See also Peter Stansky and William Abrahams, *The Unknown Orwell* (New York: Alfred A. Knopf, 1972), pp. 31-32. In my book much of the biographical information about Blair's time at school and in Burma is taken from Stansky and Abraham's book because, as the title suggests, next to Bernard Crick's *Orwell: A Life*, it is the only work so far that has shed any real light on this early period of Blair's life.

4. Orwell, *CEJL*, IV, pp. 388-89. Orwell was to describe his family as "lower-upper-middle." See George Orwell, *The Road to Wigan Pier* (Harmondsworth, England: Penguin Books [in association with Secker and Warburg], 1962), p. 106. This novel will be called "Wigan Pier" in later references. For a discussion surrounding this, see Stansky and Abrahams, *The Unknown Orwell* pp. 3-12.

5. Orwell, *CEJL*, IV, pp. 392, 401-02. There is some uncertainty as to when Orwell wrote "Such, Such Were the Joys." See Bernard Crick, *George Orwell: A Life* (London: Secker and Warburg, 1980), p. 365.

6. Crick, *George Orwell: A Life*, p. 31.

7. Orwell, *CEJL*, IV, pp. 412-13.

8. Stansky and Abrahams, *The Unknown Orwell*, p. 76.

9. Ibid., pp. 120-21, 101, 85, 105. See also Crick, *George Orwell: A Life*, p. 49.

10. Orwell, *Wigan Pier*, pp. 120–21. Stansky and Abrahams properly note that "a peculiarity of Orwell's analysis of the mood of early postwar England is that it is based almost entirely upon Blair's experience of it at Eton—that was all that he knew at first-hand, for from 1922 to 1927 he was out of England. . . ." (*The Unknown Orwell*, p. 124).

11. Christopher Gillie, *Movements in English Literature: 1900–1940* (Cambridge, England: Cambridge University Press, 1975), p. 112.

12. Stansky and Abrahams, *The Unknown Orwell*, p. 161.

13. Orwell, *Wigan Pier*, p. 126.

14. Ibid., pp. 128–29.

15. Stansky and Abrahams, *The Unknown Orwell*, pp. 176, 183.

16. Orwell, *Wigan Pier*, p. 129.

17. Peter Stansky and William Abrahams, *Orwell: The Transformation* (London: Constable, 1979), pp. 42–43.

18. Ibid., p. 4.

19. George Woodcock, *The Crystal Spirit* (Harmondsworth, England: Penguin Books, 1970), p. 51.

20. Orwell, *CEJL*, I, pp. 25–26.

21. Ibid., pp. 26, 25.

22. Ibid., IV, p. 81.

23. George Orwell, *Burmese Days* (Harmondsworth, England: Penguin Books [in association with Secker and Warburg], 1967), p. 17.

24. Stansky and Abrahams, *The Unknown Orwell*, p. 195.

25. Orwell, *Burmese Days*, p. 119.

26. Ibid., p. 66.

27. Ibid., p. 262.

28. Orwell, *Wigan Pier*, p. 126.

29. Orwell, *Burmese Days*, pp. 40, 37.

30. Ibid., p. 37.

31. Ibid., pp. 37, 41.

32. Ibid., p. 118.

33. Stansky and Abrahams, *The Unknown Orwell*, pp. 193–94.

34. Orwell, *Burmese Days*, pp. 27–28, 113.

35. Orwell, *CEJL*, III, p. 301. For the natives' acceptance of such myths as those expressed by Elizabeth, see E.M. Forster, *A Passage to India* (Harmondsworth, England: Penguin Books, 1936), p. 137, where Dr. Aziz, the native doctor, shouts to the two white women, " 'Put on your topis at once, the early sun is highly dangerous for heads. . . . Not for my thick head,' he laughed."

36. George Orwell, *Inside the Whale and Other Essays* (Harmondsworth, England: Penguin Books [in association with Secker and Warburg], 1962), pp. 154, 156. This collection will be called *Other Essays* in later references.

37. John Atkins, *George Orwell* (London: John Calder, 1954), p. 76. H. Alan C. Cairns, in *The Clash of Cultures* (New York: Frederick A. Praeger, 1965), p. 198, points out how some colonizers in fact believed that trade (though not necessarily exploitative trade) was very much a necessary tool of the Christian progress and how (to Livingstone, for example) trade seemed to be "an ethical rather than an economic concept."

38. Orwell, *Burmese Days*, p. 40.

39. Ibid., p. 44.

40. Ibid., pp. 44, 44, 37.

41. A.W. Stevens, "George Orwell and Southeast Asia," *Yearbook of Comparative and General Literature* II (1962): 133.

42. Orwell, *Burmese Days,* pp. 137, 181.

43. Ibid., pp. 66.

44. Ibid., pp. 67, 66.

45. Ibid., pp. 29, 222.

46. Ibid., pp. 69, 69, 272.

47. Woodcock, *The Crystal Spirit,* p. 76.

48. Orwell, *Wigan Pier,* p. 127.

49. Christopher Hollis, *A Study of George Orwell* (London: Hollis and Carter, 1956), p. 38. In *The Unknown Orwell,* p. 170, Stansky and Abrahams write: "If Blair had arrived in Burma a few years earlier, he would have found a much more orderly, ordinary province, appearing to function in a smooth, untroubled way under a benevolent imperial administration. It is not inconceivable that the jarring, sometimes quite trivial events that stood out so painfully when he was there would have been less noticeable, less abrasive, less guilt-producing, if they had not taken place against a background of growing confusion and uncertainty for the once so self-confident British rulers in Bruma. Paradoxically, it was the very attempts of the British government to liberalize its own administration and to allow the Burmese voice to be heard that made Orwell more conscious than he probably would have been otherwise of the Empire as a system in which he could not continue to participate and keep his self-respect." See also ibid., p. 172.

50. Orwell, *Burmese Days,* p. 221. See also James F. Guyot, "Bureaucratic Transformation in Burma," in *Asian Bureaucratic Systems Emergent from the British Imperial Tradition,* ed. Ralph Braibanti (Durham, N.C.: Duke University Press, 1966), p. 374. Guyot talks of how the club is the place where "many of the important administrative decisions, particularly those affecting the big British firms, were made in an environment free from the restraints of formal bureaucratic routine." Forster makes the same point in *A Passage to India,* p. 268. Turton, one of the club members, approaches Fielding and says coldly, "I should be glad if you will put in your appearance at the Club this evening." Fielding answers, "I have accepted re-election, sir. Do you regard it is necessary I should come? I should be glad to be excused. . . ." Turton replies, "It is not a question of your feeling, but of the wish of the Lieutenant-Governor. Perhaps you will ask me whether I speak officially. I do. I shall expect you this evening at six."

51. Orwell, *Burmese Days,* p. 32.

52. Stansky and Abrahams, *The Unknown Orwell,* p. 188.

53. Orwell, *Burmese Days,* p. 235.

54. Ibid., p. 67.

55. Orwell, *CEJL,* I, p. 265, 266, 269. Bernard Crick makes the interesting observation that "whether he [Orwell] actually shot an elephant or not does not seem quite so important as whether he saw a hanging, or was flogged for bed-wetting [about which Orwell also wrote]." See Crick, *George Orwell: A Life,* p. 96.

56. Woodcock, *The Crystal Spirit,* p. 70.

57. Ibid., p. 76.
58. Orwell, *Burmese Days,* p. 37.
59. Orwell, *CEJL,* IV, p. 90.
60. Orwell, *Burmese Days,* p. 28.
61. In *The Clash of Cultures,* p. 92, Cairns notes the existence of the same analogy in imperialist Africa and also mentions that "the most explicit indication of the denial of equality of racial and cultural status is seen in the very widespread comparison of the African to a child."
62. Orwell, *Wigan Pier,* pp. 120–34, 131.
63. Keith Alldritt, *The Making of George Orwell* (London: Edward Arnold, 1969), p. 21. See also Stevens, "George Orwell and Southeast Asia," p. 134.
64. Stansky and Abrahams, *The Unknown Orwell,* pp. 183, 201.
65. See Hollis, *A Study of George Orwell,* p. 38, where Orwell, in reference to the train journey during which he and the educational officer guiltily damned the Empire, writes, "Because he found it difficult to reveal himself to others, he thought that everybody found it difficult."

CHAPTER 2

1. Orwell, *Wigan Pier,* pp. 126, 130, 129–30.
2. Charles L.M. Mowat, *Britain Between the Wars: 1918–1940* (London: Methuen and Co. Ltd., 1966), p. 126. This volume will be called *Britain: 1918–1940* in later references.
3. The article was titled "An Enquiry Into Civic Progress in England" and subtitled "The Great Misery of the British Worker. 1. Unemployment." It appeared in Paris as one in a series of articles on unemployment and poverty in England that was published in *Progrès Civique* between December 1928 and May 1929.
4. Orwell, *Wigan Pier,* pp. 129–30.
5. Orwell, *CEJL,* I, pp. 34–35.
6. The other three Englands are cited in Mowat, *Britain: 1918–1940,* pp. 480–81.
7. Orwell, *Wigan Pier,* p. 130.
8. Alldritt, *The Making of George Orwell,* p. 17.
9. Orwell, *CEJL,* I, pp. 28, 288–89.
10. Stuart Samuels, "English Intellectuals and Politics in the 1930s," in *On Intellectuals,* ed. Philip Reiff (New York: Anchor Books, 1970), p. 247. (This article will be called "English Intellectuals" in later references.) The dichotomies between aesthetic impulse and political purpose, symbolism and utilitarianism, and aestheticism and realism are not exactly the same, of course. However, they do reflect the common tension between the belief that involvement in social and political affairs was vulgar and the beliefs that the proper function of the artist was to celebrate beauty and that "realism" was synonymous with the seamier side of life.
11. Mowat, *Britain: 1918–1940,* p. 419.
12. Samuels, *English Intellectuals,* p. 238.
13. Mowat, *Britain: 1918–1940,* p. 526.
14. Ibid., p. 4. Lloyd George used this phrase during the British general election of 1918.
15. George Orwell, *Coming Up For Air* (Harmondsworth, England: Pen-

guin Books [in association with Secker and Warburg], 1962), pp. 111–13.
16. Ibid., p. 106.
17. Ibid., p. 107.
18. Ibid., pp. 107–08.
19. Orwell, *Coming Up For Air*, pp. 113, 123.
20. Mowat, *Britain: 1918–1940*, pp. 261, 201.
21. Ibid., p. 393.
22. Noreen Branson and Margot Heinemann, *Britain in the Thirties* (St. Albans, England: Panther Books, 1973), pp. 20–21.
23. Ibid., pp. 21–28.
24. Mowat, *Britain: 1918–1940*, p. 412.
25. Samuel Hynes, *The Auden Generation: Literature and Politics in England in the 1930s* (Toronto: The Bodley Head, 1976), pp. 66–67. This book will be called *The Auden Generation* in later references.
26. Ibid., p. 75.
27. Samuels, "English Intellectuals," p. 214.
28. Hynes, *The Auden Generation*, p. 108. The writers referred to here included Auden, Spender, and Day Lewis. (See also *The Auden Generation*, p. 115.)
29. Orwell, *Wigan Pier*, p. 121.
30. Mowat, *Britain: 1918–1940*, p. 201. For comments on Orwell as a writer in the Thirties, see Mowat, pp. 486, 522, and 531.
31. Orwell, *Wigan Pier*, p. 121.
32. Orwell, *Burmese Days*, p. 64.
33. Orwell, *Wigan Pier*, p. 130.
34. Orwell, *CEJL*, I, p. 26.
35. Orwell, *Wigan Pier*, p. 129.
36. Orwell, *CEJL*, I, p. 28.
37. Stansky and Abrahams, *The Unknown Orwell*, p. 207.
38. Orwell, *CEJL*, I, p. 101.
39. Orwell, *Wigan Pier*, p. 133.
40. Stansky and Abrahams, *The Unknown Orwell*, p. 307.
41. Crick, *George Orwell: A Life*, p. 140.
42. Orwell, *Wigan Pier*, p. 131.
43. Orwell, *Wigan Pier*, p. 106.
44. Stansky and Abrahams, *The Unknown Orwell*, p. 178.
45. Orwell, *CEJL*, IV, pp. 44, 46–47.
46. Orwell, *Wigan Pier*, pp. 130–31.
47. William Ashworth, *An Economic History of England: 1870–1939* (London: Methuen and Co. Ltd., 1960), p. 425.
48. Mowat, *Britain: 1918–1940*, p. 433. Their numbers were greatest among men aged sixty to sixty-four for whom the dole would cease at age sixty-five. (See Mowat, p. 482.)
49. Woodcock, *The Crystal Spirit*, p. 128.

CHAPTER 3

1. Georgie Anne Geyer, "Margaret Thatcher No Longer Comes Across as a Woman Leader," *Vancouver Province*, March 1, 1981.
2. Orwell, *CEJL*, II, p. 108. See also p. 125.

3. Orwell, *Wigan Pier,* pp. 141–42.

4. George Orwell, *Keep the Aspidistra Flying* (Harmondsworth, England: Penguin Books [in association with Secker and Warburg], 1962), p. 217. This novel will be called *Aspidistra* in later references.

5. Orwell, *CEJL,* I, pp. 109–19. See also Stansky and Abrahams, *The Unknown Orwell,* pp. 20–21, 251, 301.

6. Orwell, *Aspidistra,* pp. 55, 54–55.

7. George Orwell, *Down and Out in Paris and London* (Harmondsworth, England: Penguin Books [in association with Secker and Warburg], 1966), pp. 15, 16, 16–18. This book will be called *Down and Out* in later references.

8. Ibid., pp. 103, 69–70, 81.

9. George Orwell, *A Clergyman's Daughter* (Harmondsworth, England: Penguin Books [in association with Secker and Warburg], 1964), pp. 112, 165.

10. Ibid., p. 135.

11. Orwell, *Wigan Pier,* p. 73.

12. Orwell, *A Clergyman's Daughter,* p. 111–12.

13. Orwell, *Down and Out,* p. 104.

14. Orwell, *Wigan Pier,* p. 34.

15. Orwell, *Down and Out,* p. 19.

16. George Orwell, *Nineteen Eighty-Four* (Harmondsworth, England: Penguin Books [in association with Secker and Warburg], 1954), p. 72.

17. Orwell, *A Clergyman's Daughter,* p. 196.

18. It is unlikely that television and movies would improve this situation very much. While the media may certainly lead to an awareness of other ways of life and may create hope through the creation of illusions and myth, their often superficial treatment does not provide many, if any, clues to the details of how certain historical changes were effected.

19. Orwell, *Wigan Pier,* p. 57.

20. Ibid., pp. 16–17.

21. Ibid., p. 78.

22. In Wigan, for example, Orwell found that of about 36,000 insured workers approximately 10,000 were unemployed at the beginning of 1936. Allowing for dependents, this meant that out of Wigan's total population of nearly 87,000, more than one in three were living on the dole ("Wigan Pier," p. 68).

23. Orwell, *Down and Out,* p. 160.

24. Mowat, *Britain: 1918–1940,* p. 484.

25. Orwell, *Wigan Pier,* p. 80.

26. Ibid., pp. 121, 80.

27. Ibid., p. 86.

28. Ibid., p. 79.

29. Ashworth, *An Economic History of England: 1870–1939,* pp. 310–11.

30. Orwell, *Wigan Pier,* pp. 81, 79–80.

31. Orwell, *Down and Out,* p. 23.

32. Orwell, *Wigan Pier,* p. 50. This is typical of the kind of remark that causes Orwell to be so consistently and rightly praised as one of the most honest writers of the age.

33. Orwell, *A Clergyman's Daughter*, p. 27.

34. In *Coming Up For Air*, for example, the whole train of events hinges on the protagonist, George Bowling, risking ten shillings on a horse race. He bets the "ten bob" on a horse that has been chosen by a fellow worker's perusal of a book entitled *Astrology Applied to Horse-racing*. (*Coming Up For Air*, p. 9.)

35. Orwell, *Nineteen Eighty-Four*, pp. 71–72.

36. Orwell, *Wigan Pier*, p. 79.

37. Ibid., p. 81.

38. In *Wigan Pier*, p. 111, Orwell wrote that through the "weapon of unemployment" in the interwar years, "the English working class have grown servile with a rather horrifying rapidity."

39. Orwell, *Down and Out*, pp. 106, 107.

40. Orwell, *Wigan Pier*, pp. 197, 137.

41. Orwell, *Down and Out*, pp. 108, 106, 106–07.

42. Ibid., p. 107.

43. Orwell, *Wigan Pier*, pp. 132–33.

44. Ibid., pp. 43–44.

45. Orwell, *CEJL*, II, pp. 181–82.

46. Orwell, *Down and Out*, pp. 61, 68–69, 63.

47. Orwell, *Wigan Pier*, p. 140.

48. Ibid., p. 131.

49. Orwell, *CEJL*, III, p. 34.

50. Ibid., II, p. 108.

51. George Orwell, "Our Opportunity," *The Left News*, January 1941, p. 1610.

52. Orwell, *Wigan Pier*, pp. 155, 43, 43, 43, 44.

53. Ibid., pp. 43, 44–45.

54. Ibid., pp. 75, 44, 137, 140, 141.

55. Orwell, "Our Opportunity," p. 1610.

56. Orwell, *CEJL*, III, p. 36.

57. Orwell, *Wigan Pier*, pp. 201, 107. In his review of Alec Brown's *The Fate of the Middle Classes*, Orwell criticizes Brown for lumping "into the middle classes the entire block of the population between dividend-drawers on the one hand and the wage-slaves on the other, . . . as though there were no serious distinctions between them except the size of their incomes. It is a method of classification about as useful as dividing the population into bald men and hairy men." (*Adelphi* [May, 1936]: 128.) Orwell, however, uses the term *middle-class* often enough (for example, see *Wigan Pier*, p. 199), and although qualification is often nearby and he does use *middle-classes* to show he is aware of "serious distinctions," some circumspection needs to be used when dealing with the term in Orwell's work.

58. Orwell, *Wigan Pier*, p. 108.

59. Orwell, *Coming Up For Air*, pp. 14, 14, 14–16.

60. Ibid., p. 14.

61. Orwell, *Wigan Pier*, p. 116.

62. Ibid., p. 108.

63. Ibid., pp. 198–99. See how middle classes combined against working

classes in the general strike, *Wigan Pier*, p. 202.
64. Orwell, *CEJL*, I, p. 81. See also *Wigan Pier*, p. 131.
65. George Orwell, in a review of Alec Brown, "The Fate of the Middle Classes," reviewed by George Orwell (*Adelphi*, May 1936, p. 128). The "private" schools are mostly middle-class versions of the rich's "public" schools.
66. Orwell, "Our Opportunity," p. 1610.
67. Orwell, *Wigan Pier*, p. 120.
68. Orwell, *Aspidistra*, pp. 45, 46.
69. Orwell, *CEJL*, IV, pp. 389, 407.
70. Orwell, *Aspidistra*, pp. 56, 49, 77.
71. Ibid., p. 54.
72. Orwell, *Wigan Pier*, p. 103. There is undoubtedly inconsistency between Orwell's claims that a "middle class person goes utterly to pieces under the influence of poverty" (*Wigan Pier*, p. 130), his conviction that in times of stress the middle classes "tend to come to the front" (*Wigan Pier*, p. 44), and his beliefs about the "heroic snobbishness" of the middle classes. However, the inconsistency is more apparent than real: one must remember that times of stress are not necessarily times of poverty. In any case, Orwell's phrase that the middle classes go "utterly to pieces" is plainly an exaggeration to convery his belief that the middle classes are much harder hit psychically by poverty than the working class is. (See also *Wigan Pier*, pp. 73, 103, 108.)
73. Orwell, *Aspidistra*, p. 49.
74. Orwell, *Coming Up For Air*, p. 108.
75. Orwell, *Aspidistra*, p. 49.
76. Orwell, *CEJL*, IV, p. 409.
77. Ibid., IV, pp. 407–08.
78. Orwell, *Wigan Pier*, p. 115.
79. This revulsion not only affected schoolboys but travelled abroad—in this case, with Assistant Superintendent Blair to Burma, where he beat Burmese and where his stomach turned at the "*lower-class* sweat of the private British soldiers." (*Wigan Pier*, p. 125.)
80. Orwell, *Wigan Pier*, p. 110.
81. Orwell, *CEJL*, III, p. 51.
82. Ibid., IV, pp. 510–11.
83. Orwell, "Our Opportunity," p. 1610.
84. Orwell, *Wigan Pier*, p. 104.
85. Orwell, *Aspidistra*, p. 49.
86. Orwell, *Wigan Pier*, p. 109.
87. Orwell, *CEJL*, II, pp. 92–93.
88. Ibid., I, pp. 511, 529, 528, 511–12.
89. Ibid., pp. 597, 511–12, 517.
90. Ibid., III, pp. 230, 230–31. In this vein, Blair's first article to appear in England, "A Farthing Newspaper" (1928) (see *CEJL*, I, pp. 34–37) was prompted by the publication of a mass daily, *Ami du Peuple*, being sold in Paris for less than a farthing a copy. Fascinated by its success at such a clearly unprofitable price, Orwell discovered that the paper, whose widely proclaimed intent was to "make war on the great trusts, to fight for a lower cost

of living and above all to combat the powerful newspapers which are strangling free speech in France," was owned by Monsieur Coty. The latter was not only "a great industrialist capitalist" but also owned *Figaro* and the *Gaulois*.

Though he liked the idea of a cheap mass paper for the poor, Orwell was concerned that mass circulation, made possible by a rich owner charging a low price, would lead to a decline in free speech, the very thing that M. Coty said he wanted to foster. He warned that precisely because one paper is so cheap it can crowd out less prosperous and smaller competitors and most importantly, can still the voices of those with opposing opinions who cannot afford to sell any paper for a farthing (ibid., p. 36). Although his general point is well taken, Orwell undoubtedly confuses here the right to free speech with the opportunity to be heard.

91. Ibid., p. 526.
92. Ibid., IV, pp. 411–12.
93. Ibid., I, p. 445.
94. Orwell, *CEJL*, II, pp. 33, 304, and III, pp. 123, 126.
95. Orwell, *CEJL*, III, p. 126.
96. Orwell, *Aspidistra*, p. 49.
97. Orwell, *Nineteen Eighty-Four*, p. 212.
98. Orwell, *CEJL*, III, p. 127. Orwell was convinced that because the belief in personal immortality, which nurtured the old sense of right and wrong, had disappeared, "man is not likely to salvage civilization unless he can evolve a system of good and evil which is independent of heaven and hell." (Ibid.)
99. Ibid.
100. Ibid., II, p. 33.
101. Orwell, "Our Opportunity," p. 1610.
102. Orwell, *Nineteen Eighty-Four*, p. 217.
103. Orwell, *CEJL*, II, p. 33.
104. *Manchester Evening News*, February 7, 1942, p. 2.
105. Orwell, *CEJL*, IV, p. 425. Also see *A Clergyman's Daughter*, pp. 50–51.
106. Orwell, *CEJL*, III, p. 456.
107. Ibid., II, pp. 102, 100.
108. *Manchester Evening News*, January 31, 1946, p. 2.
109. Orwell, *CEJL*, II, p. 32.
110. Ibid., p. 504.
111. Orwell, *A Clergyman's Daughter*, p. 259.
112. Orwell, *Wigan Pier*, p. 154.
113. Ibid., p. 189.
114. Orwell, *CEJL*, II, p. 33.

CHAPTER 4

1. Orwell, *CEJL*, I, p. 423.
2. Orwell, *Wigan Pier*, pp. 141, 126.
3. Ibid., pp. 150, 154, 199.
4. Orwell, *CEJL*, II, pp. 100–101, 126, 113, 121.
5. Ibid., III, p. 51.

6. Ibid., II, p. 120.
7. Orwell, *Wigan Pier*, p. 151.
8. Orwell, *CEJL*, II, p. 105.
9. Ibid., I, pp. 215, 583.
10. Ibid., III, p. 143.
11. Orwell, *Wigan Pier*, p. 189.
12. Orwell, *CEJL*, IV, p. 36.
13. Ibid., II, p. 101.
14. George Orwell, "Will Freedom Die With Capitalism?" *The Left News*, April 1941, pp. 1682–85.
15. Harold Laski, review of Orwell's *The Road to Wigan Pier*, *The Left News* (March 1937): 275–76.
16. Orwell, *Wigan Pier*, p. 29.
17. Orwell, *CEJL*, I, p. 456.
18. Ibid., III, p. 83.
19. Ibid., II, pp. 132, 124, 132, 132–33.
20. Orwell, *Wigan Pier*, p. 195.
21. Orwell, *CEJL*, II, p. 132.
22. Ibid., I, p. 457.
23. Orwell, *Coming Up For Air*, pp. 146, 148.
24. Orwell, *CEJL*, I, p. 583.
25. Orwell, *Wigan Pier*, p. 16.
26. Orwell, *CEJL*, I, p. 583.
27. Orwell, *Wigan Pier*, pp. 62–63, 71.
28. Orwell, *CEJL*, IV, p. 33.
29. Ibid.
30. Orwell, *Wigan Pier*, p. 173.
31. Orwell, *A Clergyman's Daughter*, p. 241.
32. Orwell, *Coming Up For Air*, pp. 177–78.
33. Orwell, *Wigan Pier*, pp. 184, 172, 165.
34. Orwell, *CEJL*, II, p. 97.
35. Orwell, *Wigan Pier*, p. 181.
36. Ibid., pp. 178–79, 170, 182.
37. Ibid., pp. 166, 178, 178, 176–77, 171.
38. Ibid., p. 172.
39. *Time*, June 16, 1975, p. 1.
40. Orwell, *Wigan Pier*, pp. 182, 179.
41. Orwell, *Other Essays*, p. 154.
42. Orwell, *CEJL*, IV, pp. 27–28, 27, 29.
43. Orwell, *Wigan Pier*, p. 179. See also ibid., p. 182.
44. Ibid., p. 88.
45. Orwell, *Coming Up For Air*, pp. 12, 158.
46. Ibid., pp. 26–27.
47. Orwell, *Wigan Pier*, pp. 179, 179.
48. Orwell, *CEJL*, II, p. 131.
49. Orwell, *Wigan Pier*, pp. 188, 164.
50. Orwell, *Aspidistra*, p. 95.
51. Orwell, *Wigan Pier*, p. 188.

52. Orwell, *A Clergyman's Daughter,* p. 258. Orwell's concern is echoed in K.R. Minogue's comment that "it is one of the major difficulties of much socialist thought that it must yoke together two quite different things: material provision on the one hand and spiritual development or happiness on the other." (K.R. Minogue, "Humanist Democracy: The Political Thought of C.V. Macpherson," *Canadian Journal of Political Science* 9, no. 3 [September 1976]: 382.)

53. Orwell, *Wigan Pier,* p. 197.

54. Orwell, *CEJL,* IV, p. 211.

55. Orwell, *Wigan Pier,* pp. 142, 141, 189.

56. Orwell, *CEJL,* IV, p. 88.

57. Ibid., II, pp. 96, 249.

58. Ibid., III, pp. 19, 39.

59. Ibid., IV, p. 211.

60. Ibid., III, p. 227. The significant point is that despite the increase in war wages and Orwell's earlier statements about the advent of an "indeterminate stratum [technicians and the like] at which the older class distinctions are beginning to break down," class remained an important factor (*CEJL,* II, p. 98). In a study conducted in England, W.G. Runciman points out, for example, that while "between 1918 and 1962 inequality of status was diminishing, . . . relative deprivation of status [was] *growing* more widespread" and that "despite all talk of workers 'becoming middle-class,' there was no evidence that the changes brought about by the prosperity of the 1950s were yet sufficient to overcome the traditional barriers of status." (W.G. Runciman, *Relative Deprivation and Social Justice* [Berkeley: University of California Press, 1966], pp. 118, 118, 115.) (The italics are mine.)

CHAPTER 5

1. Orwell, *Wigan Pier,* p. 152.

2. Ibid., p. 152. See also Alex Zwerdling, *Orwell and the Left* (New Haven: Yale University Press, 1974), p. 34.

3. Orwell, *Wigan Pier,* p. 185.

4. Orwell, *Aspidistra,* pp. 90–91.

5. Orwell, *Wigan Pier,* p. 162.

6. For the difficulty of characterizing English intellectuals as a clearly identifiable group, as opposed to the relatively easy identification of Continental intellectuals, see Anthony Hartley, "English Intellectuals: Their Power and Powerlessness," *Interplay,* April 1968, pp. 47–53. Failure to distinguish between these two targets in Orwell's work can lead us into erroneously lumping together his attacks on the middle-class leftists in the Thirties, which stem from his *Adelphi* days, and his attacks in the Forties upon the intellectual Left and intellectuals in general, such as occur in "Inside the Whale" (1940) and "The Prevention of Literature" (1946).

7. Orwell, *Wigan Pier,* pp. 142, 158, 201, 202–03.

8. Ibid., p. 138.

9. Orwell, *CEJL,* II, p. 113.

10. Orwell, *Wigan Pier,* p. 157.

11. Ibid., pp. 160–61.

12. Ibid., pp. 159–62, 166, 165, 182, 177.
13. Ibid., pp. 152, 152.
14. Orwell, *Coming Up For Air,* pp. 214–15.
15. Orwell, *Wigan Pier,* p. 153.
16. Ibid., pp. 163, 187–88.
17. Ibid., p. 151.
18. Richard Hoggart, introduction to the Heinemann edition of Orwell's *The Road to Wigan Pier,* (London: Heinemann, 1965), p. xviii.
19. Orwell, *Coming Up For Air,* p. 165.
20. Orwell, *Wigan Pier,* p. 40.
21. Orwell, *CEJL,* I, p. 591. See also *CEJL,* II, p. 131.
22. George Orwell, "Patriots and Revolutionaries," in *The Betrayal of the Left,* ed. Victor Gollancz (London: Gollancz, 1941), pp. 239–41.
23. Orwell, *CEJL,* II, p. 84.
24. Orwell, *Coming Up For Air,* pp. 42–43.
25. Orwell, *CEJL,* II, pp. 80, 76.
26. Ibid., I, pp. 117, 117, 92–93, 88, 586–87.
27. Ibid., II, pp. 117, 87, 84.
28. Ibid., III, pp. 336, 591, 592.
29. Orwell, *Aspidistra,* p. 87.
30. Orwell, *CEJL,* II, p. 115.
31. Ibid., I, p. 374. See also pp. 313, 317, 320, 369.
32. Zwerdling, *Orwell and the Left,* p. 84.
33. Orwell, *CEJL,* I, pp. 590–91.
34. Ibid., II, pp. 32, 32.
35. Orwell, *Wigan Pier,* p. 204.
36. Orwell, *CEJL,* III, pp. 411. 411.
37. Ibid., I, p. 301.
38. Julian Symons, *The Thirties* (Westport, Conn.: Greenwood Press, 1973), pp. 120–21.
39. Orwell, *CEJL,* II, p. 117.
40. Zwerdling, *Orwell and the Left,* p. 64.
41. Samuels, "English Intellectuals," p. 225.
42. Woodcock, *The Crystal Spirit,* p. 26.
43. Philip Toynbee, review of Orwell's *The Road to Wigan Pier,* in *The Critical Heritage,* ed. J. Meyers (Boston: Routledge and Kegan Paul Ltd., 1975), pp. 116–17.
44. Orwell, *Wigan Pier,* p. 104.
45. Orwell, *CEJL,* I, p. 207.
46. Hynes, *The Auden Generation,* p. 276.
47. Orwell, *Wigan Pier,* pp. 104, 204.
48. John Mander, *The Writer and Commitment* (London: Secker and Warburg, 1961), p. 91. Mander observes, "The principles of justice and liberty, the underlying ideals of Socialism, were already incarnate in the working class. It was merely a question of persuading the rest of the community to embrace these principles."
49. Arthur Calder Marshall, review of Orwell's *The Road to Wigan Pier,* reprinted in *The Critical Heritage,* p. 102.

50. Orwell, *Wigan Pier*, p. 128. See also Zwerdling, *Orwell and the Left*, pp. 74–75.

51. Zwerdling, *Orwell and the Left*, p. 51.

52. George Mayberry, review of Orwell's *The Road to Wigan Pier*, reprinted in *The Critical Heritage*, p. 110.

53. Hoggart, introduction to *Wigan Pier*, p. 42.

54. Toynbee, review of *Wigan Pier*, p. 116.

55. Woodcock, *The Crystal Spirit*, p. 125.

56. Zwerdling, *Orwell and the Left*, pp. 133, 133.

57. Orwell, introduction to the French edition of *Down and Out*, reprinted in *The Critical Heritage*, p. 40.

58. Zwerdling, *Orwell and the Left*, pp. 5, 37.

59. Samuels, "English Intellectuals," p. 213.

60. Zwerdling, *Orwell and the Left*, p. 167.

61. Hollis, *A Study of George Orwell*, p. 50.

62. Ibid.

63. Zwerdling, *Orwell and the Left*, p. 70.

64. Ibid., p. 69.

65. Orwell, *CEJL*, I, p. 374.

66. Zwerdling, *Orwell and the Left*, p. 68.

67. Orwell, *Wigan Pier*, pp. 124, 124.

68. Orwell, *Burmese Days*, p. 42.

69. Orwell, *Nineteen Eighty-Four*, p. 60.

70. Orwell, *CEJL*, III, p. 34.

71. Orwell, *Down and Out*, pp. 106–107.

72. Orwell, *CEJL*, II, p. 88.

73. Orwell, *Wigan Pier*, p. 194.

CHAPTER 6

1. Thomas A. Sancton, "The *Franquista* Coup That Failed," *Time*, March 9, 1981, pp. 30–31.

2. Hugh Thomas, *The Spanish Civil War* (Harmondsworth, England: Pelican Books, 1968). This summary draws heavily on Thomas's book, which, historically speaking, is by far the most comprehensive and best-researched book on the war.

3. Thomas, *The Spanish Civil War*, p. 34.

4. Ibid., pp. 33, 62, 34–35. Though such violence was indiscriminately directed against members of the Church, it is important to note that at the local level the priest was "usually regarded as a comparatively amiable counsellor." And while "no fate would be too unpleasant for the priest" if he showed favor to the rich over the poor, religion for the Spanish worker was, by and large, a passionate concern. (See ibid., p. 55.)

5. Ibid., pp. 35–38.

6. Franz Borkenau, *The Spanish Cockpit* (Ann Arbor, Mich.: Ann Arbor Paperbacks, 1963), p. 46.

7. Thomas, *The Spanish Civil War*, p. 39.

8. Ibid., p. 78.

9. Borkenau, *The Spanish Cockpit*, p. 48.

10. Thomas, *The Spanish Civil War,* pp. 73, 74.

11. Ibid., pp. 80, 84, 91.

12. Ibid., p. 94.

13. Ibid., pp. 96, 98.

14. Ibid., p. 113.

15. Ibid., pp. 114, 116.

16. Ibid., pp. 20, 118, 121, 76.

17. Ibid., pp. 129, 130, 134.

18. Ibid., p. 134.

19. Ibid., pp. 136–37.

20. Ibid., pp. 138–39, 140, 142.

21. Ibid., pp. 150, 159.

22. Ibid., p. 176.

23. Ibid., p. 175. Actually, this uprising took place a little before five o'clock (the prearranged time for the uprising in Spanish Morocco), once the plotters had learned that details of the plan for the takeover in Melilla had been leaked to local Republicans.

24. Ibid., pp. 193, 196.

25. Ibid., p. 193.

26. Ibid., pp. 735, 751, 790.

27. Orwell, *Aspidistra,* p. 26.

28. Orwell, *Wigan Pier,* p. 150.

29. Katherine B. Hoskins, *Today the Struggle: Literature and Politics in England During the Spanish Civil War* (Austin: University of Texas Press, 1969), p. 4. This study will be called *Today the Struggle* in later references.

30. Mowat, *Britain: 1918–1940,* p. 547.

31. Hynes, *The Auden Generation,* p. 198.

32. Frederick R. Benson, *Writers in Arms: The Literary Impact of the Spanish Civil War* (New York: New York University Press, 1967), pp. xx–xi.

33. Orwell, *CEJL,* I, pp. 589–90.

34. Samuels "English Intellectuals," p. 265, 248.

35. Hoskins, *Today the Struggle,* p. 12. See also Thomas, *The Spanish Civil War,* p. 797. On p. 794 Thomas notes that just "as very few Americans [out of about three thousand] fought for the Nationalists [Franco], . . . not more than a dozen British subjects appear to have done so."

36. Branson and Heinemann, *Britain in the Thirties,* p. 342.

37. Samuels, "English Intellectuals," p. 254.

38. Ibid., p. 253.

39. Ibid., p. 578.

40. Mowat, *Britain: 1918–1940,* p. 578.

41. Hynes, *The Auden Generation,* p. 208.

42. See Mowat, *Britain: 1918–1940,* p. 530, and Samuels, "English Intellectuals," p. 255.

43. Samuels, "English Intellectuals," p. 255.

44. Hynes, *The Auden Generation,* p. 206.

45. While it is important to note that Orwell wrote the book on commission from Victor Gollancz, and not the Left Book Club as such (the L.B.C. selected it for the March Book of the Month), it would be naive to think

that Orwell was unaware of Gollancz's position as an editor of the L.B.C. While Gollancz writes in his introduction to *The Road to Wigan Pier* (London: Gollancz, 1937), p. xii, "The Left Book Club has no 'policy': or rather it has no policy other than that of equipping people to fight against war and Fascism," it was nevertheless clear, as Richard Hoggart points out, that "The club was intended to mobilize and nourish socialist thought." (Hoggart, introduction to the Heinemann edition of *The Road to Wigan Pier*, p. v.) Benson, *Writers in Arms*, p. 91.

46. Orwell, *CEJL*, I, pp. 351–52, II, p. 456. For a discussion of the problems raised by Orwell's tendency at times to alter the sequence of events, see Crick, *George Orwell: A Life*, pp. 211, 206, 435 (fn. 10).

47. Stansky and Abrahams, *The Transformation*, pp. 141–142. Also see Chapters 15–17. Eileen O'Shaughnessy, who met Orwell in 1935, was studying for her master's degree in Educational Psychology at University College in London. For further details see ibid., Chapter 12.

48. Orwell, *CEJL*, I, p. 301.

49. George Orwell, *Homage to Catalonia* (which is bound with the essay "Looking Back on the Spanish War") (Harmondsworth, England: Penguin Books [in association with Secker and Warburg], 1966), p. 8. (This book will be called *Homage* or "Looking Back" in later references.) There is some confusion surrounding Orwell's financing of the trip. On the one hand, it has been claimed that Orwell was "under contract" with Secker and Warburg to produce a book on the Civil War (Jenni Calder, *Chronicles of Conscience: A Study of George Orwell and Arthur Koestler* [Pittsburgh: University of Pittsburgh Press, 1968], p. 99) and on the other, that he got an "advance" from Secker and Warburg for a book about his Spanish experiences (Brander, *George Orwell*, pp. 128–29). In any event, Warburg did not sign a contract for *Homage to Catalonia* until September 1, 1937, after it had been rejected by Gollancz. (Frederic Warburg, *All Authors Are Equal: the Publishing Life of Frederic Warburg, 1936–1971* [London: Hutchison, 1973], p. 98). See also ibid., pp. 8–9.

50. P.O.U.M. (Partido Obrero de Unificacion Marxista) consisted of semi-Trotskyists who, as mentioned earlier, started out as members of the Workers and Peasants Alliance. (See Thomas, *The Spanish Civil War*, p. 131.) Seeing their fight as primarily a struggle between socialism and capitalism, they held strongly to the anarchist slogan "The war and revolution are inseparable." (See Orwell, *Homage*, p. 69, and Thomas, *The Spanish Civil War*, p. 494.)

51. Orwell, *Homage*, p. 114.

52. Mowat, *Britain: 1918–1940*, p. 577.

53. Orwell, *CEJL*, I, pp. 312, 319, 323. Irrespective of whether Orwell had received an advance from Secker and Warburg for a book on his Spanish experiences, though refusing to publish *Homage to Catalonia*, Gollancz "had options under his contract with Orwell for his next two full-length novels, and clearly wanted to preserve them." As Bernard Crick notes "Never has a publisher tried harder to keep his hooks into an author whose best books he cordially disliked." (Warburg, *All Authors Are Equal*, p. 40.) For Orwell's comment on Gollancz's options on the next two books, see *CEJL*, IV, p. 444.

CHAPTER 7

1. Thomas, *The Spanish Civil War,* p. 77. Thomas describes anxious unemployed assembling at dawn "as in a slave market." See also ibid., pp. 52–53. In the golden century of Spain, when she was the great power, it was not unusual, for example, for "noblemen to serve as privates in the Army." The Church in Spain was actively committed for a time to an egalitarian spirit and practice: not only did it argue for a "more equal distribution of land," but it was noticeably hostile to commerce. Its "precommercial" (rather than socialistic) stance, however, petered out after the Napoleonic Wars, when it began resisting the spirit of liberalism and fell increasingly under the influence of Rome—particularly from the Jesuits.

2. Orwell, *Homage,* pp. 48, 30.

3. Orwell, *CEJL,* II, p. 306.

4. Orwell, *Homage,* p. 245.

5. Ibid., pp. 8–9. See also poet John Cornford's remarkably similar description of his arrival in Barcelona (Peter Stansky and William Abrahams, *Journey to the Frontier* [Boston: Little, Brown and Co., 1966] p. 316.)

6. Orwell, *Homage,* p. 9.

7. Orwell, *CEJL,* I, p. 207.

8. Orwell, *Homage,* p. 9.

9. Thomas, *The Spanish Civil War,* pp. 461, 622, 767.

10. Orwell, *Homage,* pp. 108, 238.

11. Ibid., pp. 9, 10, 12, 36.

12. Ibid., pp. 12, 12–13.

13. I have used Orwell's spelling of Saragosa.

14. Orwell, *Homage,* pp. 18, 19, 19, 21, 24, 22.

15. Ibid., pp. 25, 101, 103, 103.

16. Ibid., p. 101.

17. Ibid., pp. 29, 28, 23.

18. Ibid., pp. 30, 30, 30, 28–29, 29. Orwell notes that some "boys of fifteen were being brought up for enlistment by their parents" simply for the militiaman's wage of ten pesetas a day and for the bread their offspring could smuggle home from the barracks. (Orwell, *Homage,* p. 15.)

19. Thomas, *Spanish Civil War,* pp. 153, 227.

20. While there was, no doubt, much violence involved in these actions, the term *non-military* is used to indicate the difference between the battle against Franco's forces and the attempts to restructure society behind the anti-Franco front line.

21. Orwell, *Homage,* pp. 49, 50.

22. Thomas, *The Spanish Civil War,* p. 248.

23. Orwell, *Homage,* p. 50.

24. Thomas, *The Spanish Civil War,* pp. 248–49.

25. Ibid., p. 250.

26. Orwell, *Homage,* pp. 60–61.

27. Thomas, *The Spanish Civil War,* p. 463.

28. Orwell, *CEJL,* II, p. 108, I, pp. 358–59.

29. Orwell, *Homage,* pp. 29–30. However, in 1942, in "Notes on the War,"

he would write that "if whole armies had to be coerced, no war could ever be fought." (Orwell, *CEJL*, II, p. 32.)

30. George Orwell, "Caesarian Section in Spain," *The Highway* 31(March 1939): 145–47, 146, 146.

31. Ibid., p. 146. The words *childish, democratic,* and *spirit* I have quoted are also taken from ibid., p. 146.

32. Orwell, "Ceasarean Section in Spain," p. 147.

33. Ibid.

34. George Orwell, review of *Home Guard for Victory,* by Hugh Slater, in *Horizon* (March, 1941), pp. 219–20.

35. Orwell, "Caesarean Section in Spain," p. 147.

36. Orwell, *CEJL,* II, p. 232.

37. Orwell, "Caesarean Section in Spain," p. 147.

38. Orwell, *Homage,* p. 102.

39. Ibid., pp. 101–102.

40. Orwell, *Homage,* p. 103. The closest he comes to this tone elsewhere, though in muted form, is in his near obsessive tracts about the revolutionary potential of the English Home Guard in World War II. For just a few examples of this see his articles on the Home Guard in *The Tribune,* December 20, 1940; *The Observer,* October 15, 1943; *The Observer,* May 9, 1944.

41. Ibid., p. 184.

42. Ibid., pp. 226, 228.

43. Orwell, *Wigan Pier,* p. 127.

44. Orwell, *Homage,* p. 227.

45. Ibid., p. 9.

46. Ibid., p. 189.

47. Orwell, *CEJL,* I, pp. 583, 28.

48. Orwell, *Homage,* pp. 55, 102, 102–103.

49. Ibid., pp. 51, 304.

50. Orwell, *Homage,* p. 195. For the suppression of the P.O.U.M. see Thomas, *The Spanish Civil War,* pp. 494, 578–79, 622. For suppression of the Anarchists see *The Spanish Civil War,* pp. 601–602.

51. Thomas, *The Spanish Civil War,* p. 494.

52. Orwell, *Homage,* pp. 171, 125–26.

53. Thomas, *The Spanish Civil War,* pp. 550, 581.

54. Orwell, *Homage,* p. 207. See also Orwell, "Looking Back on the Spanish War," *CEJL,* II, pp. 286–306.

CHAPTER 8

1. Orwell, *Homage,* pp. 103, 46–47.

2. Ibid., pp. 57, 47.

3. Ibid., pp. 48, 50.

4. Ibid., pp. 48, 50, 51.

5. Orwell, *CEJL,* I, p. 318.

6. Orwell, *Homage,* pp. 51, 66. Orwell writes, "Please notice that I am saying nothing against the rank-and-file Communists, least of all against the thousands of Communists who died heroically round Madrid. But those were not the men who were directing party policy. As for the people higher

up, it is inconceivable that they were not acting with their eyes open." (Ibid., p. 67.)

7. Ibid., pp. 50–51.

8. Ibid., pp. 51, 64.

9. Orwell, *CEJL*, I, pp. 314. See also ibid., p. 311, for reference to Borkenau's *Spanish Cockpit*.

10. Orwell, *Homage*, pp. 234.

11. Arthur Koestler, cited in Phillip Knightley, *The First Casualty* (New York: Harcourt Brace Jovanovich, Harvest Book, 1976), p. 195.

12. Orwell, *Homage*, pp. 65, 156–57.

13. Ibid., p. 228.

14. Ibid.

15. Orwell, *CEJL*, I, pp. 28, 331–32.

16. Orwell, *Homage*, p. 18.

17. Ibid., p. 43.

18. Uncharacteristically, given his usual care with language, Orwell has used the words *intellectuals* and *intelligentsia* interchangeably, particularly in his comments about patriotism (see Orwell, *CEJL*, II, p. 95; *CEJL*, III, p. 53; *CEJL*, IV, p. 207). However, as he is clearly referring to people who inhabit (even if they do not actually earn their living in) a world of "ideas," I will use the word *intellectual* unless either directly quoting or paraphrasing Orwell's use of the word *intelligentsia*.

19. George Orwell, "Political Reflections on the Crisis." *The Adelphi*, December 1938, pp. 110–11.

20. Orwell, *Other Essays*, pp. 15, 17.

21. Ibid., p. 40.

22. Ibid., p. 18.

23. Ibid., p. 35.

24. Ibid.

25. Ibid., p. 36.

26. Orwell, *CEJL*, IV, p. 468.

27. *Other Essays*, p. 35.

28. Ibid., pp. 32, 32, 34.

29. Ibid., II, p. 2. In large measure it is this lack of patriotism among the leftist intellectuals that, despite the common ground shared with fellow middle-class socialists, separates not only them from the middle class but Orwell's attack upon them from his attack on the middle class in general and the middle-class socialists in particular. A middle-class socialist himself, Orwell, we recall, had written that patriotic tradition, even at its "stupidest and most sentimental," was "a comelier thing than the shallow self-righteousness of the left-wing intelligentsia." But while his major attack upon the middle-class socialists took place in 1936 in *The Road to Wigan Pier*, his most virulent attack on the leftist, often middle-class, intellectuals took place in the 1940s.

30. Orwell, *Other Essays*, p. 36.

31. Orwell, "Political Reflections on the Crisis," *The Adelphi*, December 1938, p. 110. This work will be called "Political Reflections" in later references.

32. Orwell, *Other Essays*, p. 37.

33. Peter Stansky, lecture on Orwell delivered in February 1976 at Simon Fraser University, Vancouver, Canada.

34. George Orwell, annotations on Randall Swingler, "The Right to Free Expression," *Polemic*, September–October 1946, p. 47.

35. Orwell, "Political Reflections," p. 110.

36. W.H. Auden, "Spain 1937," *The English Auden: Poems, Essays & Dramatic Writings, 1927–1939*, p. 210.

37. Orwell, *Other Essays*, p. 36.

38. Ibid., p. 37.

39. Orwell, *CEJL*, III, p. 178. For a study of how the totalitarian methods of Soviet Russia were accepted outside England, see David Caute, *The Fellow-Travellers* (London: Weidenfeld and Nicolson, 1973), p. 108.

40. Orwell, *Other Essays*, pp. 39, 33. Though in retrospect Orwell's skepticism and disgust with the reporting of the war have been justified, there is undoubtedly some truth in Lawrence Brander's observation that in *Homage to Catalonia* Orwell "does not concern himself with the obvious difficulty [especially in wartime] of the most conscientious reporter." (Brander, *George Orwell*, p. 145.)

41. Orwell, *Homage*, pp. 235, 235, 236. The estimates of the number of Russians "went as high as half a million," whereas Thomas (in *The Spanish Civil War*, p. 797) records the figure was more accurately around one thousand.

42. Orwell, *Homage*, p. 236.

43. Orwell, *CEJL*, IV, p. 86.

44. Ibid., II, p. 131.

45. Ibid.

46. Orwell, *Homage*, p. 236.

47. Orwell, *CEJL*, II, p. 131.

48. Ibid., IV, p. 85.

49. Orwell, *CEJL*, I, pp. 374–75.

50. Ibid., IV, p. 468.

51. Ibid., p. 467.

52. Orwell, "Political Reflections," p. 111.

53. Orwell, *CEJL*, IV, p. 93.

54. Ibid., I, p. 404.

55. Ibid., II, p. 470.

56. Orwell, *CEJL*, IV, p. 218.

57. Ibid., I, pp. 347–48.

58. Orwell, *Homage*, p. 236.

59. Ibid.

60. Orwell, *Nineteen Eighty-Four*, p. 223.

61. Ibid.

62. Orwell, *CEJL*, I, p. 301.

63. Orwell, *Nineteen Eighty-Four*, p. 68.

64. Orwell, *Homage*, pp. 236, 237.

65. Ibid., p. 15.

66. Ibid., p. 7.

67. Benson, *Writers in Arms*, p. 172.

68. Orwell, *Homage*, p. 102.

69. Ibid., p. 47.

70. In *Homage*, p. 238, Orwell does write, "In the long struggle that has followed the Russian Revolution it is the manual workers who have been defeated, and it is impossible not to feel that it was their own fault. Time after time, in country after country, the organized working-class movements have been crushed by open, illegal violence, and their comrades abroad, linked to them in theoretical solidarity, have simply looked on and done nothing." This is still no closer to an examination of inherent administrative weaknesses and the like within the revolutionary structures, but only tells of a lack of solidarity abroad—though it does say something about international brotherhood.

71. Orwell, *Homage*, pp. 232, 50.

72. Ibid., p. 240.

73. Jeffrey Meyers, *A Reader's Guide to George Orwell* (London: Thames and Hudson, 1975), p. 117.

74. Orwell, *Homage*, p. 153.

75. Mander, *The Writer and Commitment*, p. 72.

76. Lionel Trilling, introduction to *Homage to Catalonia* (New York: Harcourt, Brace and World Co., 1952), pp. xxii–xxiii.

77. Orwell, *Homage*, pp. 245, 233.

78. Brander, *George Orwell*, p. 102.

79. Orwell, *Wigan Pier*, p. 145.

80. Orwell, *CEJL*, IV, p. 486.

81. Orwell, *Homage*, pp. 48, 174.

82. Ibid., pp. 135, 220.

83. Orwell, *CEJL*, I, pp. 576–77.

84. Hynes, *The Auden Generation*, pp. 379–80.

85. Orwell, *Homage*, pp. 220, 245, 245.

86. Zwerdling, *Orwell and the Left*, pp. 77, 9–10, 9, 8.

87. Orwell, *CEJL*, I, p. 583.

88. Ibid., II, pp. 140–41.

CHAPTER 9

1. Orwell, *CEJL*, IV, p. 287.

2. Hollis, *A Study of George Orwell*, p. 107.

3. The loan, given anonymously at the time, was from the novelist L.H. Meyers. See Orwell, *CEJL*, I, p. 600.

4. Orwell, *Coming Up For Air*, pp. 158, 233, 156, 154, 155.

5. Orwell, *CEJL*, I, p. 406.

6. Orwell, *Coming Up For Air*, p. 149.

7. Ibid., p. 160.

8. Orwell, *CEJL*, II, pp. 407, 45.

9. No trace of this pamphlet has been found. See Orwell, *CEJL*, I, p. 395.

10. Orwell, *Other Essays*, p. 40.

11. Orwell, *Coming Up For Air*, pp. 143, 151–52.

12. Alldritt, *The Making of George Orwell*, pp. 130–34. Alldritt is particu-

larly good in showing how "Inside the Whale" is an important autobiographical piece as well as a literary criticism of the Thirties. Miller's position was not really pacifism but rather that involvement in such things as the Spanish War should not be motivated from a sense of duty to others. See Orwell, *Other Essays*, p. 40.

13. Orwell, *CEJL*, I, p. 400.

14. Orwell, *Other Essays*, pp. 48, 17.

15. Orwell, *CEJL*, II, pp. 42–45, 108.

16. George Orwell, "Too Hard on Humanity an imaginary interview between GEORGE ORWELL and JONATHAN SWIFT," *The Listener*, November 26, 1942, p. 693.

17. Orwell, *CEJL*, III, p. 71.

18. Ibid., IV, p. 323.

19. Ibid., I, pp. 339, 340, 369.

20. Ibid., pp. 314, 306, 318, 425, 425.

21. Ibid., III, p. 272.

22. Ibid., IV, p. 138.

23. Lionel Trilling, "George Orwell and the Politics of Truth," in *George Orwell: A Collection of Critical Essays* (Englewood Cliffs, N.J.: Prentice-Hall, 1974), p. 65.

24. Orwell, *CEJL*, IV, pp. 321–22.

25. Ibid., p. 322.

26. Zwerdling notes, "We find him [Orwell], for example, using many of the essays of the forties to investigate a phenomenon that we have seen disturbed him deeply: the lust for power . . . 'Raffles and Miss Blandish,' . . . 'Wells, Hitler and the World State,' and 'Lear, Tolstoy and the Fool.' " (Zwerdling, *Orwell and the Left*, p. 180.) Zwerdling also notes, "He [Orwell] consistently uses popular literature as a tool of sociological investigation." (Ibid., p. 189.)

27. Owell, *CEJL*, II, p. 99.

28. Ibid., pp. 240–41.

29. Orwell, *CEJL*, III, pp. 264, 262–63. For more impressions from his war correspondence, see William Steinhoff, *George Orwell and the Origins of 1984* (Ann Arbor: University of Michigan Press, 1975). pp. 114–15.

30. George Orwell, "The British General Election," *Commentary*, November 1945, p. 69.

31. Orwell, *CEJL*, IV, pp. 312–13. For an excellent account of the literary forbears of *Nineteen Eighty-Four*, see William Steinhoff's *George Orwell and the Origins of 1984*.

32. Hugh Trevor-Roper, "The Germans and the Jews," a review of Walter Laqueur's *The Terrible Secret* (London: Weidenfeld, 1980) in *The Listener*, Jan. 1, 1981, pp. 19–20.

33. Orwell, *CEJL*, IV, p. 520.

34. Ibid., III, p. 458.

35. Ibid., pp. 237, 458.

36. Stansky and Abrahams, *The Transformation*, pp. 138, 162, 165.

37. Orwell, *CEJL*, III, p. 459.

38. Warburg, *All Authors Are Equal*, p. 42.

39. Ibid., p. 41.
40. Orwell, *CEJL*, III, p. 207.
41. Warburg, *All Authors Are Equal*, pp. 42, 48. For Bernard Crick's reservations about Warburg's account, see Crick, *George Orwell: A Life*, p. 318.
42. Ibid., pp. 48–49.
43. Ibid., p. 48.
44. Bernard Crick, "Freedom of the Press," *Times Literary Supplement*, September 15, 1972, p. 1040.
45. Orwell, *CEJL*, III, p. 47.
46. Ibid., p. 177. The idea of superstates owes much to Orwell's reading of James Burnham's *Managerial Revolution* (see CEJL, III, p. 374).
47. Orwell, *Other Essays*, p. 48.
48. Orwell, *CEJL*, IV, p. 355.
49. Warburg, *All Authors Are Equal*, p. 355.
50. Orwell, *CEJL*, IV, p. 459. For Orwell, like most writers, rough drafts were "just a mess and don't have much relationship to the final draft." (Orwell, *CEJL*, IV, p. 448.)
51. Orwell, *CEJL*, IV, p. 36.
52. Orwell, *Nineteen Eighty-Four*, p. 162.
53. Ibid., pp. 163, 164. See also Orwell, *Wigan Pier*, p. 157.
54. Orwell, *Nineteen Eighty-Four*, pp. 137, 164–65.
55. Orwell, *Wigan Pier*, p. 188.
56. Orwell, *Nineteen Eighty-Four*, p. 168.
57. Ibid., pp. 167–68.
58. Orwell, *CEJL*, II, p. 120.
59. Orwell, *Nineteen Eighty-Four*, pp. 210–11.
60. Ibid., p. 414.
61. Bernard Crick, "Lost Illusions," review of Alex Zwerdling's *Orwell and the Left* in *New Review* 1, no. 9, (December 1974): 63.
62. Orwell, *CEJL*, IV, p. 211.
63. Orwell, *Nineteen Eighty-Four*, p. 164.
64. Orwell, *CEJL*, I, p. 419.
65. Ibid.
66. Orwell, *Nineteen Eighty-Four*, p. 6. At one point in Goldstein's theory, it is asserted that "Oceania . . . is not centralized in any way." (Ibid., p. 167.) This is an obvious and gross contradiction of the overwhelming fact that London is the "chief city of Airstrip One" and is so completely dominated by the four ministries.
67. Ibid., pp. 6–7.
68. Ibid., p. 160.
69. Orwell, *Coming Up For Air*, p. 160.
70. Orwell, *Nineteen Eighty-Four*, pp. 5, 8, 8, 20.
71. Ibid., pp. 62–63. See *Wigan Pier*, pp. 16–17.
72. Orwell, *CEJL*, II, pp. 161–64. In *The English People* (written in May 1944), Orwell expressed a belief that the "change-over to a centralized economy . . . does of itself guarantee greater equality" (Orwell, *CEJL*, III, p. 50), but clearly he saw the dangers beyond a certain point, for in the same essay he calls for less centralization (*CEJL*, III, pp. 51–52), arguing that not only

would this be good for English agriculture, but that diversity "would strengthen national unity rather than weaken it." (*CEJL*, III, p. 52.)

73. Orwell, *CEJL*, II, p. 162.
74. Orwell, *Nineteen Eighty-Four*, pp. 9, 166.
75. Orwell, *CEJL*, I, p. 418.
76. Ibid., II, pp. 163, 164.
77. Orwell, *Burmese Days*, p. 67.
78. Orwell, *Nineteen Eighty-Four*, p. 223.
79. Ibid., p. 224.
80. Orwell, *Animal Farm*, pp. 12–13, 120.
81. Ibid., pp. 120, 31, 114.
82. Orwell, *CEJL*, IV, p. 156.
83. Orwell, *Animal Farm*, pp. 16, 114.
84. Ibid., pp. 111, 110.
85. Ibid., pp. 57, 77, 77, 23, 60, 23, 78.
86. Ibid., p. 22.
87. Soviet dissident Andrei Sakharov said in an interview with a *Time* correspondent, "The problem is that in order to achieve the good life here [in Russia], one necessarily develops a certain conformist mentality. *For most people, there is no opportunity to compare the system here with systems outside.* The material side of life has improved here and people know it. *So humans work, live and exist here, not knowing of any other kind of life.*" (The italics are mine.) (*Time*, February 21, 1977, p. 17.) See also Orwell, *Nineteen Eighty-Four*, p. 170.
88. Orwell, *Animal Farm*, pp. 83, 99.
89. Orwell, *CEJL*, IV, p. 86.
90. In his study of Stalin, Boris Souvarine notes, "The only things that matter are the latest writings of Stalin, the most recent speeches of his spokesmen, the newspaper articles setting forth the perishable truth of the day, up-to-the-minute texts which render seditious and obsolete the orthodox publications of the day before, finally the current sources of information such as the Soviet Encyclopaedias, . . . which must be thrown on the scrapheap, . . . despite the many expurgations repeated by the many successive censorships, despite the many falsifications introduced in the very course of printing." (Boris Souvarine, *Stalin*, 1939, p. 622, quoted in Jennifer McDowell, "1984 and Soviet Reality," *University of California Graduate Journal* no. 1 [Fall 1962]: 18.)
91. Orwell, *CEJL*, II, p. 463.
92. Orwell, *Homage*, p. 170.
93. Orwell, *Animal Farm*, pp. 68–69.
94. Orwell, *Nineteen Eighty-Four*, p. 14.
95. Orwell, *Animal Farm*, pp. 114, 107.
96. Orwell, *Nineteen Eighty-Four*, pp. 251, 245, 167, 242, 171, 172, 250, 241.
97. Ibid., pp. 45, 44, 165, 250.
98. Ibid., pp. 45, 242, 248, 146–48.
99. Orwell, *CEJL*, III, pp. 166, 43, 166, 162, 43–44.
100. Orwell, *Nineteen Eighty-Four*, p. 46.
101. Orwell, *CEJL*, IV, pp. 165–66.

102. Orwell, *Nineteen Eighty-Four*, pp. 46–47.
103. Ibid., pp. 146–47.
104. Ibid., pp. 147–48.
105. Ibid., p. 200.

CHAPTER 10

1. Orwell, *Other Essays*, p. 48.
2. Orwell, *CEJL*, IV, p. 82.
3. Orwell, annotations on Randall Swingler, "The Right to Free Expression," p. 47.
4. Orwell, *Nineteen Eighty-Four*, p. 149.
5. Orwell, *CEJL*, III, p. 224.
6. Ibid., II, pp. 465–66.
7. Ibid., IV, pp. 83, 85, 86.
8. Orwell, *Nineteen Eighty-Four*, p. 107.
9. Orwell, *CEJL*, IV, pp. 92, 96.
10. Ibid., p. 91.
11. Orwell, *CEJL*, III, pp. 266, 293. Orwell points to Trollope as the exception to the rule. He notes, however, that "as he [Trollope] also hunted three days a week and was usually playing whist till midnight, I suspect that he did not overwork himself in his official [Post Office] duties." (Orwell, *CEJL*, III, p. 293.)
12. Orwell, *CEJL*, III, p. 265.
13. Ibid., I, p. 568.
14. Ibid., III, p. 178.
15. Orwell, *Nineteen Eighty-Four*, p. 185.
16. Orwell, *CEJL*, IV, p. 91.
17. Rigorously imposed censorship has, of course, often encouraged the development of certain art forms that might otherwise have lain dormant. One can think of the art of mime: for example, The Black Theatre of Prague, Czechoslovakia, has received world acclaim.
18. Orwell, *Nineteen Eighty-Four*, p. 113.
19. Ibid., pp. 83–84.
20. Ibid., p. 176.
21. Orwell, *CEJL*, III, p. 43.
22. Ibid., IV, p. 94. In her *1984 and Soviet Reality* (p. 18) Jennifer McDowell writes, "It may surprise some readers to learn that 'two plus two equals five' was an optimistic slogan for the first Five Year Plan meaning the fulfillment of the Five Year Plan in four years." It is also noted how Eugene Lyons reported having seen the slogan "in electric lights on Moscow housefronts."
23. Orwell, *Nineteen Eighty-Four*, p. 154.
24. Ibid.
25. Ibid., p. 160.
26. Orwell, *CEJL*, IV, p. 294.
27. Orwell, *Nineteen Eighty-Four*, p. 161.
28. Orwell, *Animal Farm*, p. 50.
29. Orwell, *CEJL*, II, p. 29.
30. Ibid.

31. Orwell, *Nineteen Eighty-Four*, p. 237.
32. Ibid., pp. 156, 157, 157.
33. Ibid., pp. 156–57.
34. Orwell, *CEJL*, IV, pp. 88, 28.
35. Ibid., p. 30.
36. Orwell, *Nineteen Eighty-Four*, pp. 244, 249.
37. Ibid., pp. 63, 66, 63, 66.
38. Ibid., pp. 170, 171.
39. Ibid., p. 32.
40. Ibid., p. 200.
41. Ibid., p. 68.
42. Orwell, *Wigan Pier*, p. 173.
43. Orwell, *Nineteen Eighty-Four*, p. 80.
44. Orwell, *CEJL*, I, p. 28.
45. Orwell, *Nineteen Eighty-Four*, p. 68.
46. Ibid., p. 213.
47. Orwell, *CEJL*, IV, pp. 300–302.
48. Orwell, *A Clergyman's Daughter*, p. 240.
49. Orwell, *Nineteen Eighty-Four*, pp. 67, 213, 200.
50. Ibid., pp. 204, 38, 38, 149.
51. Ibid., p. 45.
52. Orwell, *Homage*, p. 237.
53. Orwell, *CEJL*, IV, pp. 381, 382, 383, 382, 401.
54. Ibid., p. 401.
55. Orwell, *CEJL*, IV, p. 388.
56. History was, of course, taught but Orwell's point was that the way it was taught, it made little or no sense. "History was a series of unrelated, unintelligible but—in some way that was never explained to us—important facts. . . .

      '1857?'
      'Massacre of St. Bartholomew!'
      '1707?'
      'Death of Aurangzeeb!' " (Orwell, *CEJL*, IV, p. 387.)

57. Orwell, *CEJL*, IV, p. 421.
58. Ibid., p. 411.
59. Orwell, *A Clergyman's Daughter*, pp. 240–41.
60. Orwell, *Nineteen Eighty-Four*, p. 136.
61. Ibid., pp. 205, 195, 19.
62. Orwell, *Coming Up For Air*, pp. 148–49.
63. Orwell, *Nineteen Eighty-Four*, pp. 13, 15.
64. Ibid., p. 177.
65. Ibid., pp. 181, 181.
66. Ibid., p. 187.
67. Ibid., pp. 217, 205.
68. Ibid., p. 216.
69. Orwell, *CEJL*, II, p. 23.
70. Orwell, *Homage*, p. 237.

71. Orwell, *Nineteen Eighty-Four,* pp. 19, 39.
72. Ibid., pp. 169, 9, 169, 169.
73. Ibid., pp. 169, 128.
74. Ibid., pp. 101, 101.
75. Ibid., pp. 109, 109, 109.
76. Vladimir Gsovski writes in a *Pravda* editorial of May 28, 1936, that "marriage receives its full lifeblood and value for the Soviet State only if there is the birth of children." (McDowell, *1984 and Soviet Reality,* p. 16.)
77. Orwell, *Nineteen Eighty-Four,* pp. 212, 212, 212.
78. Orwell, *CEJL,* II, pp. 32, 33, 78.
79. Orwell, *Nineteen Eighty-Four,* pp. 218, 204, 222–23.
80. Ibid., p. 225.
81. Ibid., pp. 225, 227–28.
82. Bob Edwards, the British M.P. who fought with Orwell in Aragon, recalls in an introduction to *Homage to Catalonia* that Orwell "had a great phobia against rats and, whilst most of us got used to them even when they gnawed at our boots at night, Orwell could never feel comfortable in their presence." See the Folio Society edition of *Homage to Catalonia* (London: Folio Society, 1970), p. 90.
83. Orwell, *Nineteen Eighty-Four,* p. 230.
84. Ibid., pp. 203, 215, 239.
85. Orwell, *CEJL,* III, pp. 159, 159, 159, 160.
86. Ibid., pp. 159, 160.
87. Orwell, *Nineteen Eighty-Four,* p. 59.
88. Ibid., pp. 59, 60, 61.
89. Ibid., pp. 61, 60.
90. Ibid., p. 63.
91. For example, when Lysenko's wheat experiments, which stressed the influence of environment rather than genes (encouraging Stalin's belief in the creation of a Soviet Man), failed to produce bumper crops, blame could be placed elsewhere than where it belonged—that is, upon the essential fallacies of Lysenko's theory.
92. Orwell, *Nineteen Eighty-Four,* p. 11.
93. Ibid., pp. 113, 116, 113.
94. Ibid., pp. 169, 135, 176.
95. Ibid., pp. 166, 175.
96. Ibid., p. 176.
97. Orwell, *CEJL,* III, p. 43.
98. Orwell, *Nineteen Eighty-Four,* p. 101.
99. Ibid., pp. 126, 102.
100. Ibid., p. 110.
101. Orwell, *CEJL,* IV, p. 175.

CHAPTER 11

1. George Orwell, "Will Freedom Die with Capitalism?" *The Left News,* April 1941, pp. 1684, 1683.
2. Orwell, *CEJL,* III, p. 365.
3. Orwell, *CEJL,* III, p. 142.
4. Brander, *George Orwell,* p. 204.

5. Bernard Crick, "Lost Illusions," pp. 61–74.

6. Orwell, *CEJL*, IV, p. 428.

7. Ibid., p. 564.

8. Steinhoff, *George Orwell and the Origins of 1984*, p. 199. Here I endorse Richard Vorhees, Philip Rahv, William Steinhoff, and George Woodcock in believing that Orwell's last novel is unequivocally a warning and not a prophecy.

9. Gabriel Gersh, "A Reactionary Radical," review of *CEJL*, in *Modern Age*, Summer 1969, p. 12. Bernard Crick suggests that the climate of Jura did not do Orwell any harm. I find this implausible. Despite Islanders agreeing that "the climate was no harm to him (local pride?), I give more weight to William Dunn, another Island resident, who, as Crick reports, firmly believes that "the dampness was obviously harmful." Certainly, Orwell's farmhouse, Barnhill, was remote—away from the kind of medical attention his condition warranted. See Bernard Crick, *George Orwell: A Life*, pp. 368–69.

10. Orwell, *CEJL*, II, p. 127.

11. Ibid., I, p. 591.

12. Orwell, *CEJL*, IV, p. 344.

13. George Orwell, "Too Hard on Humanity," p. 693.

14. Orwell, *CEJL*, I, p. 469.

15. Ibid., I, p. 311.

16. Ibid., I, p. 577.

17. Richard J. Vorhees, *The Paradox of George Orwell* (Lafayette, Ind.: Purdue University Press, 1961), p. 90.

18. Zwerdling, *Orwell and the Left*, p. 3.

19. Malcolm Muggeridge, "Books," review of *CEJL* in *Esquire*, March 1969, p. 2.

20. Woodcock, *The Crystal Spirit*, p. 49.

21. Orwell, *CEJL*, I, pp. 25–26.

22. Orwell, *Wigan Pier*, p. 130.

23. Zwerdling, *Orwell and the Left*, p. 64.

24. Woodcock, *The Crystal Spirit*, Preface.

25. Ibid., p. 50.

26. Orwell, *Other Essays*, p. 150.

27. Muggeridge, "Books," p. 3.

28. Orwell, *CEJL*, IV, p. 166.

29. Bernard Crick, *In Defence of Politics*, rev ed. (Harmondsworth, England: Pelican Books, 1964), p. 63.

30. Orwell, *CEJL*, IV, p. 167.

31. Ibid., I, p. 28.

32. Ibid., IV, p. 94.

33. Warburg, *All Authors Are Equal*, pp. 101–102.

34. Orwell, *CEJL*, IV, p. 573.

35. Warburg, *All Authors Are Equal*, pp. 102–103.

36. Orwell, *CEJL*, IV, pp. 536, 519.

37. Ibid., IV, pp. 548, 549.

38. Ibid., IV, p. 557.

39. Personal conversation with Julian Symons, March 22, 1981.

SELECTED BIBLIOGRAPHY

Note: References to two or more works by the same author (or authors) are listed by date of publication.

Atkins, John. *George Orwell*. London: John Calder, 1954; New York: Riverrun Press, 1981.

Auden, W.H. *The English Auden: Poems, Essays & Dramatic Writings, 1927–1939*, edited by Edward Mendelson. New York: Random House, 1968.

Belloc, H. *The Servile State*. 2nd ed. London: T.N. Foulis, 1913; New York: Library of America, 1977.

Benson, Frederick R. *Writers in Arms–The Literary Impact of the Spanish Civil War*. New York: New York University Press, 1967.

Borkenau, Franz. *The Spanish Cockpit*. Ann Arbor, Mich.: Ann Arbor Paperbacks, 1963.

Bottomore, T.B. *Classes in Modern Society*. 5th imp. London: George Allen and Unwin Ltd., 1970; New York: Random House, 1968.

Braibanti, Ralph, ed. *Asian Bureaucratic Systems Emergent from the British Imperial Tradition*. Durham, N.C.: Duke University Press, 1966.

Brander, Laurence. *George Orwell*. London: Longmans, Green and Co., 1954.

Branson, Noreen, and Heinemann, Margot. *Britain in the Thirties*. St. Albans, England: Panther Books, 1973.

Brome, Vincent. *The International Brigades*. London: Heinemann, 1965.

Cairns, H. Alan C. *The Clash of Cultures*. New York: Frederick A. Praeger, 1965.

Calder, Jenni. *Chronicles of Conscience: A Study of George Orwell and Arthur Koestler*. Pittsburgh, Pa.: University of Pittsburgh Press, 1968.

Cook, Richard. "Rudyard Kipling and George Orwell." *Modern Fiction Studies*, 7 (Summer 1961): 125–35.

Crick, Bernard. *In Defence of Politics*. Rev. ed. Harmondsworth, England: Pelican Books, 1962; Chicago: University of Chicago Press, 1972.

———. "Coming Up To Orwell." (Review of *The World of George Orwell*, edited by Miriam Gross.) *New Statesman*, October 8, 1971, pp. 478–79.

———. An accompanying commentary on the hitherto unpublished article "The Freedom of the Press" (by George Orwell). *Times Literary Supplement*, September 15, 1972, pp. 1039–40.

———. "Lost Illusions." (Review of *Orwell and the Left*, by Alex Zwerdling.) *New Review* 1, no. 9 (December 1974): 61–64.

————. *Orwell: A Life*. London: Secker and Warburg, 1980; Boston: Little, Brown, 1981.

Dahrendorf, Ralf. *Class and Class Conflict in Industrial Society*. Stanford: Stanford University Press, 1959.

Davidson, James F. "Political Science and Political Fiction." *American Political Science Review* 55(December 1961): 851–60.

Deutsch, Karl. "The Performance of Political Systems." In *Politics and Government: How People Decide Their Fate*. New York: Houghton Mifflin, 1970; London: Houghton Mifflin, 1980.

Dooley, D.J. "The Limitations of George Orwell." *University of Toronto Quarterly* 28(1958–59): 291–300.

Edwards, R. Introduction to *Homage to Catalonia*, by George Orwell. London: The Folio Society, 1970, pp. 5–11.

Emerson, Thomas J. *Toward a General Theory of the First Amendment*. New York: Random House, 1963.

Foot, Michael. "Orwell Uncovered." (Review of *The World of George Orwell*, edited by Miriam Gross.) *Evening Standard*, October 12, 1971.

Ford, Boris. *The Modern Age*. Vol. 7 of *The Pelican Guide to English Literature*, vol. 7. Rev. ed. Harmondsworth, England: Penguin Books, 1964; New York: Penguin, 1984.

Forster, E.M. *A Passage to India*. Harmondsworth, England: Penguin Books, 1936; New York: Lightyear Press, 1981.

Furnival, J.S. *Colonial Policy and Practice*. New York: New York University Press, 1956.

Geertz, Clifford. *The Social History of an Indonesian Town*. Cambridge, Mass.: M.I.T. Press, 1965.

Gersh, Gabriel. "A Reactionary Radical." (Review of *The Collected Essays, Journalism and Letters of George Orwell*, edited by Sonia Orwell and Ian Angus.) *Modern Age*, Summer 1969, pp. 308–13.

Gillie, Christopher. *Movements in English Literature: 1900–1940*. Cambridge, England: Cambridge University Press, 1975; New York: Cambridge University Press, 1975.

Gollancz, Victor. Introduction to *The Road to Wigan Pier*, by George Orwell. London: Gollancz, 1937, pp. xi–xxiv.

Goodman, Walter. "Homage to Orwell." *The New Leader*, November 27, 1972.

Gross, Miriam, ed. *The World of George Orwell*. New York: Simon and Schuster, 1971.

Hartley, Anthony. "English Intellectuals: Their Power and Powerlessness." *Interplay*, April, 1968, pp. 47–53.

Hennesy, Peter. "Bernard Crick: 'a pretty potent piece of artillery letting fly in all directions.'" *The [London] Times Higher Education Supplement*, November 29, 1974, pp. 7–8.

Hobson, J.A. *Imperialism—A Study*. 3d rev. ed., 5th imp. London: George Allen and Unwin Ltd., 1954; Ann Arbor: University of Michigan Press, 1965.

Hoggart, Richard. *The Uses of Literacy*. Harmondsworth, England: Pelican Books, 1958.

————. Introduction to *The Road to Wigan Pier,* by George Orwell. London: Heinemann, 1965, pp. v–xxvi.

Hollis, Christopher. *A Study of George Orwell.* London: Hollis and Carter, 1956.

Homans, George C. *The Human Group.* New York: Harcourt Brace, 1950; London: Routledge, Keegan, Paul, 1975.

Hoskins, Katherine B. *Today the Struggle: Literature and Politics in England During the Spanish Civil War.* Austin, Texas: University of Texas Press, 1969.

Howe, Irving. "Orwell: History as Nightmare." *The American Scholar* 25, no. 2 (Spring 1956): 193–207.

Hynes, Samuel. *The Auden Generation: Literature and Politics in England in the 1930s.* Toronto: The Bodley Head, 1976; New Jersey: Princeton University Press, 1982.

Kateb, G. "The Road to 1984." *Political Science Quarterly* 81(1966): 564–80.

Kirsch, Robert. "George Orwell—Continuing Conscience of the World." (Second part of a review of *The Collected Essays, Journalism and Letters of George Orwell,* edited by Sonia Orwell and Ian Angus.) *Los Angeles Times,* November 19, 1968, Part 4, p. 19.

Knightley, Phillip. *The First Casualty.* New York: A Harvest Book, Harcourt Brace Jovanovich, 1976; London: Quartet Books, 1978.

Koebner, Richard, and Schmidt, Helmut Dan. *Imperialism: The Story and Significance of a Political Word 1840–1960.* Cambridge, England: Cambridge University Press, 1964.

Landau, Martin. *Political Theory and Political Science: Studies in the Methodology of Political Inquiry.* New York: Macmillan Company, 1972; Brighton, England: Harvester Press, 1979.

Laski, Harold J. Review of *The Road to Wigan Pier,* by George Orwell. *The Left News,* March 1937, pp. 275–76.

Laslett, Peter. *The World We Have Lost.* London: Methuen and Co. Ltd., 1965; New York: Scribner Book Co., 1971.

Lee, Robert A. "Symbol and Structure in *Burmese Days:* A Revaluation." *Texas Studies in Literature and Language* 11(1969): 819–35.

Lichtheim, George. *Imperialism.* New York: Frederick A. Praeger, 1971.

McDowell, Jennifer. "1984 and Soviet Reality." *University of California Graduate Journal,* no. 1 (Fall 1962): 12–19.

McLellan, David. *The Thought of Karl Marx.* London: Macmillan, 1971.

Mander, John. *The Writer and Commitment.* London: Secker and Warburg, 1961; Westport, Conn.: Greenwood Press, 1975.

Mannoni, O. *Prospero and Caliban.* Translated by P. Powesland. New York: Frederick A. Praeger, 1956.

Meyers, Jeffrey, ed. *George Orwell: The Critical Heritage.* Boston: Routledge and Kegan Paul Ltd., 1965; London: Routledge, 1975.

————. *A Reader's Guide to George Orwell.* London: Thames and Hudson, 1975; New Jersey, Littlefield, Adams, 1977.

Minogue, K.R. "Humanist Democracy: The Political Thought of C.B. Macpherson." *Canadian Journal of Political Science* 9(1976): 377–422.

Mowat, Charles L.M. *Britain Between the Wars: 1918–1940.* London: Methuen

and Co. Ltd., 1956; Chicago: University of Chicago Press, 1955.
Muggeridge, Malcolm. Review of *The Collected Essays, Journalism and Letters of George Orwell*, edited by Sonia Orwell and Ian Angus. *Esquire*, March 1969.
———. *The Thirties*. London: Fontana Books, 1972.
Myrdal, Gunnar. *Asian Drama*. Vol. 2. New York: Random House, 1968.
Nadel, George H. *Imperialism and Colonialism*. Introduced by G.H. Nadel and Perry Curtis. New York: Macmillan Company, 1964.
Nye, J.S. "Corruption and Political Development: A Cost–Benefit Analysis." *American Political Science Review* 61(1967): 417–27.
O'Donnell, Donal. "Orwell Looks at the World." *Observer*, May 26, 1961, pp. 837–38.
Orwell, George. *Animal Farm*. Harmondsworth, England: Penguin Books (in association with Secker and Warburg), 1951; New York: Harcourt Brace Jovanovich, 1954.
———. *Nineteen Eighty-Four*. Harmondsworth, England: Penguin Books (in association with Secker and Warburg), 1954; New York: Harcourt Brace Jovanovich, 1949.
———. *The Orwell Reader*. Compiled with an introduction by Richard H. Rovere. New York: Harcourt Brace Jovanovich, 1956.
———. *Coming Up For Air*. Harmondsworth, England: Penguin Books (in association with Secker and Warburg), 1962; New York: Harcourt Brace Jovanovich, 1969.
———. *Inside the Whale and Other Essays*. Harmondsworth, England: Penguin Books (in association with Secker and Warburg), 1962.
———. *Keep the Aspidistra Flying*. Harmondsworth, England: Penguin Books (in association with Secker and Warburg), 1962; New York: Harcourt Brace Jovanovich, 1969.
———. *The Road to Wigan Pier*. Harmondsworth, England: Penguin Books (in association with Secker and Warburg), 1962; New York: Harcourt Brace Jovanovich, 1972.
———. *Down and Out in Paris and London*. Harmondsworth, England: Penguin Books (in association with Secker and Warburg), 1966; New York: Harcourt Brace Jovanovich, 1972.
———. *Homage to Catalonia*. Harmondsworth, England: Penguin Books (in association with Secker and Warburg), 1966; New York: Harcourt Brace Jovanovich, 1969.
———. *Burmese Days*. Harmondsworth, England: Penguin Books (in association with Secker and Warburg), 1967; New York: Harcourt Brace Jovanovich, 1962.
———. "The Freedom of the Press." *Times Literary Supplement*, September 15, 1972.
Orwell, Sonia, and Angus, Ian, eds. *The Collected Essays, Journalism and Letters of George Orwell*. 4 vols. Harmondsworth, England: Penguin Books (in association with Secker and Warburg), 1970; New York: Harcourt Brace Jovanovich, 1971.
Parkin, Frank. *Class Inequality and Political Order*. Reprinted ed. St. Albans, England: Granada Publishing Ltd., 1973.

Pelling, Henry. *Modern Britain: 1885–1955.* London: Sphere Books, 1969; New York: W.W. Norton, 1966.

Polanyi, Karl. *The Great Transformation.* Boston: Beacon Press, 1957.

Potts, Paul. "Don Quixote on a Bicycle: In Memoriam George Orwell (1903–50), for Richard, his Son." In *Dante Called You Beatrice.* London: Eyre and Spottiswoode, 1960, pp. 71–87. (Reprinted from *London Magazine,* vol. 4, no. 3 [1957], pp. 39–47.)

Pritchett, V.S. "George Orwell." In *Living Writers.* Edited by Gilbert Phelps. London: Sylvan Press, 1947, pp. 106–15.

Runciman, W.G. *Relative Deprivation and Social Justice.* Berkeley: University of California Press, 1966; London: Routledge, 1966.

Samuels, Stuart. "English Intellectuals and Politics in the 1930s." In *On Intellectuals.* Edited by Philip Rieff. New York: Anchor Books, Doubleday and Company, Inc., 1970.

Sandison, Alan. *The Last Man in Europe.* New York: Macmillan, 1974.

Scott, James C. "The Analysis of Corruption in Developing Nations." *Comparative Studies in Society and History,* 2(June 1969): 315–41.

————. "Patron–Client Politics and Political Change in Southeast Asia." *American Political Science Review,* 66(March 1972): 91–113.

Sedgwick, Peter. "Orwell: Honesty, Courage and Faith in the 'Proles.'" (Review of *The Collected Essays, Journalism and Letters of George Orwell,* edited by Sonia Orwell and Ian Angus.) *Socialist Worker,* November 9, 1968, p. 3.

————. "George Orwell International Socialist–1: The Development of Orwell's Socialism." *International Socialism,* June–July 1969, pp. 28–34.

Slater, Ian. "Orwell, Marcuse and the Language of Politics." *Political Studies* 23(December 1975): 459–74.

Small, Christopher. *The Road to Miniluv: George Orwell, the State and God.* London: Victor Gollancz Ltd., 1975.

Spegele, Roger D. "Fiction and Political Theory." *Social Research* 38(Spring 1971): 108–37.

Stansky, Peter, and Abrahams, William. *Journey to the Frontier.* Boston: Little Brown, 1966; London: Constable, 1973.

————. *The Unknown Orwell.* New York: Alfred A. Knopf, 1972; London: Constable, 1972.

————. *Orwell: The Transformation.* London: Constable and Co., 1979; Chicago: Academy Chicago Ltd., 1981.

Steinhoff, William. *George Orwell and the Origins of 1984.* Ann Arbor: University of Michigan Press, 1975; London: Weidenfeld and Nicolson *(The Road to 1984),* 1975.

Stevens, A.W. "George Orwell and Southeast Asia." *Yearbook of Comparative and General Literature,* 11(1962): 133–41.

Sutherland, R.W., Jr. "The Political Ideas of G. Orwell: A Liberal's Odyssey in the Twentieth Century." Unpublished Ph.D. dissertation, Duke University, 1964.

Swingler, Randall. "The Right to Free Expression." Annotated by George Orwell. *Polemic* no. 5(September–October 1946): 45–53.

Symons, Julian. Introduction to *Nineteen Eighty-Four,* by George Orwell.

London: Heron Books, 1970, pp. xi–xiii.
————. *The Thirties.* Westport, Conn.: Greenwood Press, 1973; London: Faber and Faber, 1975.
Thomas, Hugh. *The Spanish Civil War.* Harmondsworth, England: Pelican Books, 1968; New York: Harper and Row, 1977.
Thornton, A.P. *Doctrines of Imperialism.* New York: John Wiley and Sons Inc., 1965.
Van Dyke, Vernon. *Political Science; A Philosophical Analysis.* Stanford, Calif.: Stanford University Press, 1960.
Verba, Sidney. *Small Groups and Political Behavior: A Study of Leadership.* Princeton, N.J.: Princeton University Press, 1961.
Vorhees, Richard J. *The Paradox of George Orwell.* Lafayette, Ind.: Purdue University Press, 1961.
Wain, John. "Here Lies Lower Binfield." *Encounter* 17(October 1961): 70–83.
Warburg, Frederic. *All Authors are Equal: The Publishing Life of Frederic Warburg, 1936–71.* London: Hutchinson, 1973.
Watson, George. "Were the Intellectuals Duped?" *Encounter* vol. 41, no. 6(December 1973): 20–30.
Weintraub, Stanley. *The Last Great Cause.* New York: Weybright and Talley Inc., 1968.
Williams, Raymond. *Orwell.* London: William Collins and Co. Ltd., 1971; New York: Columbia University Press, 1981.
————, ed. *George Orwell: A Collection of Critical Essays.* Englewood Cliffs, N.J.: Prentice-Hall, 1974.
Woodcock, George. *The Crystal Spirit.* Harmondsworth, England: Penguin Books, 1970.
Woodruff, Philip [Philip Mason]. *The Men Who Ruled India.* Vol. 2, *The Guardians.* London: Jonathan Cape, 1963.
Zwerdling, Alex. *Orwell and the Left.* New Haven: Yale University Press, 1974; London (Bedford Square): Yale University Press, 1974.

The following were among those sources consulted at the Orwell Archive, University College, London.

Orwell, George. "The Fate of the Middle Classes." (Review of *The Fate of the Middle Classes,* by Alec Brown.) *Adelphi,* May 1936, pp. 127–28.
————. "The Lure of Profundity." *The New English Weekly,* December 30, 1937, pp. 235–36.
————. "The Lure of Atrocity." *New English Weekly,* June 23, 1938, p. 210.
————. "Political Reflections on the Crisis." *Adelphi,* December 1938, pp. 108–12.
————. "Caesarean Section in Spain." *The Highway* 31(March 1939).
————. "Unwillingly to School." (Reviews of: (1) *The Backward Son,* by Stephen Spender; (2) *Royal Highness,* by Thomas Mann; (3) *Iron Gustav,* by Hans Fallada; (4) *Sons and Fathers,* by Maurice Hindus; (5) *The Way*

to Santiago, by Arthur Calder-Marshall; (6) *A Book of Miracles*, by Ben Hecht; (7) *Bethel Merriday*, by Sinclair Lewis.) *The Tribune*, May 24, 1940, pp. 14–15.

———. "The Great Dictator." (Review of the film, *The Great Dictator*, starring Charlie Chaplin.) *Time and Tide*, December 21, 1940, p. 1250.

———. "Our Opportunity." *The Left News*, January 1941, pp. 1608–11.

———. "The People's Army." (Review of *Home Guard for Victory!* by Hugh Slater.) *The New Statesman and Nation*, February 15, 1941, p. 168.

———. "Patriots and Revolutionaries." In *The Betrayal of the Left*. Edited by Victor Gollancz. London: Gollancz, 1941, pp. 234–45.

———. "Home Guard for Victory!" (Review of *Home Guard for Victory!* by Hugh Slater.) *Horizon*, March 1941, pp. 219–21.

———. "Will Freedom Die with Capitalism?" *The Left News*, April 1941, pp. 1682–85.

———. "Too Hard on Humanity: An imaginary interview between GEORGE ORWELL and JONATHAN SWIFT." *The Listener*, November 26, 1942, pp. 692–93.

———. "George Orwell on Jack London." A broadcast in a B.B.C. series on American literature, March 5, 1943. The transcript is approximately eight pages of double-spaced typescript.

———. "Three Years of Home Guard: Unique Symbol of Stability." *Observer*, May 9, 1943, p. 3.

———. "Revolt in the Urban Desert." (Review of *Reflections on the Revolution of Our Time*, by Harold J. Laski.) *Observer*, October 10, 1943, p. 3.

——— "In the Firing Line." (Review of *Armies and the Art of Revolution*, by K.C. Chorley.) *Observer*, January 2, 1944, p. 3

———. "Why Machiavellis of To-Day Fall Down." (Review of *The Machiavellians*, by James Burnham.) *Manchester Evening News*, January 20, 1944, p. 2.

———. "Back to the Land." (Review of *Selections from the Works of Gerrard Winstanley*, edited by Leonard Hamilton.) *Observer*, September 3, 1944, p. 3.

———. "Home Guard Lessons for the Future." *Observer*, October 15, 1944, p. 5.

———. "Conquer Nature or Care for It?" (Review of *The Natural Order: Essays on the Return to Husbandry*, by H.J. Massingham.) *Manchester Evening News*, January 25, 1945.

———. "A Muffled Voice." (Review of *Christianity and Democracy*, by Jacques Maritain.) *Observer*, June 10, 1945, p. 3.

———. "The British General Election." *Commentary*, November 1945, pp. 65–70.

———. "London Letter." (An account of mistaken analysis in the early part of World War II and an attack upon left wing intellectuals.) *Partisan Review*, Winter 1945, pp. 77–82.

———. "What Is Socialism?" *Manchester Evening News*, January 31, 1946, p. 2.

———. Annotation of "The Right to Free Expression," by Randall Swingler. *Polemic*, no. 5 (September–October, 1946): 45–53.

———. "Marx and Russia." (Review of *What Is Communism?*, by John Plamenatz.) *Observer*, February 15, 1948, p. 4.

———. "Britain's Struggle for Survival: The Labour Government After Three Years." *Commentary*, October 1948, pp. 343–49.

ADDENDUM TO BIBLIOGRAPHY, 2003

Bowker, Gordon. *George Orwell*. New York, London: Little, Brown, 2003.

Buitenhuis, Peter and Nadel, Ira B. *George Orwell: A Reassessment*. London: MacMillan, 1988.

Davison, Peter, ed. *Keeping our Little Corner Clean 1942-1943*. London: Secker & Warburg, 2001.

———, ed. *Orwell and the Dispossessed*. London: Penguin Books, 2001.

———, ed. *Orwell's England*. London: Penguin Books, 2001.

———. ed. *Two Wasted Years 1943*. London: Secker & Warburg, 2001.

Gottlieb, Erika. *Dystopian Fiction East and West: Universe of Terror and Trial*. Montreal and Kingston: McGill-Queen's University Press, 2001.

———. *The Orwell Conundrum*. Ottawa: Carleton University Press, 1992.

Hitchens, Christopher. *Why Orwell Matters*. New York: Basic Books, 2002.

Meyers, Jeffrey. *Orwell: Wintry Conscience of a Generation*. New York, London: W. W. Norton, 2000.

Rodden, John. *The Politics of Literary Reputation. The Making and Claiming of 'St. George' Orwell*. New York, Oxford: Oxford University Press, 1989.

Savage, Robert L., Combs, James, and Nimmo, Dan, eds. *The Orwellian Moment*. Fayetteville and London: The University of Arkansas Press, 1989.

Shelden, Michael. *Orwell: The Authorized Biography*. London: Heinemann, 1991.

INDEX